David Del Tredici
Piano Album III

Notes from the Editor

The first time I heard David Del Tredici perform was in 2001 at the *A Great Day in New York* Festival. David's daring virtuosity and uninhibited expressiveness left me both breathless and in awe. The piano writing was brilliant and imaginative, exploring the entire range of the instrument replete with lush harmonies and fantastical intricacies of counterpoint and rhythm.

In 2004 we met and began a long, meaningful collaboration and friendship. The timing was fortuitous for me because it was a period in David's compositional life when he was returning with great vigor to compose for solo piano. At our first meeting he gave me a copy of his *Gymnopodie No. 1*, which had been recently engraved. I was immediately drawn to its idiomatic piano writing and poignancy. When I returned to play it for him, he gave me valuable interpretive and technical suggestions. And that is how it all started.

Some of my favorite experiences were playing concerts with David in programs of solo and four-hand works. We presented his music as well as nineteenth-century four-hand repertoire at venues around New York City and San Francisco. One experience in particular epitomizes David's personality, ethos and devilish wit. This performance put his celebration of gay sexuality on full display.

One of our gigs was at a bar in Brooklyn in which we closed our set, as we often did, with his sexy four-hand tango *Carioca Boy*. Since we were in a bar, David gave an oral program note about a former boyfriend, of questionable virtue, who wanted David to write music for his newly choreographed strip tease act. David thought a tango would work best. Most program notes are heavy on the exegesis, David's was not. It was a unique moment to say the least. The audience reaction, as well as my own, ranged from laughter and blushing-and in the case of one older patron-to staring straight ahead disbelief. I told him I was surprised I never heard this story and he informed me he made it up on the spot! Ever unpredictable and entertaining, David's life and music reflects his insatiable and provocative creative energy.

It has been a great honor and the opportunity of a lifetime to work so closely with David these past several years, both performing and recording his work. I am privileged to have such a unique vantage point into the world of his piano repertoire which has grown threefold since our first meeting.

Here are a few personal observations about the pieces contained in this volume.

Ray's Birthday Suit from 2008 is a suite of six pieces written for the 60th birthday of David's former husband Ray Warman. David's first performance, for which I turned pages, took place at Ray's birthday bash in their West Village apartment. This grand opus unfolded as the guests listened with rapt attention to a musical biographical journey of Ray's life.

Various melodies including Ray's theme of childhood Catholic innocence and David's own *Final Alice* theme are intertwined throughout this cyclical piece and developed and imitated in all kinds of inventive contrapuntal ways. David explores a pianistic panorama of styles including a relentless etude, an elaborate fugue using Yale tunes as subjects, an achingly romantic love song, seduction music including optional paddle whack sounds from the page turner, all climaxing in a majestic tour de force finale.

Many Hands was composed in 2009 and came from my suggestion that he write a piece celebrating what two hands can do in various combinations. This fired David up and he began by writing the movement for left hand, which combines a rather austere opening with a seductive middle section that suggests music for a toreador. He followed with a right-hand piece, a movement of astonishing baroque invention and finger twisting gymnastics which includes a canon for five fingers. Who would have imagined so much counterpoint was possible with just the right hand?

Next came the *Bank Street Prelude* and *Perry Street Fugue*, inspired by two locations in New York City that hold special significance for David. With all its contrapuntal ingenuity, lush sequences, and dramatic flair, one of his greatest joys is writing fugues, and this one is exciting to play. The final movement, *Quodlibet/ Finale*, combines themes from the hands alone movements and closes in a grand over the top romantic style with two hands playing thundering octaves at triple forte.

Many Hands demands a pianist's unbridled virtuosity and boundless imagination, making it an extremely effective and engaging work to program. Premiering the piece was one of the highlights of my career.

Fantasy on a Cherished Name from 2010 is an homage to composer Andrew Imbrie with whom David studied musical analysis at the University of California at Berkeley in 1958. The work has an elegiac, almost Brahmsian quality with rich inner voice leading and expressive themes conceived from the musical letters in Andrew Imbrie's name.

As I was preparing to record the *Fantasy*, David expressed reservations about the piece, an unusual attitude for him, and asked me to work my pianistic magic. Even though I had studied and performed the piece, it was in the recording session that I fully realized the profundity and poignancy of the music. I called and told him the magic was already right there in the score.

Late in the Game, which David humorously used to call *Long in the Tooth*, is nonetheless a serious piece. For a while the four pieces drifted about without connection. David did not like this until he hit upon the idea of combining them into a set that memorializes friends who have left his life. To unite them he composed musical connections between the first three pieces, with the final work *Monk* being a stand alone. The piece most altered in the process was *Bittersweet*, which became much larger and more enthralling. Just days before the premiere, I received a phone call saying part of the middle section of *Bittersweet* had been completely rewritten. After taking a deep breath I pasted the new measures over the old and went on practicing as though the former music never existed. *Late in the Game* can be performed both as a set and as individual pieces.

Ode to Music from 2015 has an interesting history. After hearing a rehearsal of David's wind quintet *The Most Beautiful Song in the World*, based on Shubert's *An die Musik*, I asked him if I could have a copy of the score to attempt a solo piano transcription. I worked on it for a few months and took it to David for his comments and suggestions. A couple of weeks later he called and said he had done his own work on the piece and that his name would probably need to be added as a transcriber. I had no problem with that. A few weeks later he called and said that my original transcription was no longer recognizable, and my name no longer needed to appear on the score. He effectively recomposed my transcription! I was deeply honored, and the result is truly masterful and magical. *Ode to Music* retains the soulful melodic essence of Schubert's song, combined with unabashed Lisztian bravura, making it a stunning concert piece.

—Marc Peloquin

Notes from the Composer

Ode to Music

Ode to Music was first performed February 21, 2015 at the Tenri Cultural Institute, New York by Marc Peloquin

Composer note:
Having written a wind quintet for the Dorians, upon which they lavished playing of great precision and elegance, I was warmly disposed towards them. So it was no surprise when, in a burst of friendship I blurted out, "Is there a piece of music you all wished-no dreamed-had been written for wind quintet? I will transcribe for your Quintet anything you choose".
After much conversation the players settled upon Shubert's song "An die Musik" - a little miracle in two verses which is often the last song sung on the last recital of a distinguished lieder singer's concluding career.
My dear friend and piano-champion, Marc Peloquin, heard this arrangement and posited: "David, I think it would also sound well on the piano". He began then to transcribe my transcription which started me thinking: Could this become the basis of a grand piano fantasy much as, in 1978, I transmuted my chaste *Acrostic Song* into a gleaming, grandiose *Virtuoso Alice*? Yes, I decided, it could work and set to the task quickly and with passion.
To Music is the result- 10 minutes that Franz Schubert might have written had he been enamored of Richard Wagner and at the same time a piano student of Franz Liszt!

Fantasy on a Cherished Name (In Memoriam, Andrew Imbrie)

Fantasy on a Cherished Name was first performed March 25, 2011 at Old First Church, San Francisco by David Del Tredici

Composer note:
In 1958 I was an undergraduate at the University of California at Berkeley. Hell-bent on becoming a concert pianist and not yet interested in composing – I took my first musical analysis course from a Mr. Andrew Imbrie. What a revelation it was! My eyes and ears were opened to the intricacies of a musical composition. To this point, I had thought that somehow music dropped fully-formed from heaven. I still remember, 40 plus years later, some of the pieces Imbrie had chosen to investigate (Bartok, *String Quartet No. 4*, Milhaud, *Douzieme String Quartet*). Andrew's passion for music, his skill at taking apart a piece – jeweler-like – and admiring its various facets, inspired me to the point where, one year later, I would myself decide to abandon the piano and become a composer.
With this memorial piece I wanted to write something with an analytical flourish that Andrew himself might have enjoyed. So I took the letters of his name which coincided with musical notes – A, D, E, B, E (in the order that they occur) – and used them as my theme. This 9-minute piece is a restless chromatic journey in A-major. As well, I twice quote from his 1947 *Sonata for Piano*. The first – three quarters of the way in, after a climactic moment – is the ghostly theme from the Sonata's first movement. In the final Postlude the chromatic writhings, now so familiar, are transformed into quietly ecstatic music which rises to a climax affirming at last an uncomplicated A-major tonality. *Fantasy on a Cherished Name* is dedicated to Barbara Imbrie.

Late in the Game

Late in the Game was first performed February 6, 2016 at the Tenri Cultural Institute, New York by Marc Peloquin

Written between 2009 and 2012, then revised in 2015, these four disparate piano pieces make up *Late in the Game*-- the title being a reference to the composer's great age. Curiously, once composed, the traditional silent spaces between pieces began to erode and fill with notes. Ultimately, *Farewell, R.W.* and *Gloss* (1 and 2) are connected--with an ironic, mood-changing quote from Beethoven's Ode to Joy. *Gloss* and *Bittersweet* (2 and 3) are also linked. *Monk*, the final piece is the only stand alone. The effect of all these elisions is to fuse the four movements together allowing the ear to hear a single arc.

Composer note:

Farewell, R.W. is my solo piano arrangement of the third movement of *Facts of Life*, a four movement work for solo guitar commissioned and premiered by David Leisner in 2010. I quote from my program note written for the premiere: "Movement 3, *Farewell, R.W.* is the slow movement and 'soul' of the work. Tranquil even ecstatic, it was inspired one afternoon by painful feelings surrounding a recent relationship break up."

Gloss. One weekend I invited my friend Drew Paralic to come visit. He arrived with a piano piece he had just composed and promptly played it. It haunted me. The next morning I awoke with a weird feeling: I wanted to "do something" to that piece. After Drew left, I began to rewrite the piece in my own image-- extending phrases, re-harmonizing chords, dramatizing structure. I was terrified to show it to Drew thinking he would be offended with all my tamperings. But he was pleased, even flattered- said it was like two views of the same source. *Gloss* moves at a moderate tempo and has a definite jazzy quality-- in line with what is Drew's own musical specialty.

Bittersweet (In memoriam John Dare). John Dare was my first love. We travelled for three days by train from California to New York City, living on 52 tuna fish sandwiches John had made. But it was love really that sustained us- at age 22 you can do that. Not bittersweet then but certainly now-- 50 years later-- the piece seesaws with a steady almost Bachian tread between chromatic progressions and spikily Baroque cadences. Only towards the end does an unalloyed Romanticism force its way forward melting away all rhythmic rigidity.

Monk (In memoriam Suzanne Nahalka). I told Suzanne some months before she died (of pancreatic cancer in 2011) that I would write her a memorial piece and that it would contain the musical letters of her name. Thus *Monk*. Her name yields the letters/notes AEAAA and so with these notes as a steady ever-pulsating accompaniment figure my piece begins. The name Monk refers not to the famous jazz pianist but to the lead character in a 10 year old TV detective series that Suzanne and I watched (in reruns) almost daily via telephone. She loved the quirky, neurotic, genius-detective Monk and he became, in those last months, our bond. Monk (the piano piece) is not mournful but - by turns Romantic, passionate, serene-- a reflection of Suzanne's own lively personality.

Many Hands

Many Hands was first performed September 7, 2017 at Symphony Space, New York by Marc Peloquin

Composer note:

It may seem obvious but hands are the unsung heroes of piano playing. Where would a pianist be without at least two of them? Of course there's four-hand piano (two people usually) and even 6 or 8 hands (try *March Slav* for an especially festive occasion). But essentially it is two hands that bear the brunt of pianistic labors. However, *Many Hands* takes hands in the opposite direction—reducing their number. Movement I uses only the left hand and movement IV only the right (it is particularly rare to have a right-handed piece). All but one of the movements is dedicated to concert -pianist friends of mine who have premiered earlier DDT works. The original idea for the set came to me via an imaginative suggestion of Marc Peloquin. Thus he is the first dedicatee.

For the Left Hand is in three parts: a craggy opening section is followed by a Spanish toreador dance—the middle of which builds to a (yes!) bullish climax before returning to the opening music, now warmed by the addition of a cantabile coda.

Bank Street Prelude follows (for two hands). It was written in memory of Emery W. Harper and commissioned by Luigi Terruso. I live on Bank Street in the West Village of New York City—a once easy-going, pan-sexual community whose profile has lately been sharply up-scaled--due no doubt to the arrival of the Whitney Museum, the High Line Park and the Standard Hotel. However, my short, bustling prelude is more an evocation of that earlier time.

The Prelude is followed without pause by the *Perry Street Fugue*-- another geographical inspiration. This is dedicated to Stephen Gosling. Note: Perry Street is parallel to Bank Street, but two blocks away. The street is meaningful in my life because of one address-- 50 Perry. This tiny room where shoes were once shined has been my emotional buttress for nearly 30 years. Why? How? More I cannot say. . .

Writing fugues is my joy and this one with its grand gestures, high energy and considerable length, did not come easy. Its wild chromaticism bends this way and that, till one hardly knows (tonality-wise) what is up. Midway through (surprise!) material from the *Prelude* returns followed by a rich reworking of the fugue theme, a grand climax and a swirl of glissandos in both hands. (Glissandos are a relatively rare use of the other side of the pianist's hands.) The movement glides then to a quiet end.

For the Right Hand (theme and six variations dedicated to Steven Beck). Without pause, a new theme—hushed, tremulous—grows out of the fugue's last murmurings. Three variations follow without interruption. The pianist's unused left hand flutters to his lap as the right hand begins to shoulder all pianistic responsibility. Variation 4 is a canon at the octave at the distance of a quarter note (which is very little distant). The two voices pile up—one atop the other (and all in one hand!). Variation 5 with its steady 32nd note figuration is reminiscent of the theme. The 6th and final variation is a chorale-prelude whose stately theme is continually interrupted by, and enhanced with, pianistic filigree.

Quodlibet/ Finale for Orion Weiss. A quodlibet is described as the juxtaposition of diverse, unexpected elements. In this case the two hands are reunited--each bringing with them their characteristic music: the left hand plays music from movement I and the right hand from movement IV. These then are contrapuntally combined and lead to the finale--an unrepentant orgy of octaves and triple fortes. Sometimes you just have to let it all out! What was earlier presented delicately for a single hand is now jacked up to a frenetic level for both hands together. And so the piece ends, leaving you, dear reader, with only one thing more to do—place your hands together and at the appropriate moment . . . clap!

Ray's Birthday Suit

Ray's Birthday Suit was first performed March 23, 2012 at Bargemusic, New York by David Del Tredici

Composer note:

Ray's Birthday Suit was written in celebration of my (then) husband Ray Warman's 60th birthday. I took the six decades of his life and wrote a piece to characterize each. Ray did not like to say he was turning 60. Instead he chose to say he was turning 50/10 – the number that whimsically comes right after 59. "It sounds younger," he'd say.

In the score, before each piece, I wrote a descriptive sentence which I will reproduce here.

I. 10 Radiant Child
"Ray, a beautiful child, is taught to embrace the Catholic Church."
A quietly contrapuntal texture introduces the Ray theme. Halfway through, woven into the texture, appears the hymn, "Tantum Ergo."

II. 10/10 Yale Fugue
"Ray, the Yale man, enters a new world that will forever change his life."
The subject of this particular fugue is the opening phrase of "Bright College Years," a Yalie song. In the course of the fugue two other Yale tunes appear: The "Wiffenpoof Song" and "Bulldog" – a fight song. At the very end, "Bright College Years" is heard in complete form (albeit highly embellished).

III. 20/10 Lawyer Etude
"Ray, the hot, hard working young lawyer takes on Gotham City."
Fast and furious to the end, the etude epitomizes Ray's struggle to make it as a lawyer in the "big time."

IV. 30/10 Domesticated/Seduced
"Ray, married and domesticated hears a new and seductive call......(WHACK!)"
This above sentence bears explanation. After twenty years of marriage and two kids, Ray felt an urge to experiment in submission to female dominatrices. They subjected him to all sorts of exotic torture. After two years of this activity, Ray felt "broken open" and realized that he was–had always been–gay. The piece is in two parts. A gentle gracious movement comes first, suggesting stability and conformity. "Salome's Dance" suddenly appears to shake things up. Ray engages with her. At the very end there is the unmistakable suggestion of a whip cracking.

V. 40/10 Love Duet
"Ray Meets David, hist first male lover"
This duet combines David's theme (from the composer's work "Final Alice") with Ray's theme. The mood is ecstatic, though the piece does end ominously and tentatively.

VI. 50/10 A Grand Occasion
"The great birthday finally arrives. There is a joyful noise heard throughout the land."
This piece is appropriately majestic and is much longer and more developed than any of the preceding movements. It contains another fugue and much tumultuous movement. There is even a highly romantic rendering of Ray's theme late in the piece. However, for the actual ending, the music revs up once more – clangorously and triumphantly combining David's theme and Ray's theme with the ending of Beethoven's "Ode to Joy".

CONTENTS

	Duration	*Page*
ODE TO MUSIC	10 min.	1
FANTASY ON A CHERISHED NAME	9 min.	20
LATE IN THE GAME	(24 min.)	
I. FAREWELL, R.W.	5 min.	37
II. GLOSS	6 min.	43
III. BITTERSWEET	7 min.	53
IV. MONK	6 min.	68
MANY HANDS	(36 min.)	
I. FOR THE LEFT HAND	7 min.	79
II. BANK STREET PRELUDE	4 min.	91
III. PERRY STREET FUGUE	12 min.	99
IV. FOR THE RIGHT HAND	7½ min.	123
V. QUODLIBET – FINALE	5½ min.	139
RAY'S BIRTHDAY SUIT	(35 min.)	
I. Radiant Child	4 min.	155
II. Yale Fugue	8 min.	160
III. Lawyer Etude	4 min.	177
IV. Domesticated / Seduced	5 min.	184
V. Love Duet	4 min.	193
VI. A Grand Occasion (Finale)	10 min.	199

Inspired by and dedicated to Marc Peloquin

ODE TO MUSIC
(fantasy on Franz Schubert's song, *An die Musik*)

DAVID DEL TREDICI

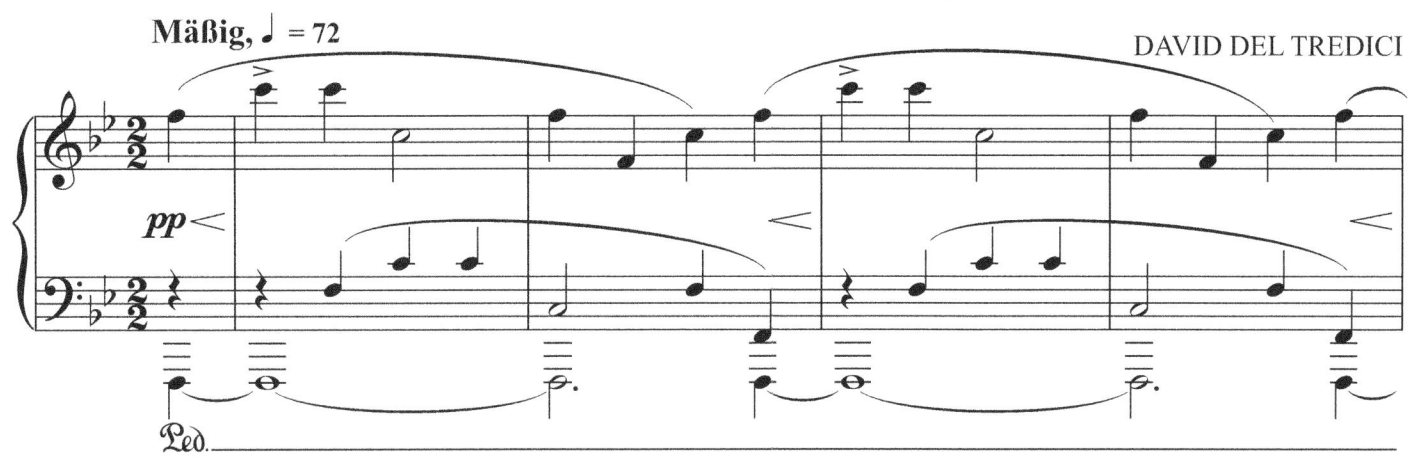

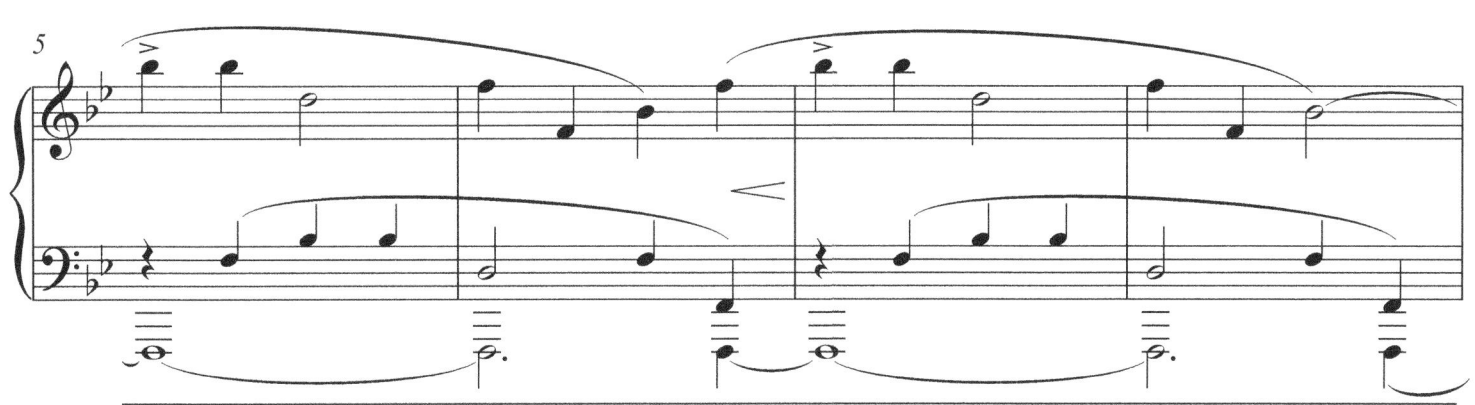

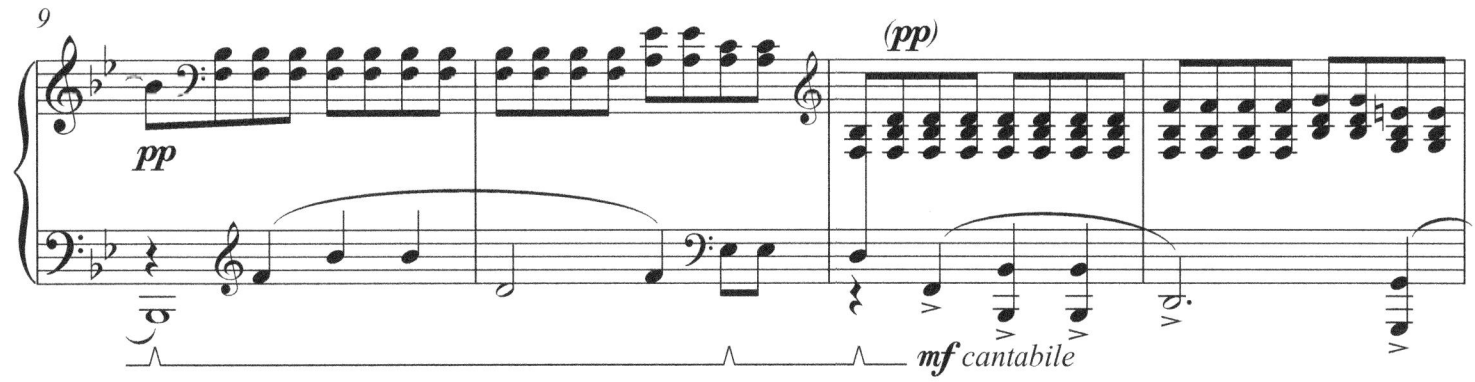

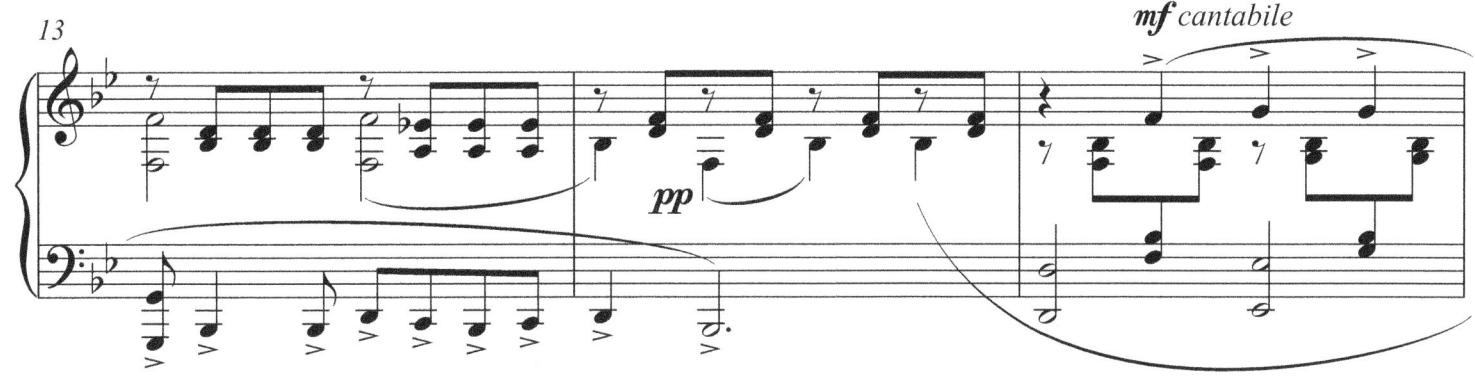

© Copyright 2014 by Boosey & Hawkes, Inc.
International copyright secured. All rights reserved.

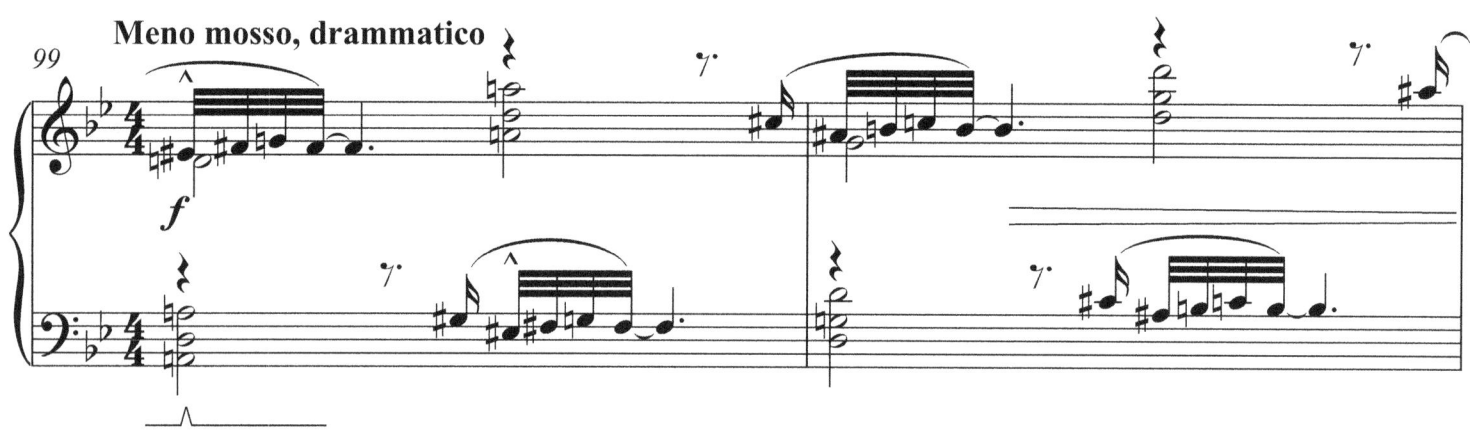
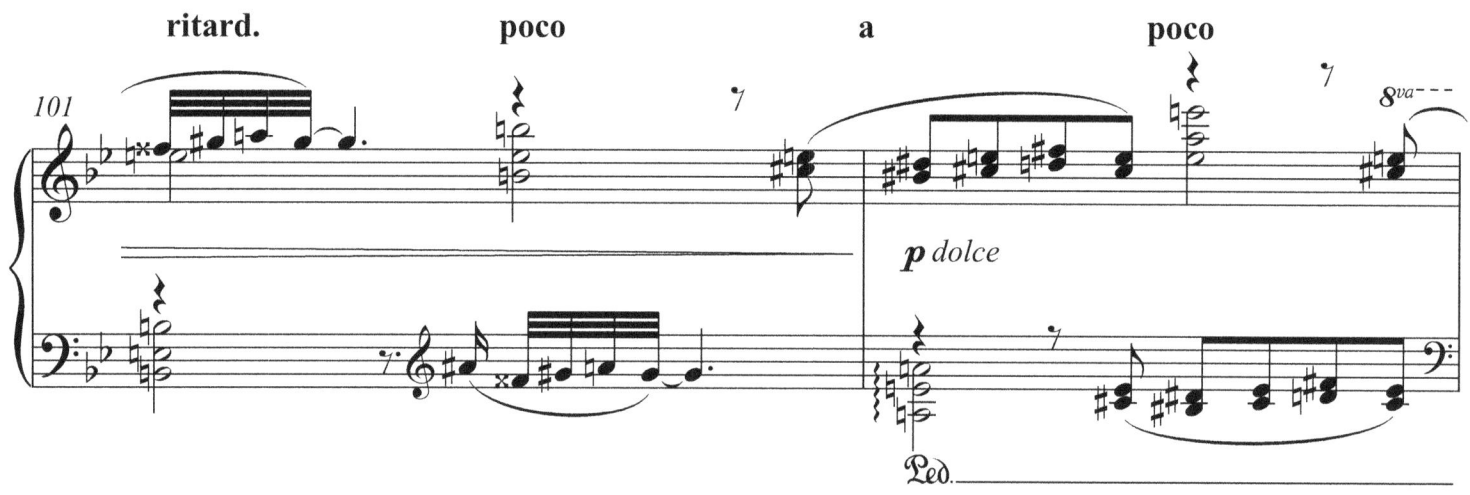
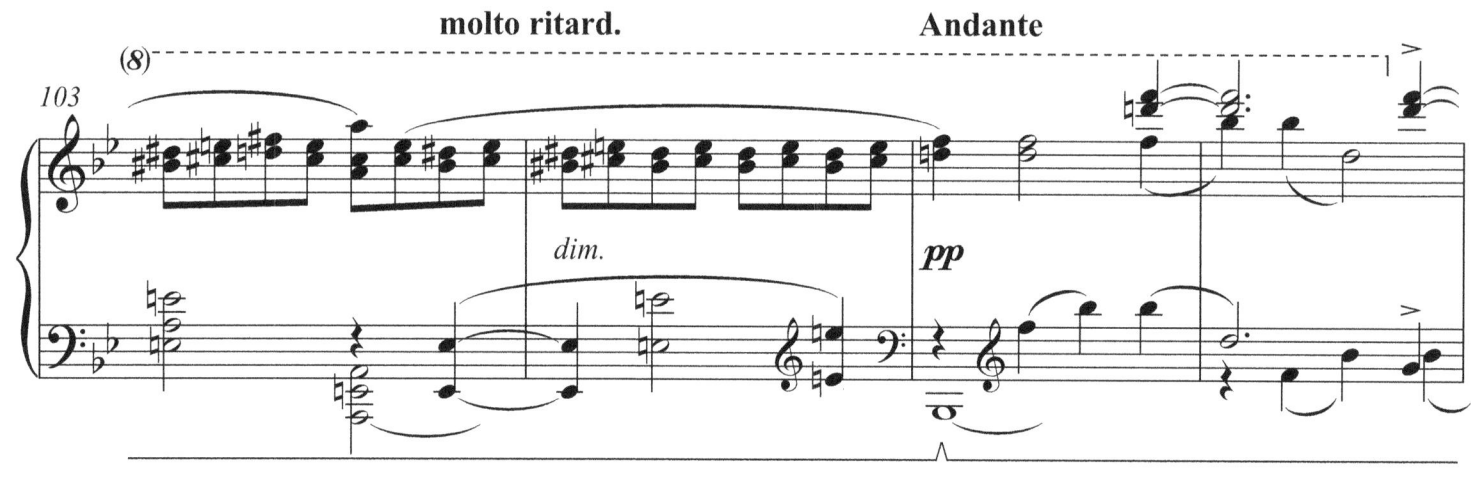

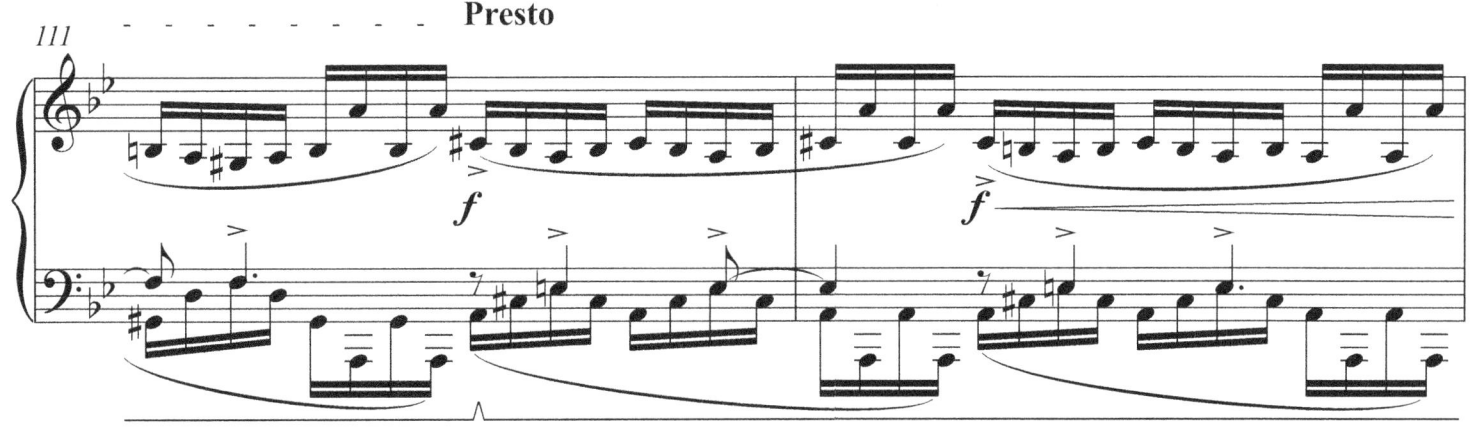

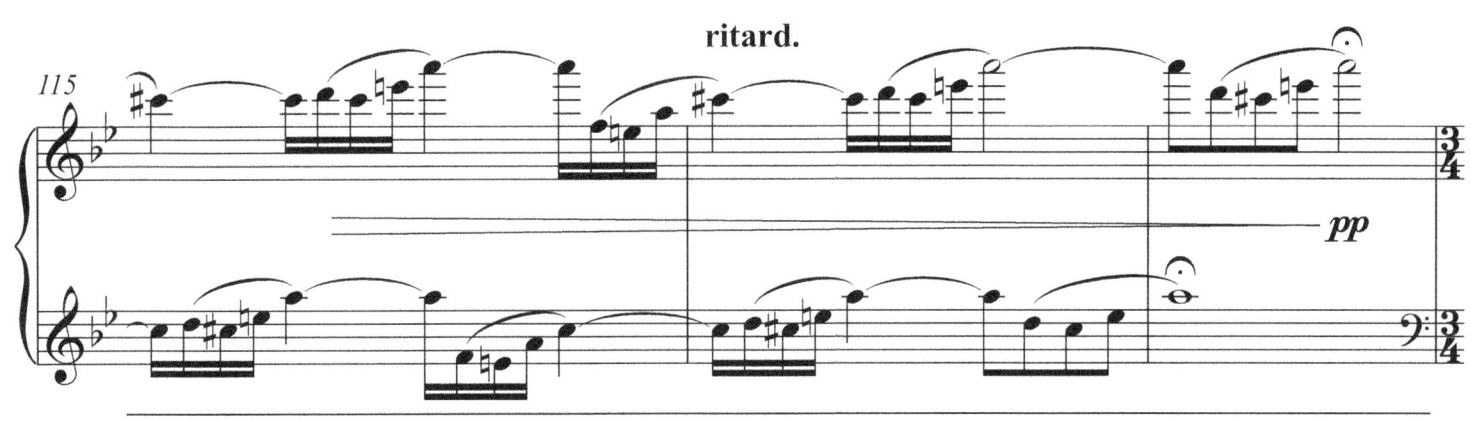

(no changes)

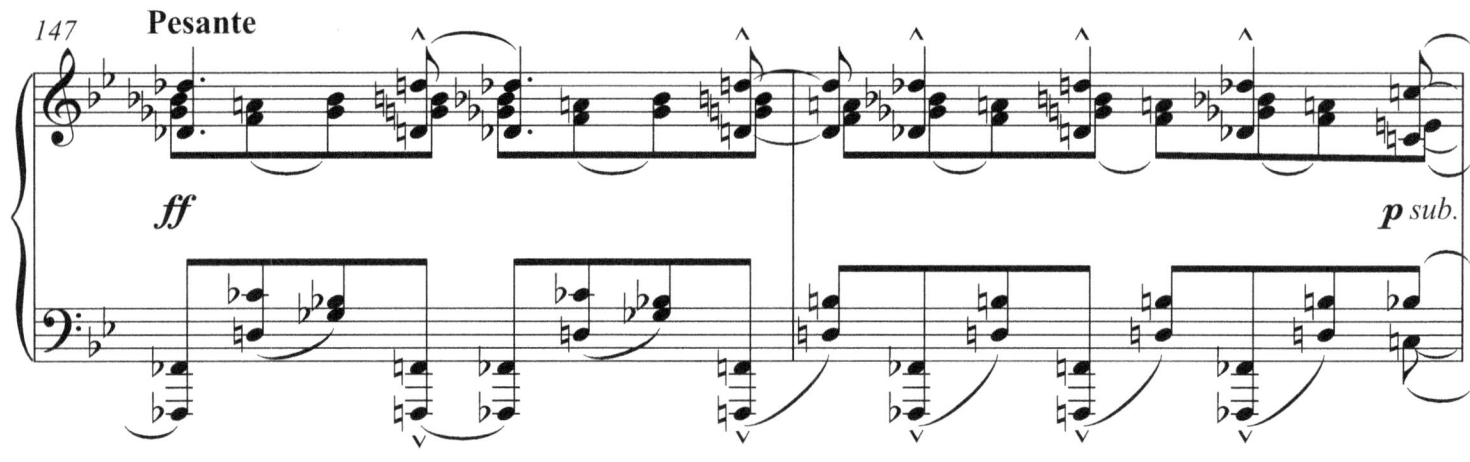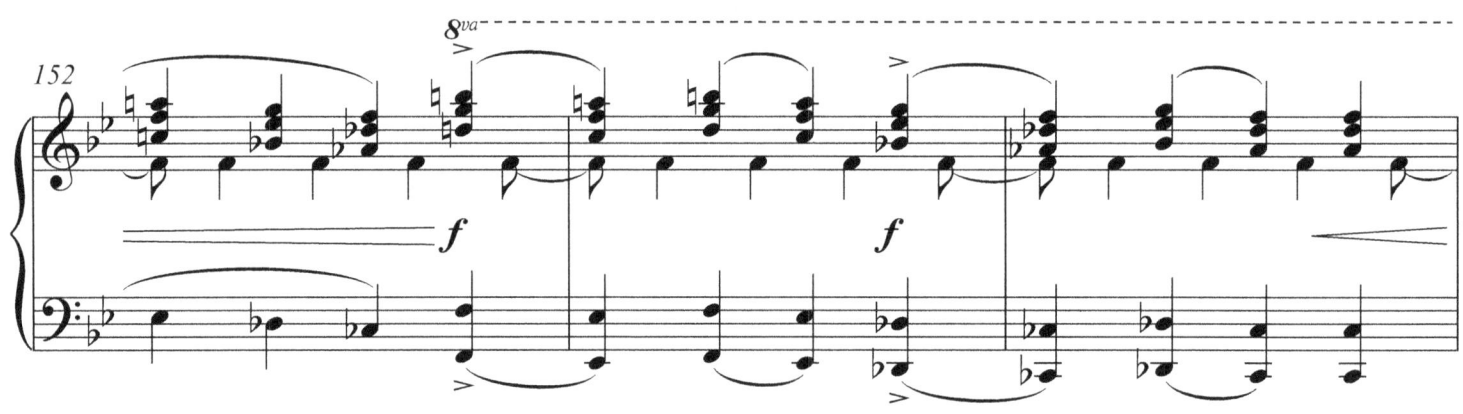

for Barbara Imbrie

Fantasy on a Cherished Name
(In Memoriam, Andrew Imbrie)

DAVID DEL TREDICI
(2010)

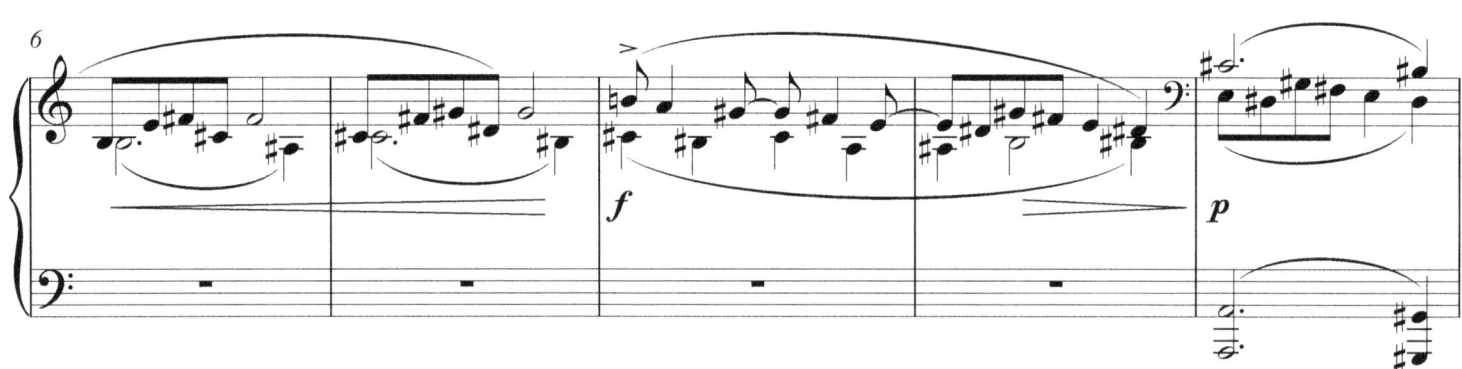
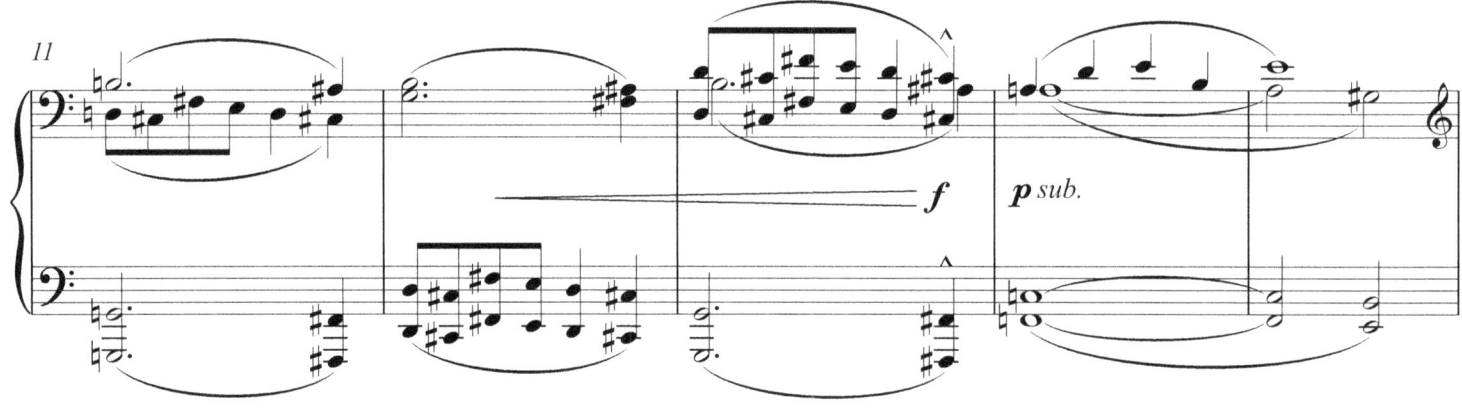
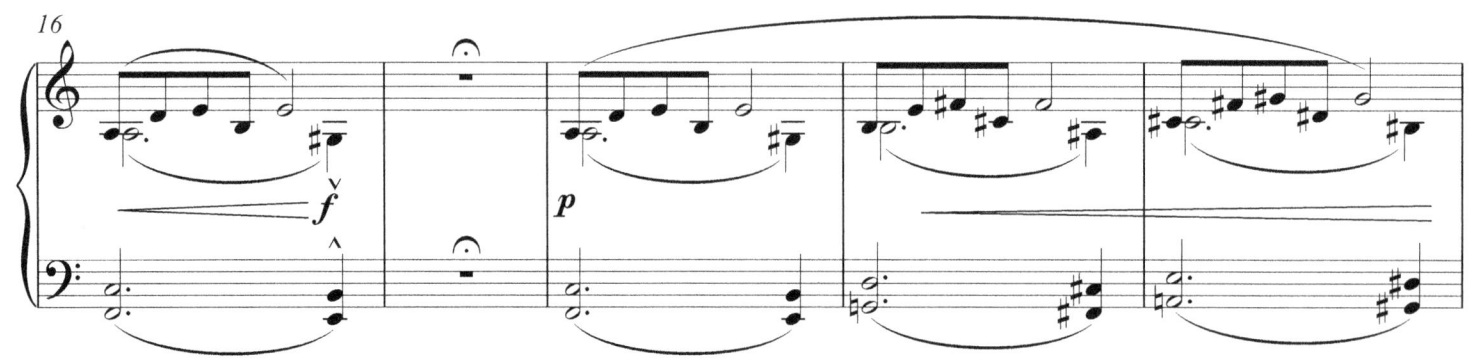

© Copyright 2010 by Boosey & Hawkes, Inc.
International copyright secured. All rights reserved.

Fantasy on a Cherished Name

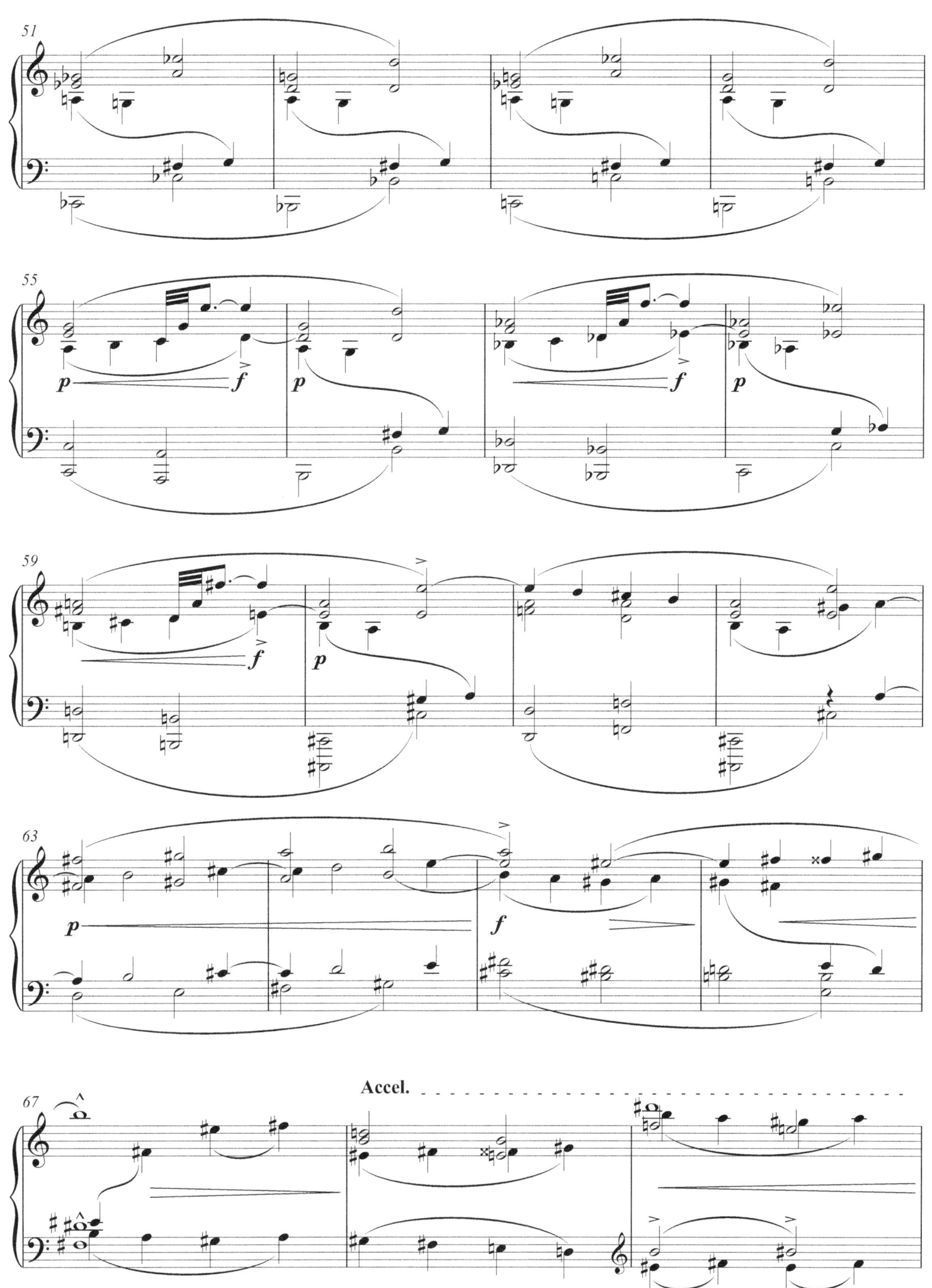

Fantasy on a Cherished Name

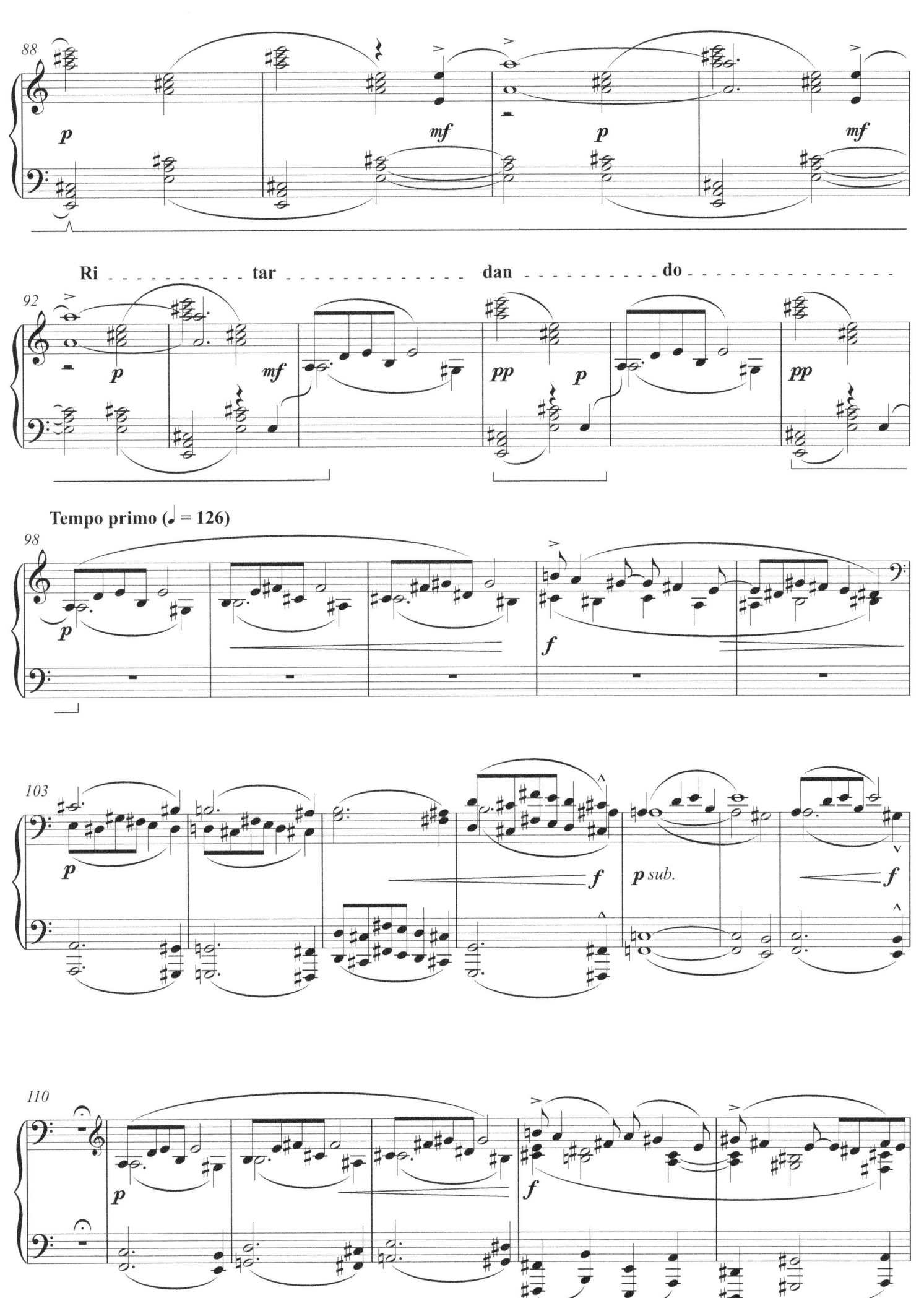

26 FANTASY ON A CHERISHED NAME

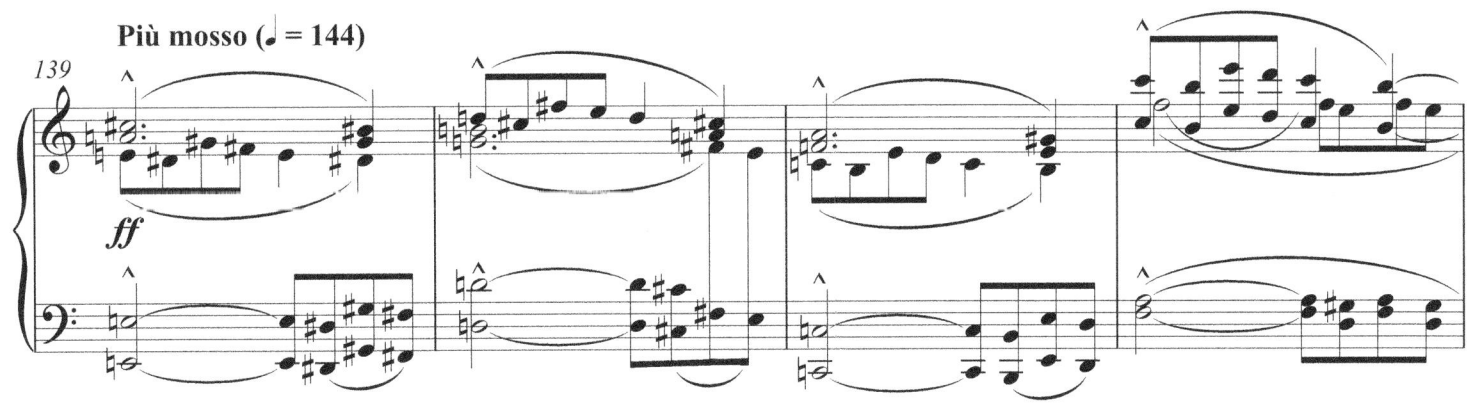

Fantasy on a Cherished Name

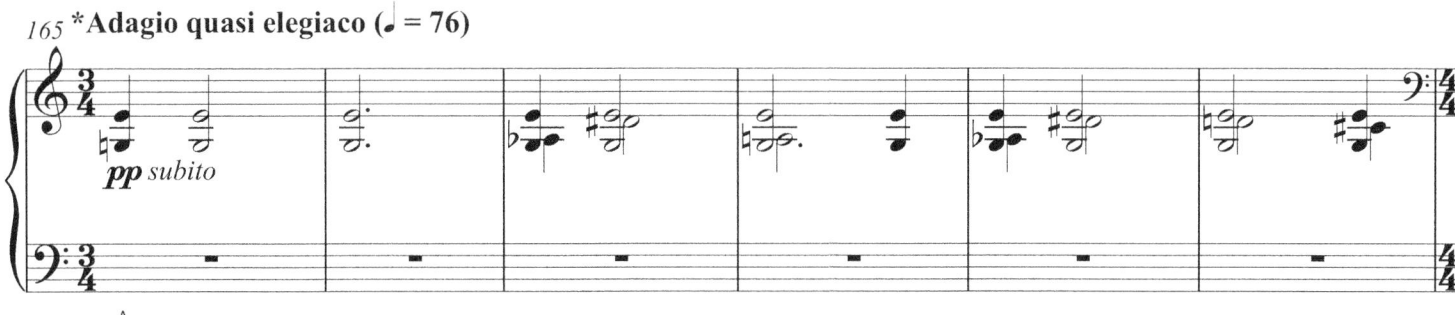

*Andrew Imbrie, Sonata for Piano (1947), Movt. 2

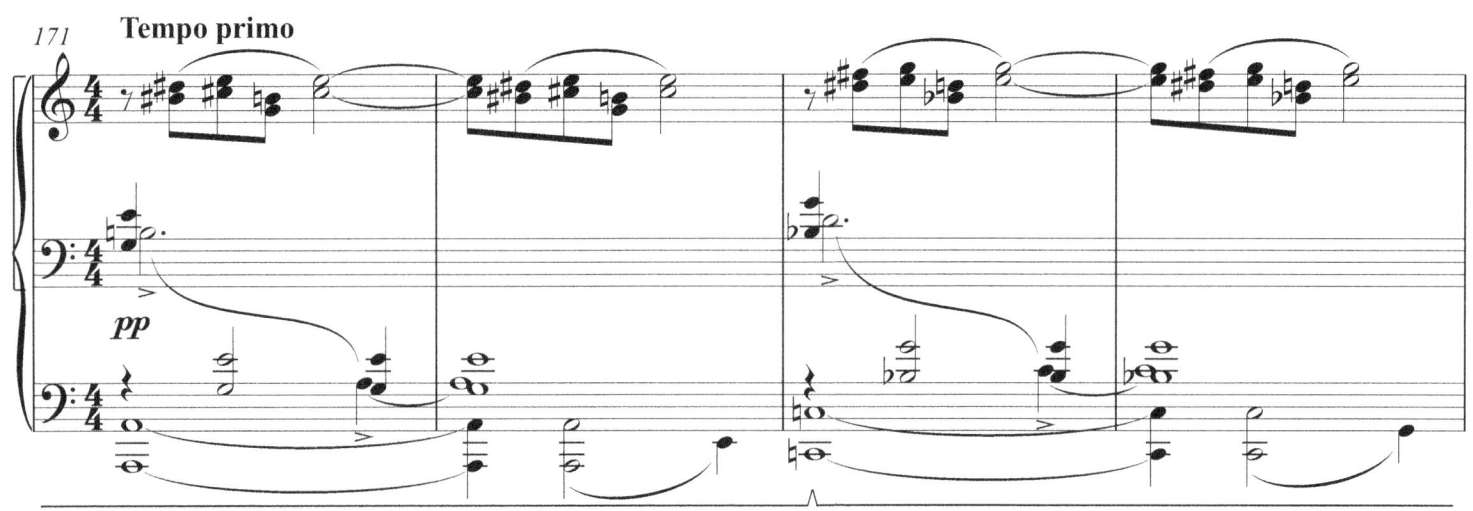

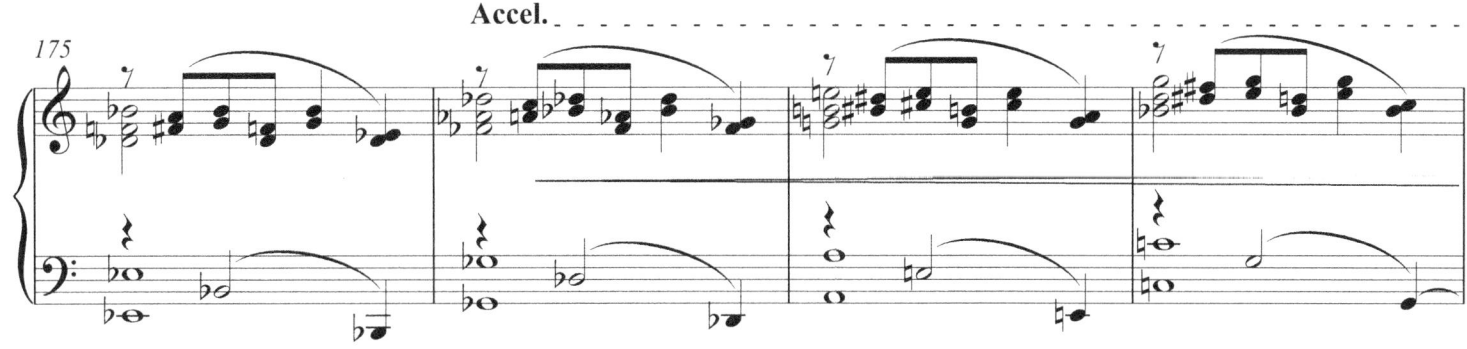

Fantasy on a Cherished Name

Fantasy on a Cherished Name

*Andrew Imbrie, <u>Sonata</u> for piano (1947), Movt. 1

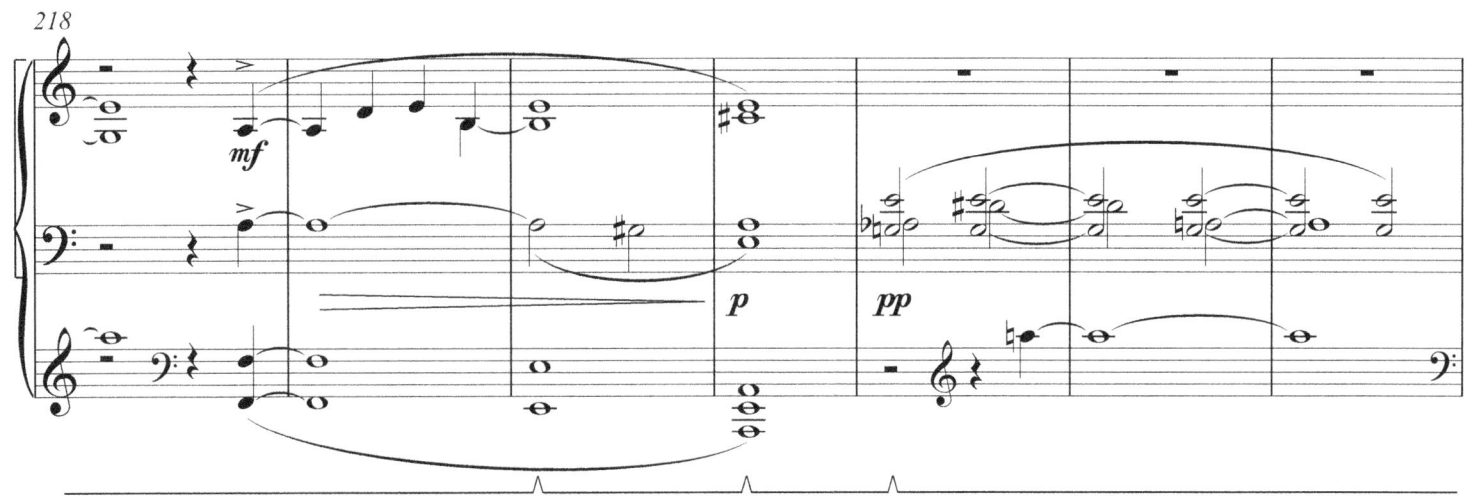

Fantasy on a Cherished Name

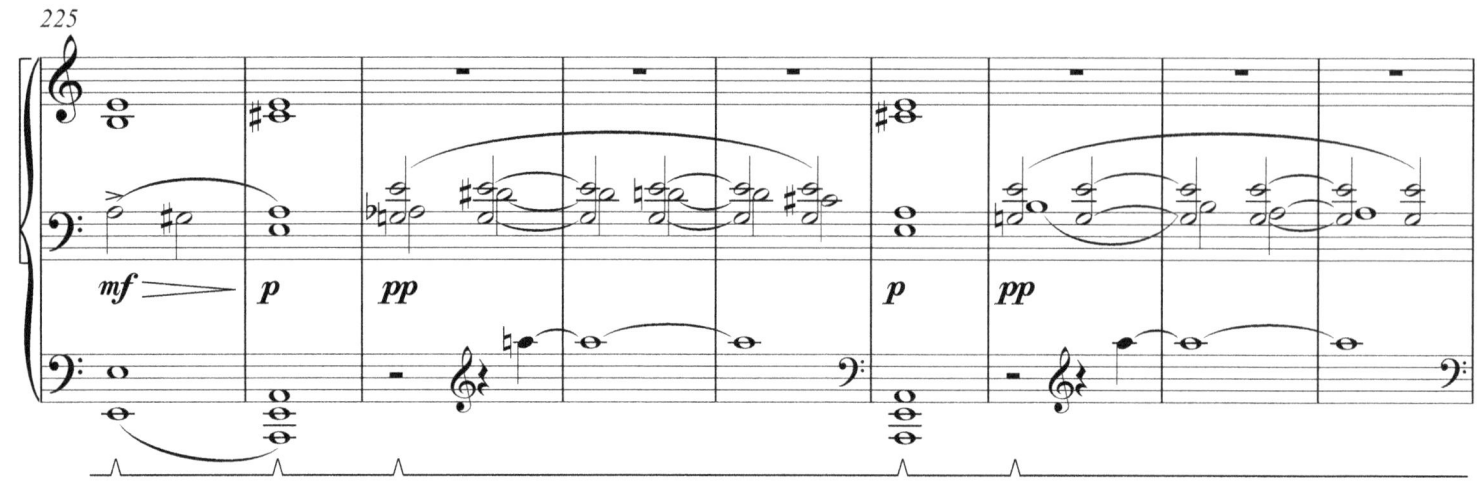

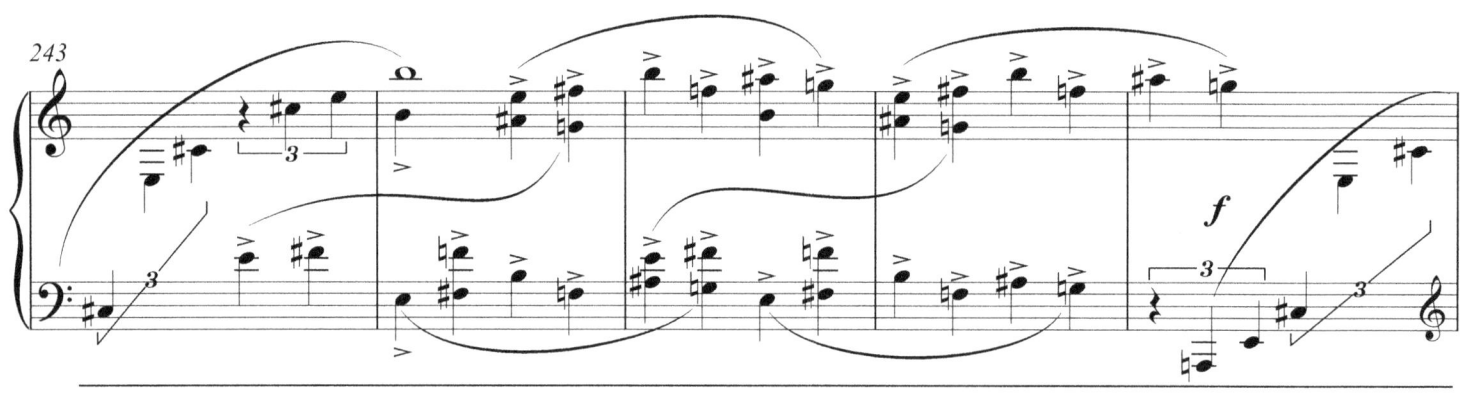

Fantasy on a Cherished Name

POSTLUDE:

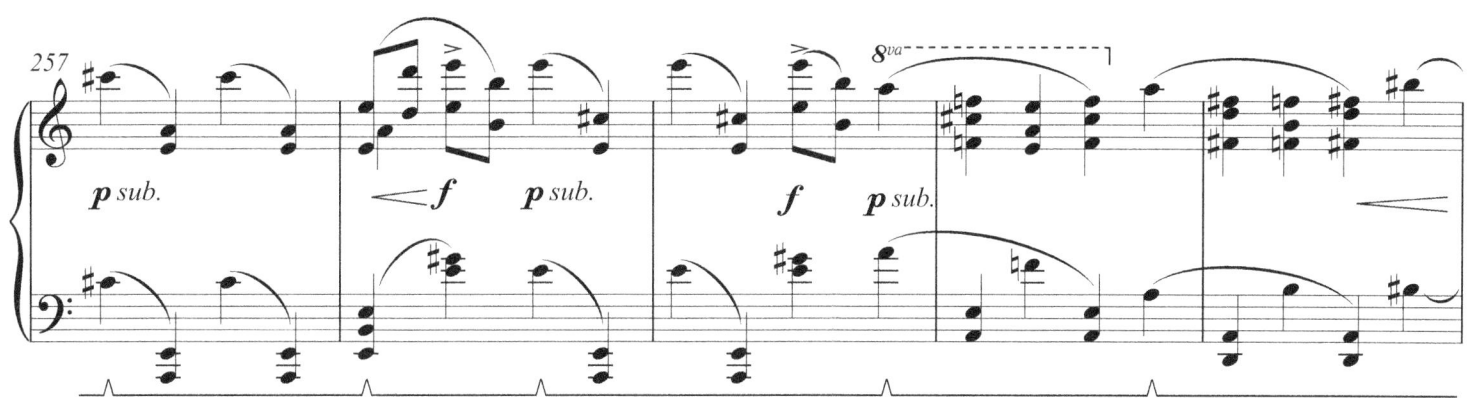

Con gran espressione

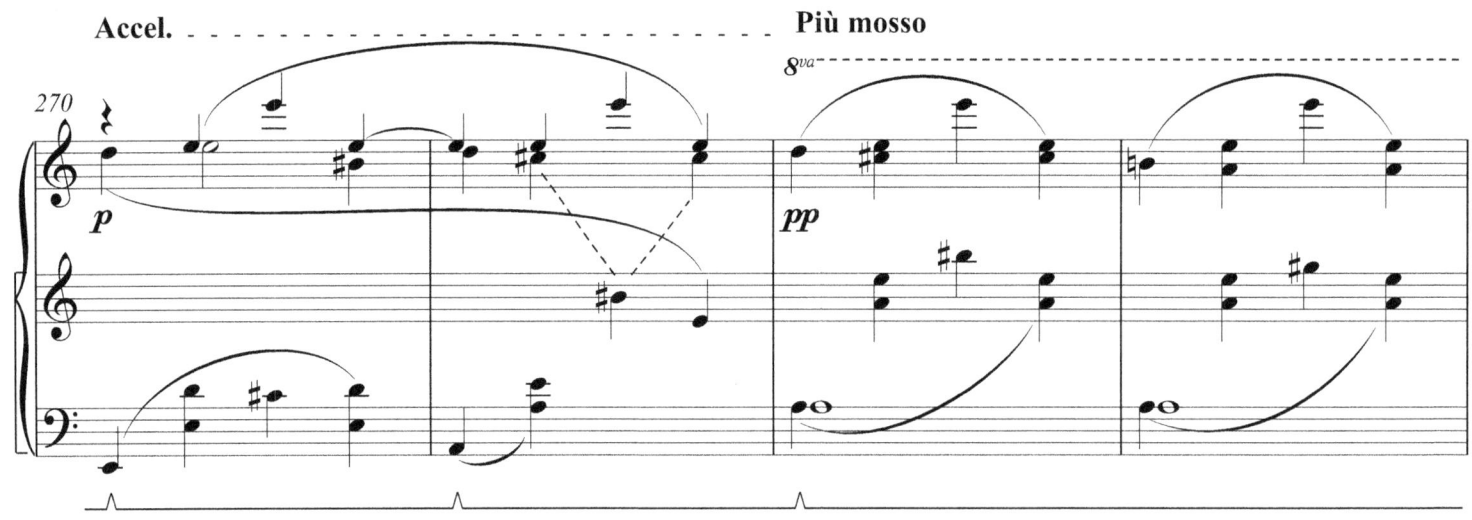
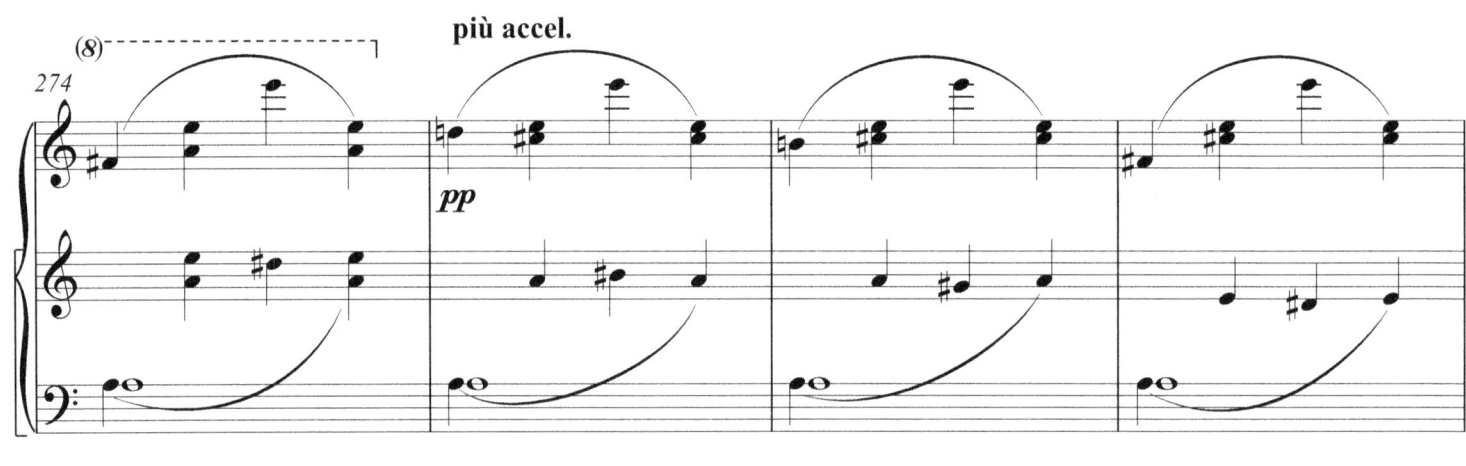

Fantasy on a Cherished Name

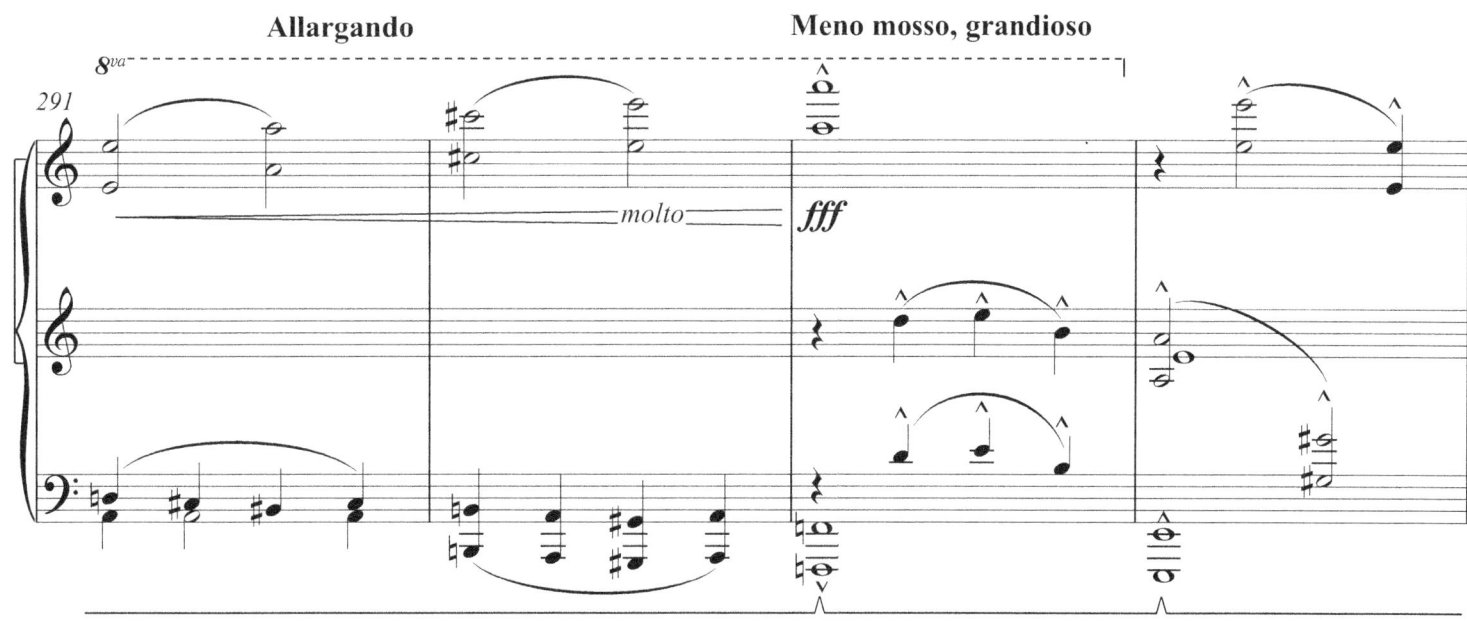
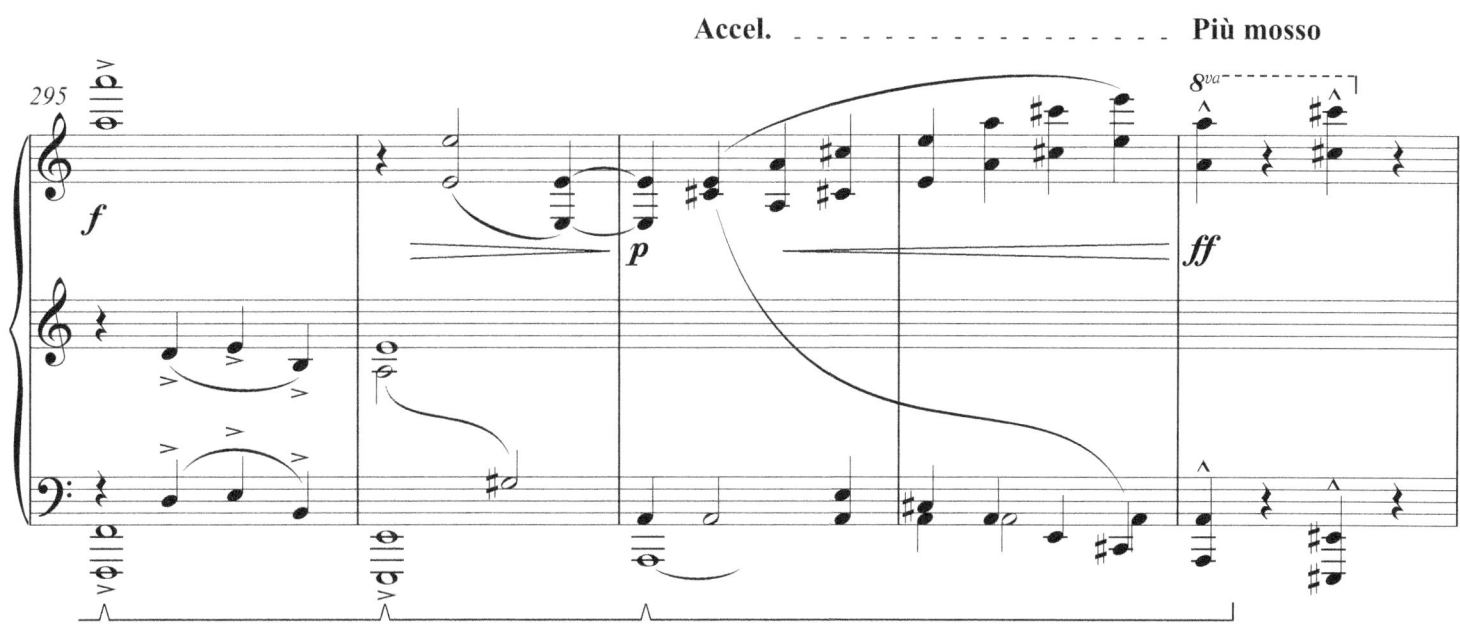

36 — Fantasy on a Cherished Name

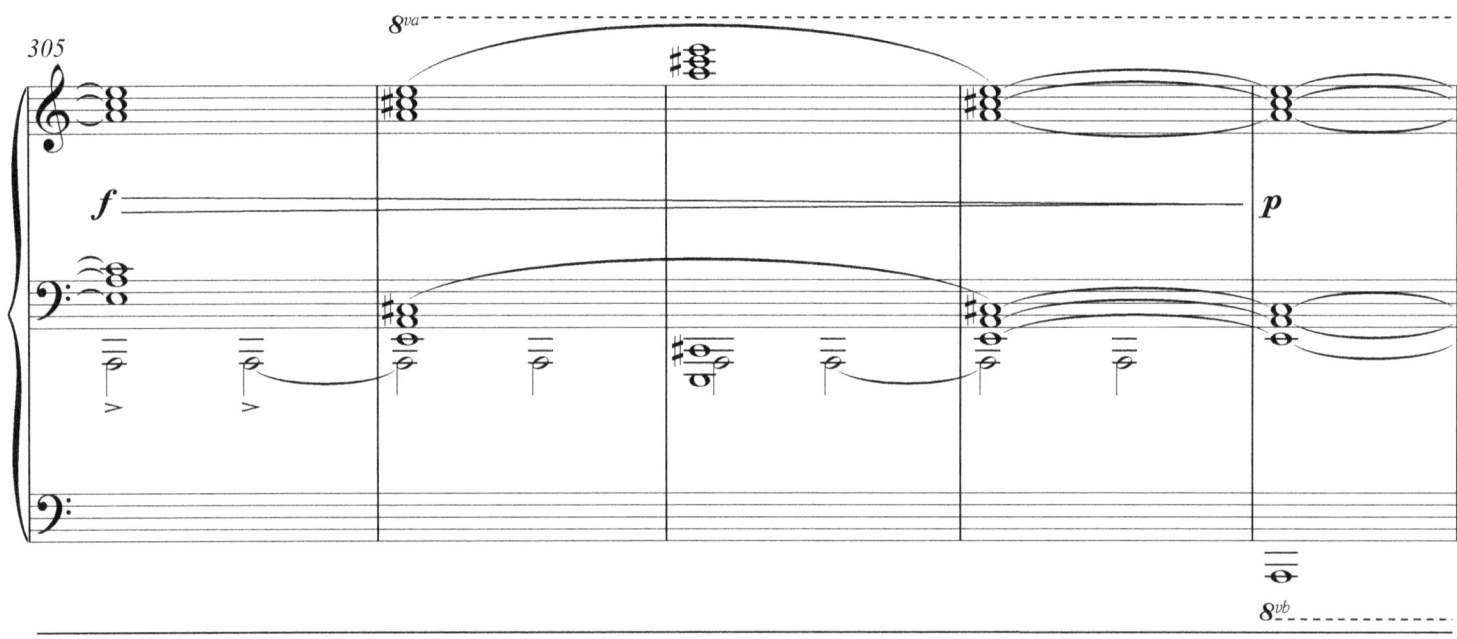
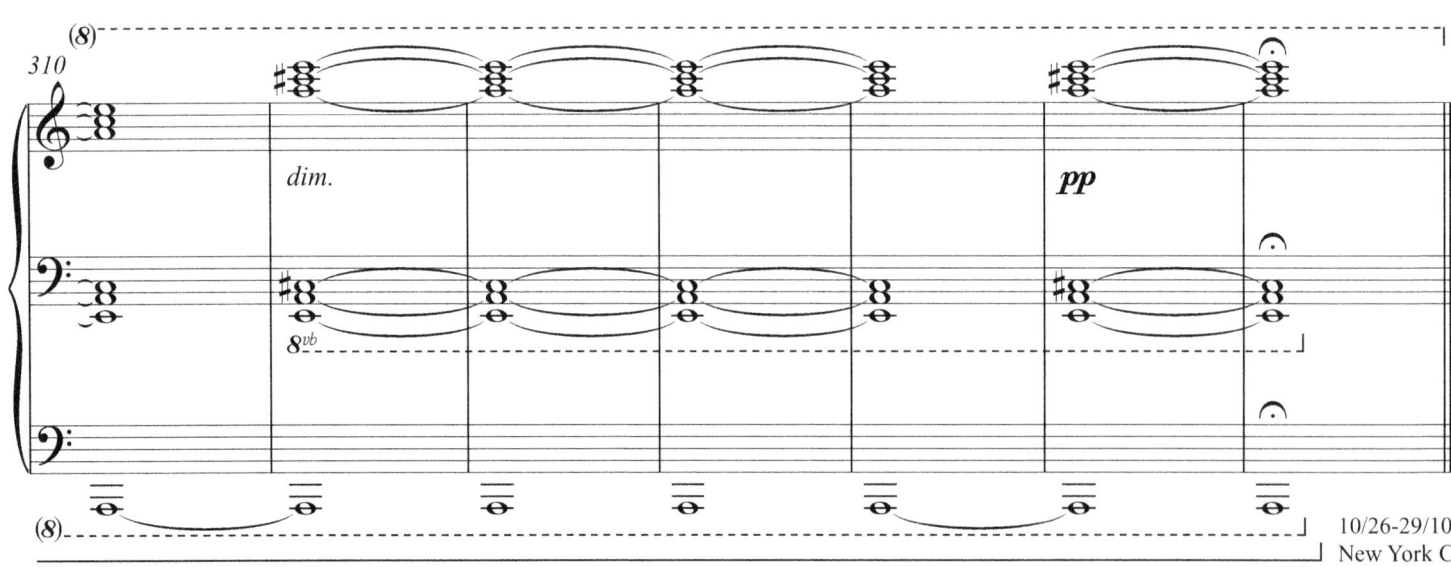

10/26-29/10
New York City

for Ray Warman

LATE IN THE GAME

I. Farewell, R.W.

DAVID DEL TREDICI
(2009, rev. 2015)

© Copyright 2016 by Boosey & Hawkes, Inc.
International copyright secured. All rights reserved.

(Revised January 2016)

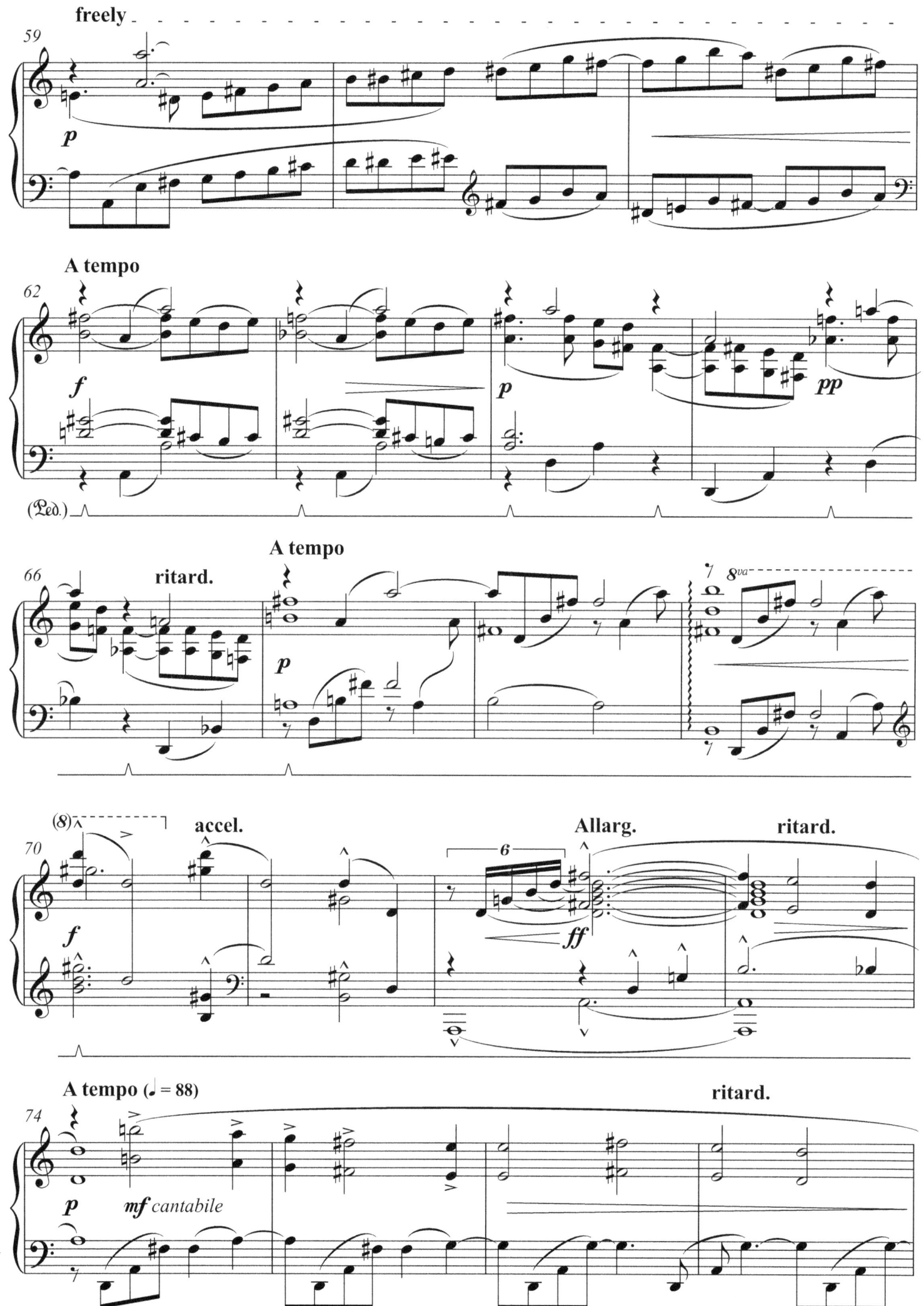

Late in the Game

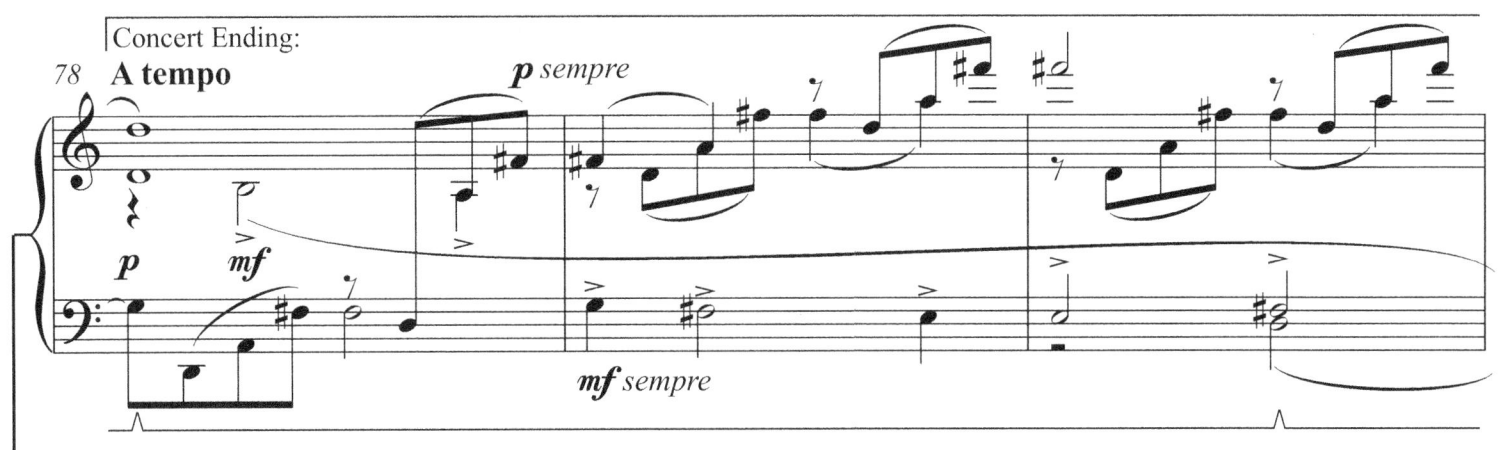

Concert Ending:

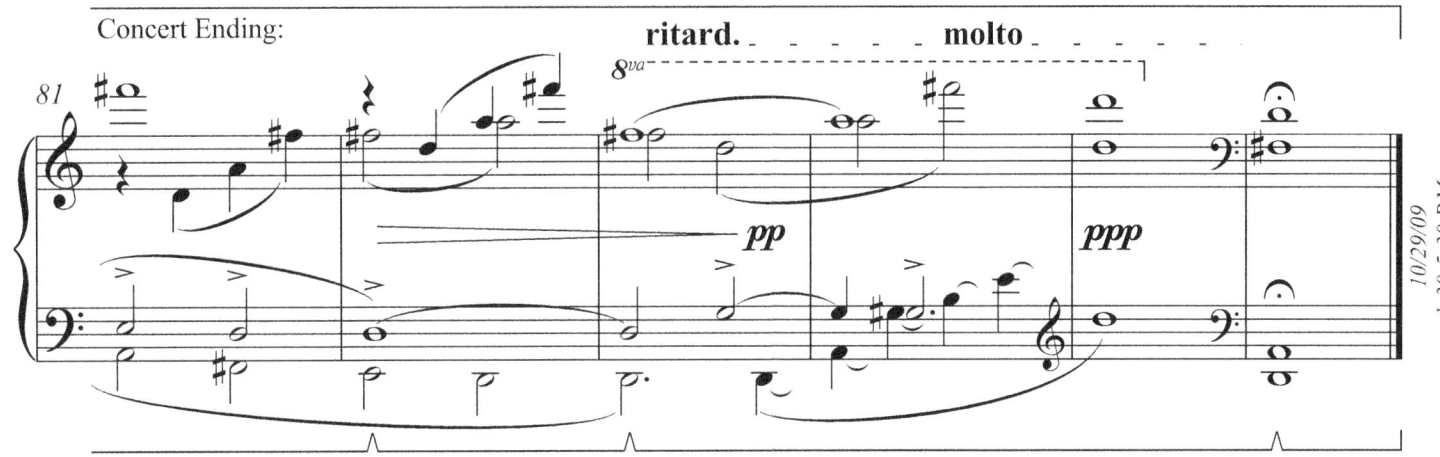

Concert Ending:

Continuation:

10/29/09
1:30-5:30 P.M.

for Drew
II. Gloss
(a gloss on *Prélude d'Ennui* by Drew Paralic)

N.B. ♪ = ♪ (triplet) thus they are played together.

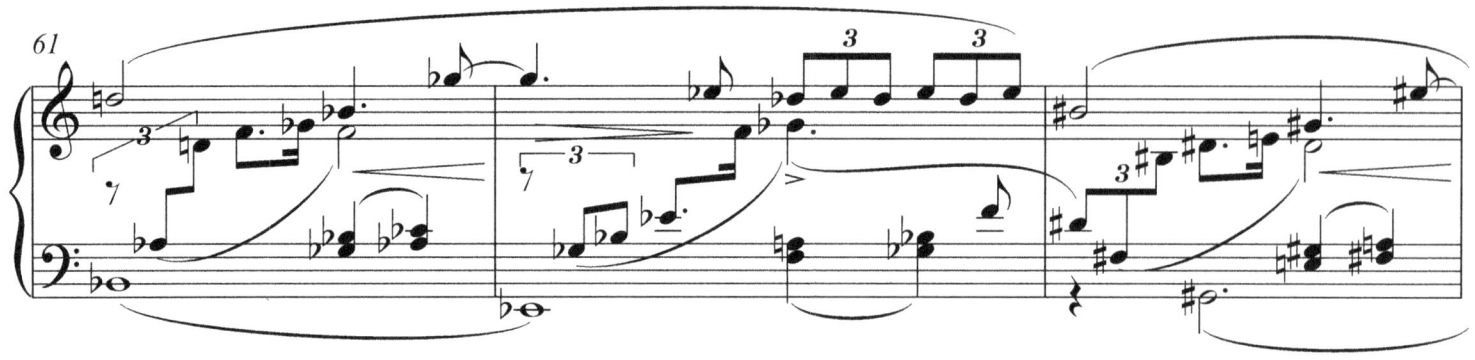
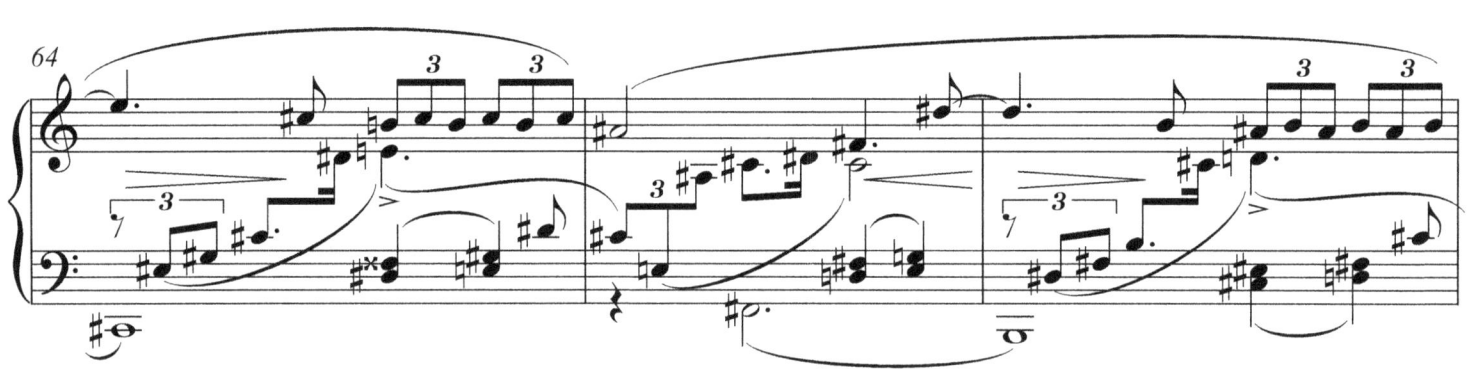
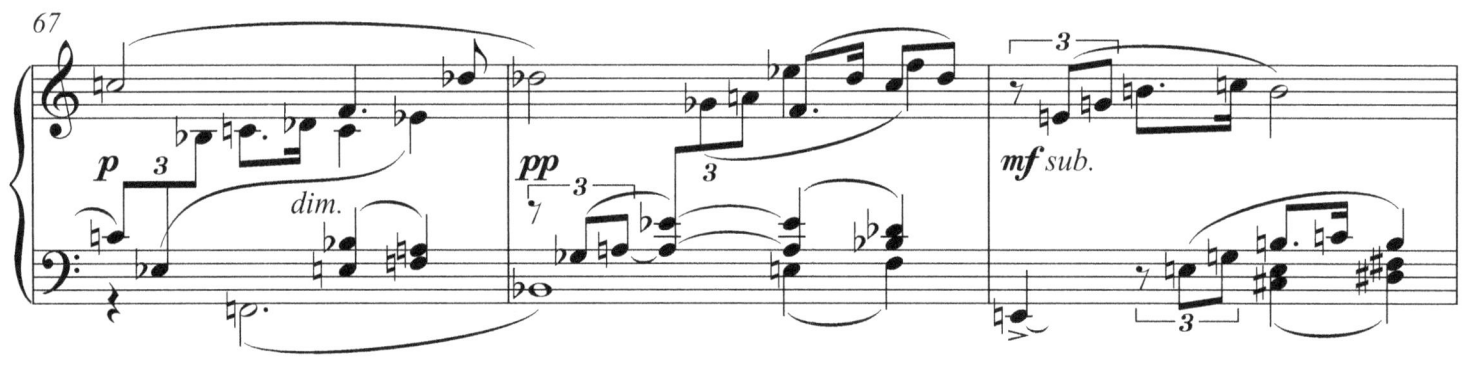

48

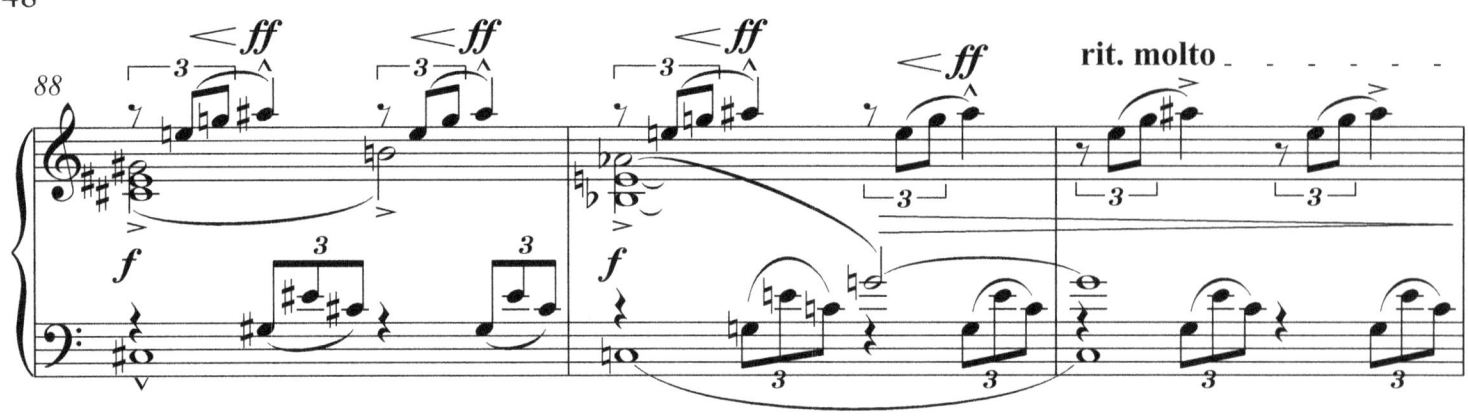

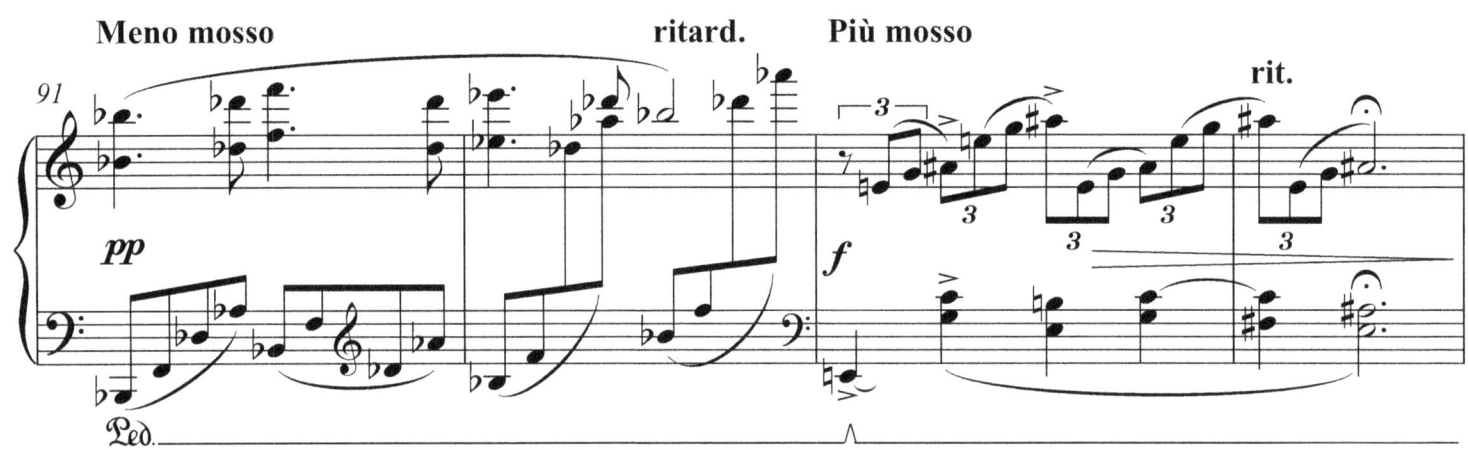

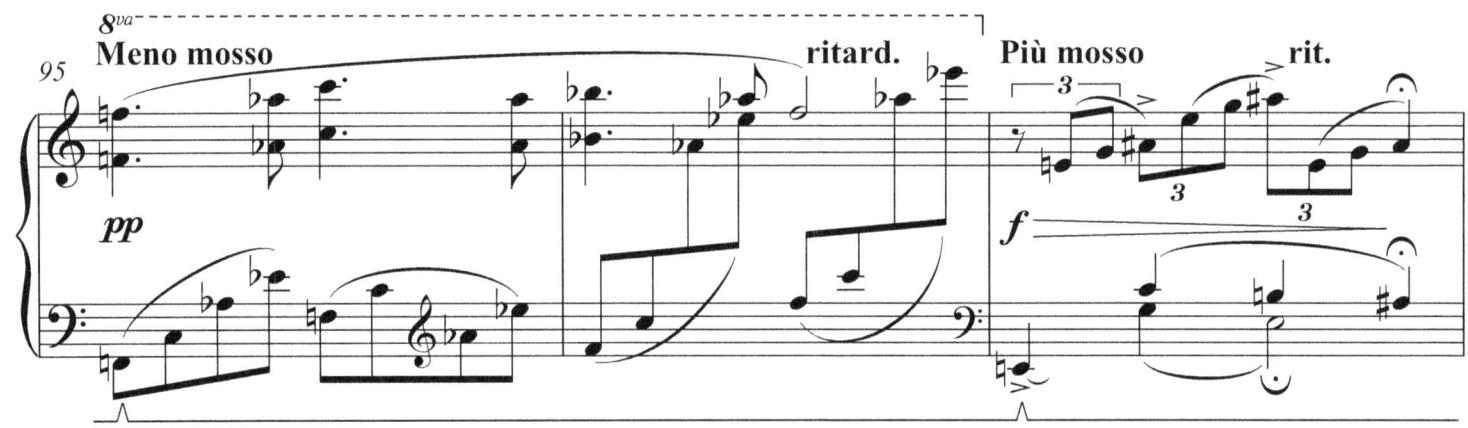

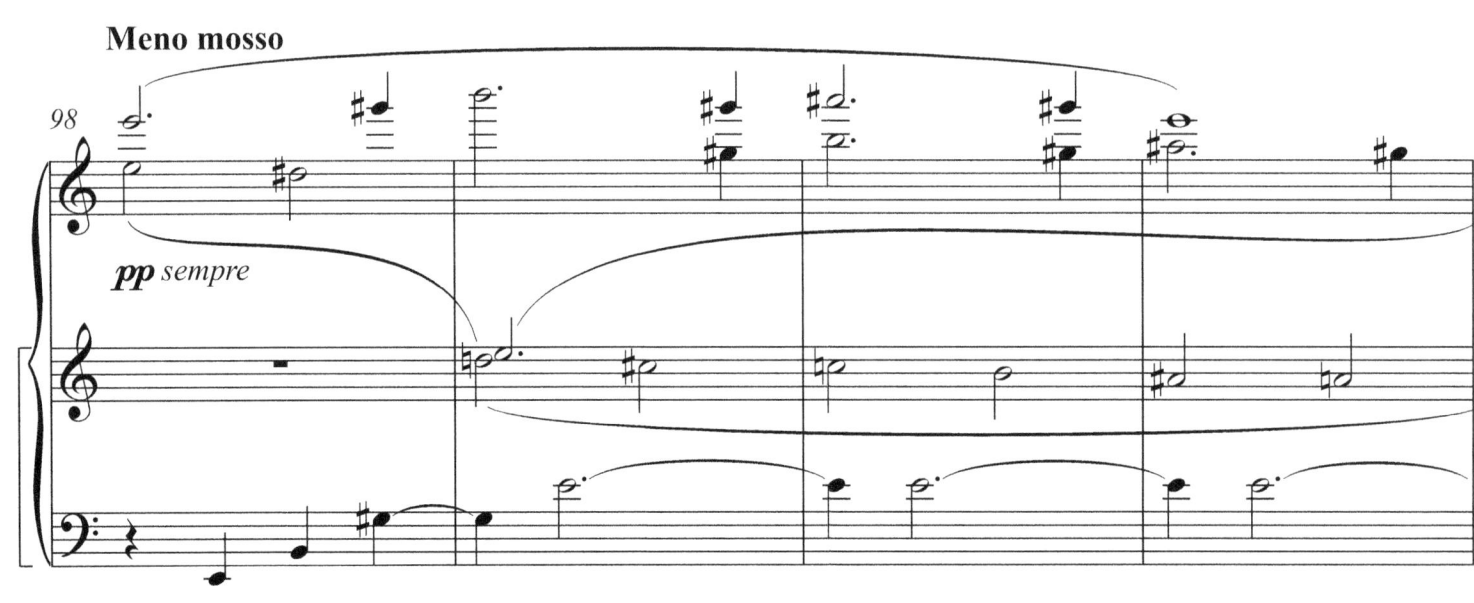

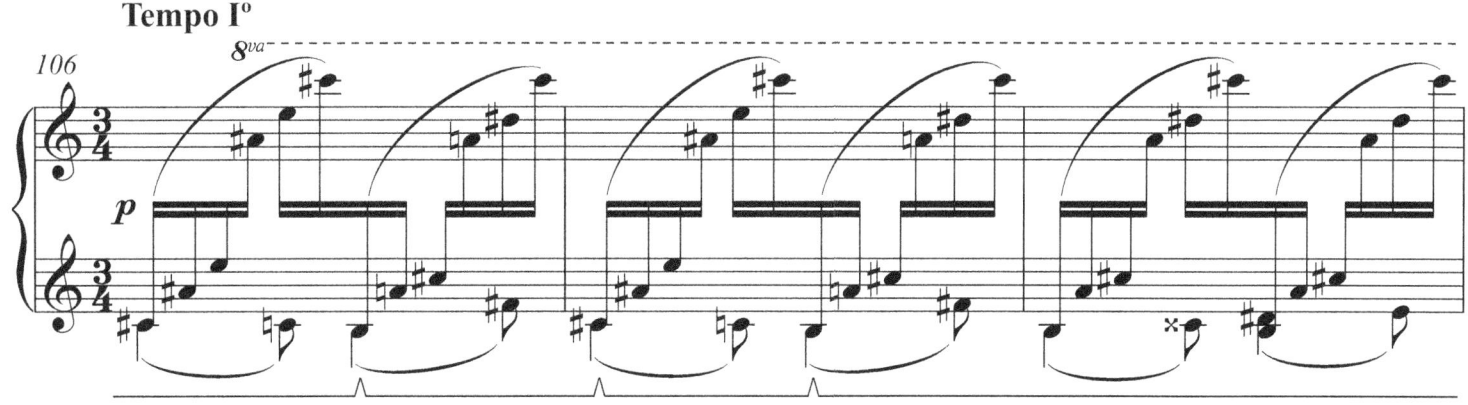
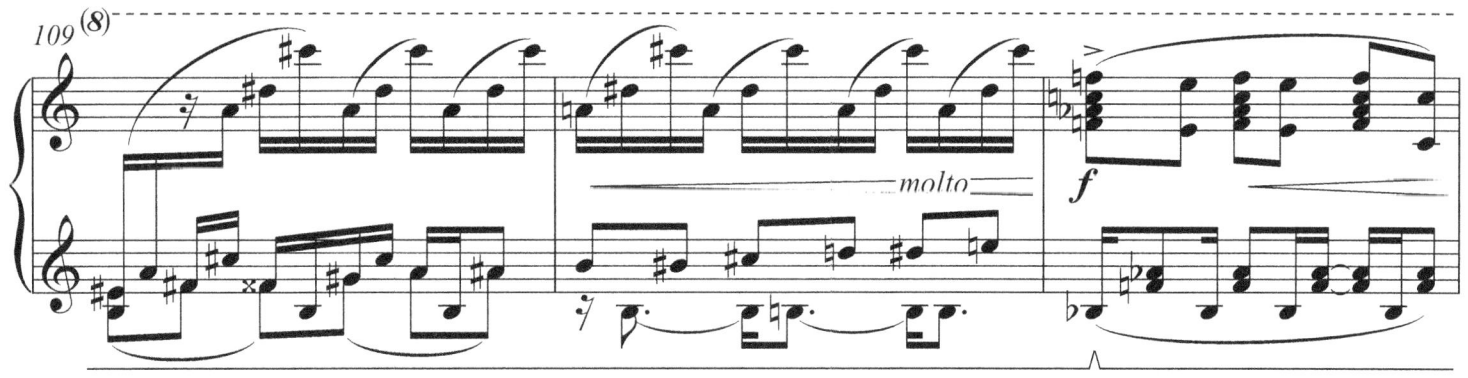
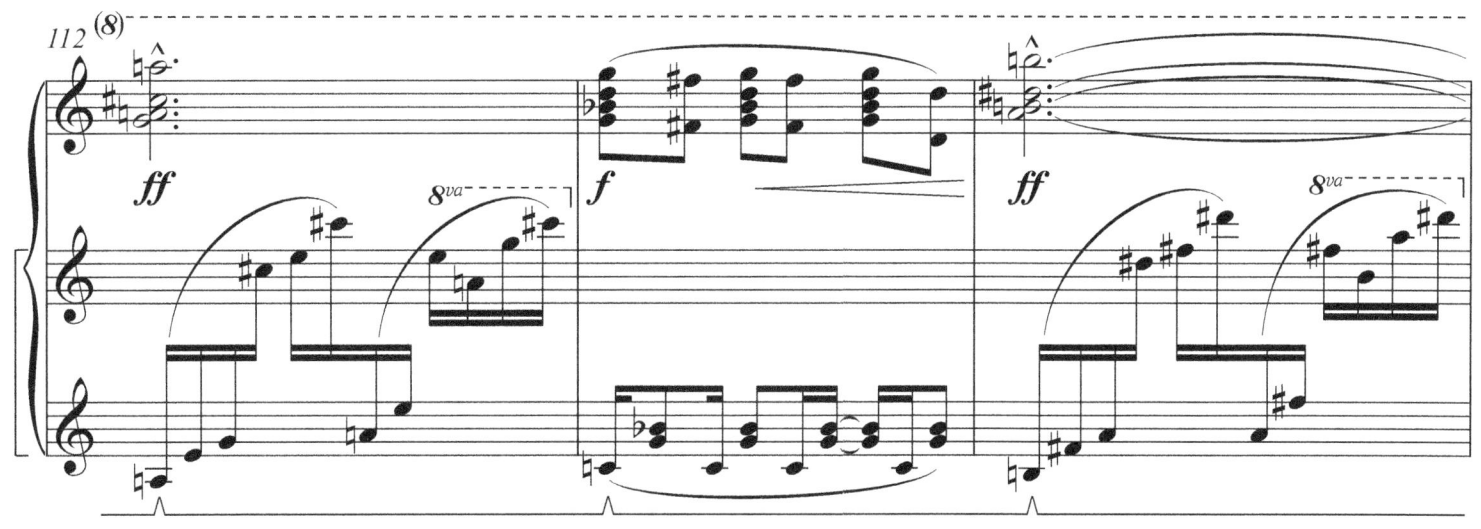

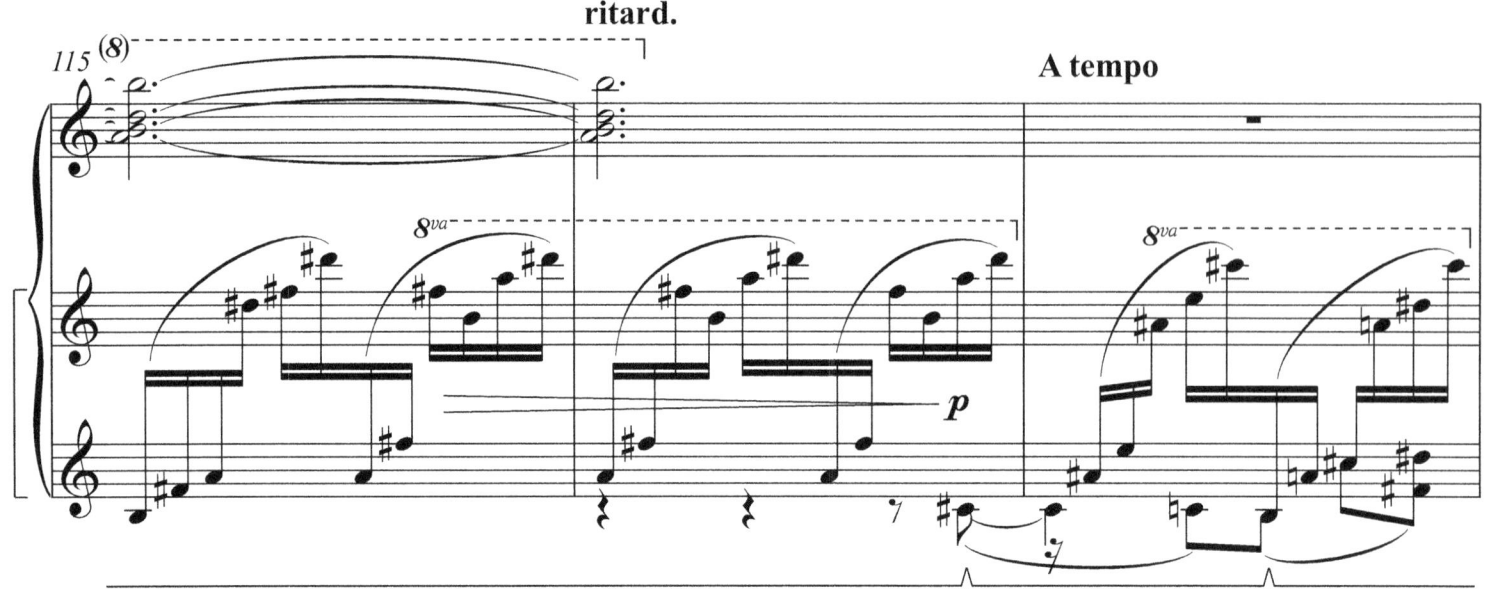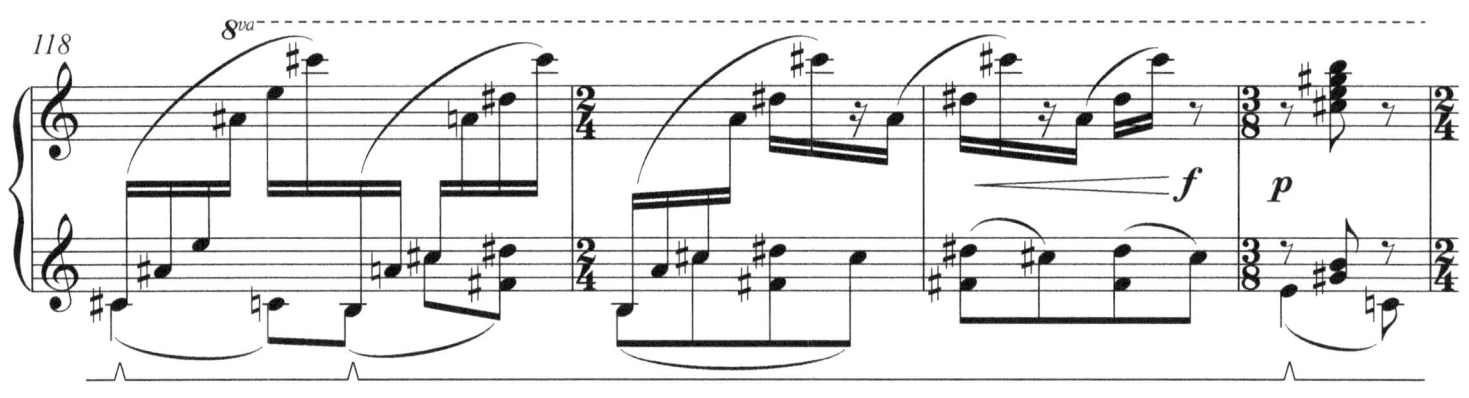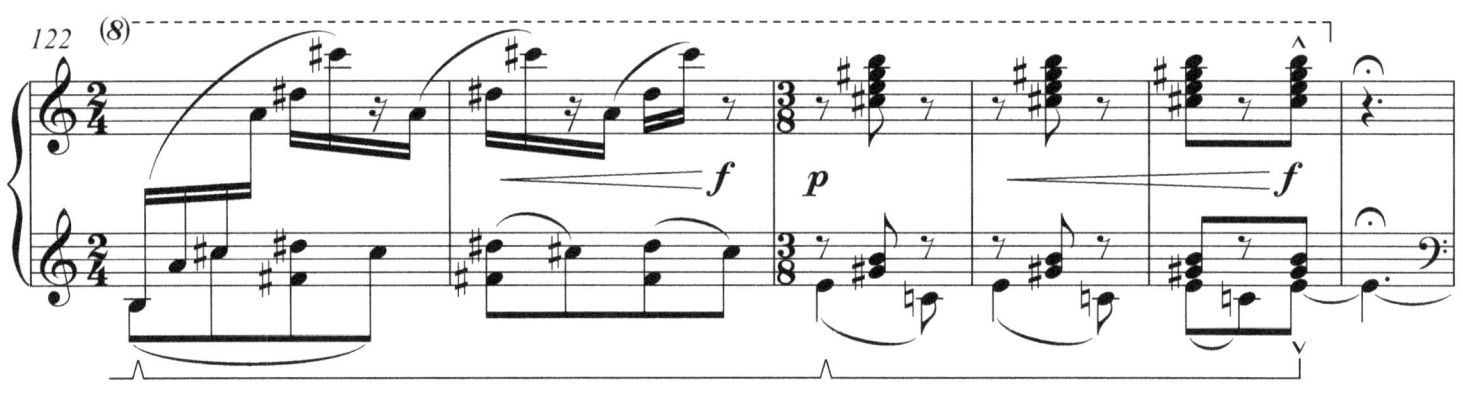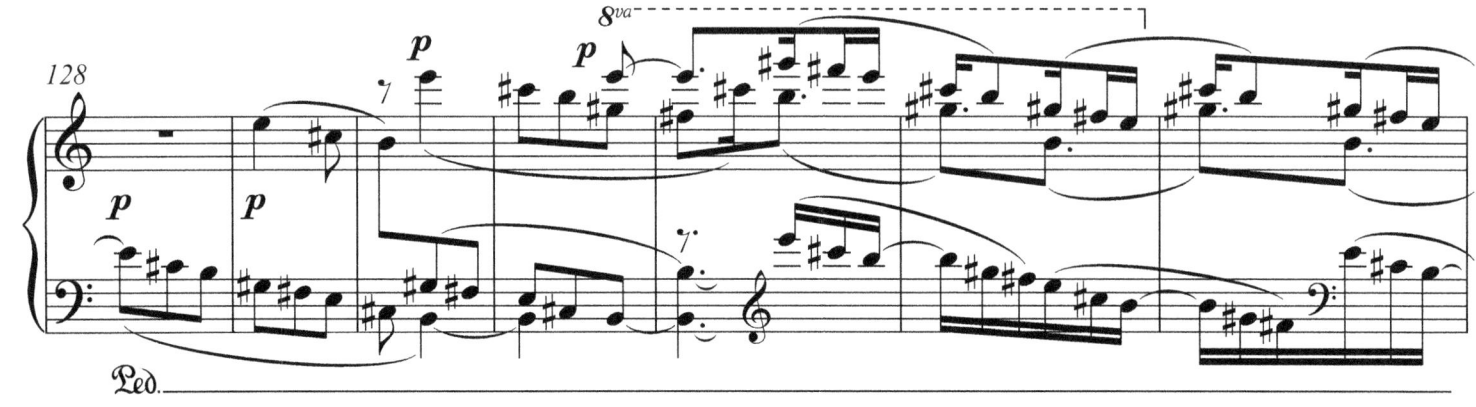

Late in the Game

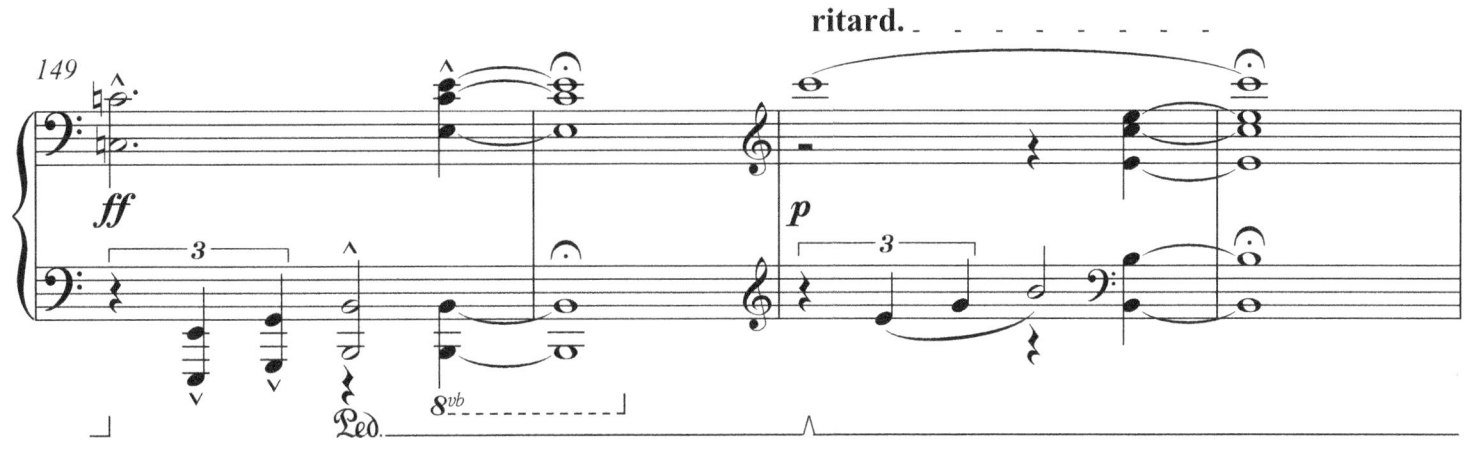

LATE IN THE GAME

In Memoriam: John Dare
Commissioned by and dedicated to Beth Levin, with admiration

III. Bittersweet

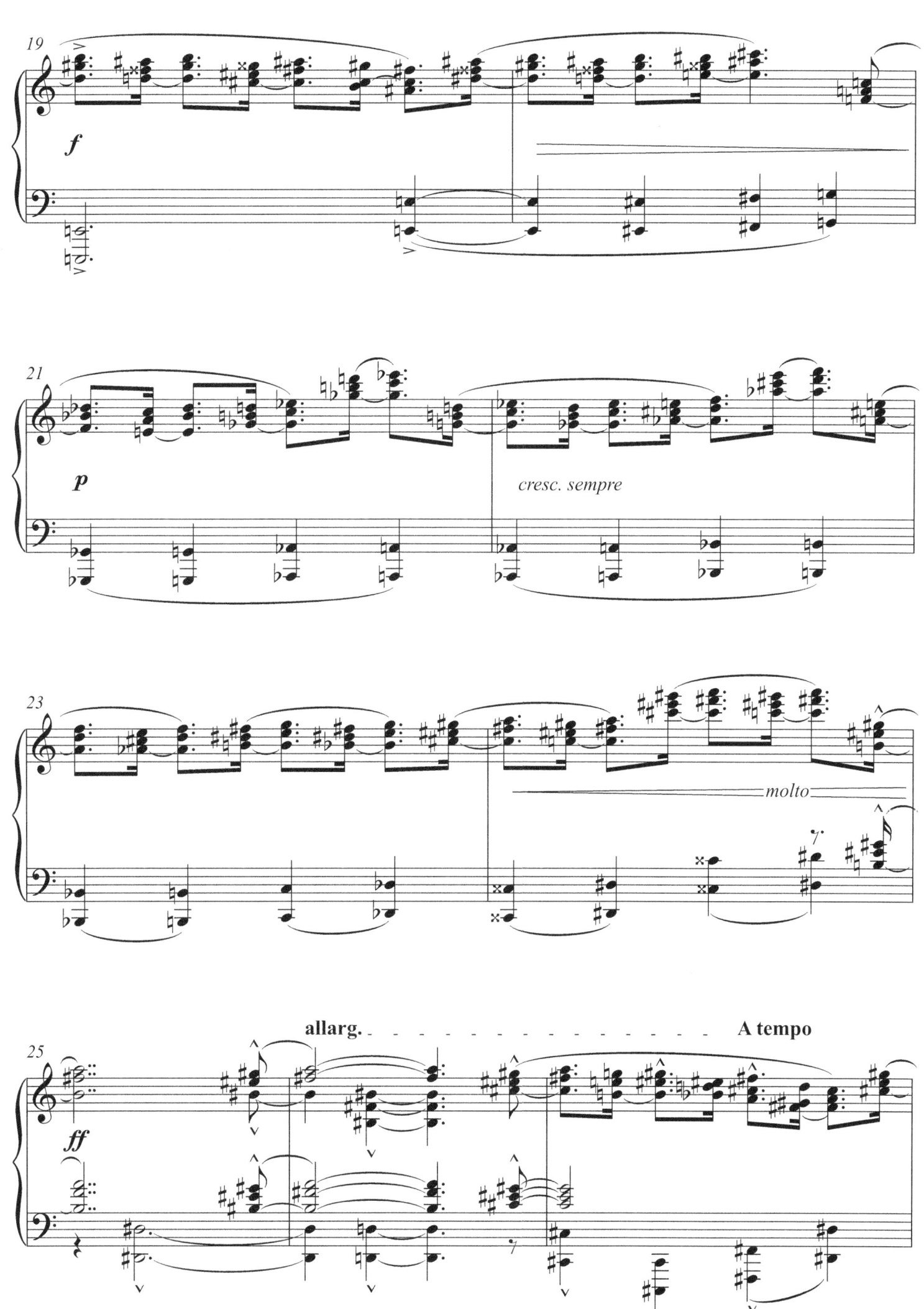

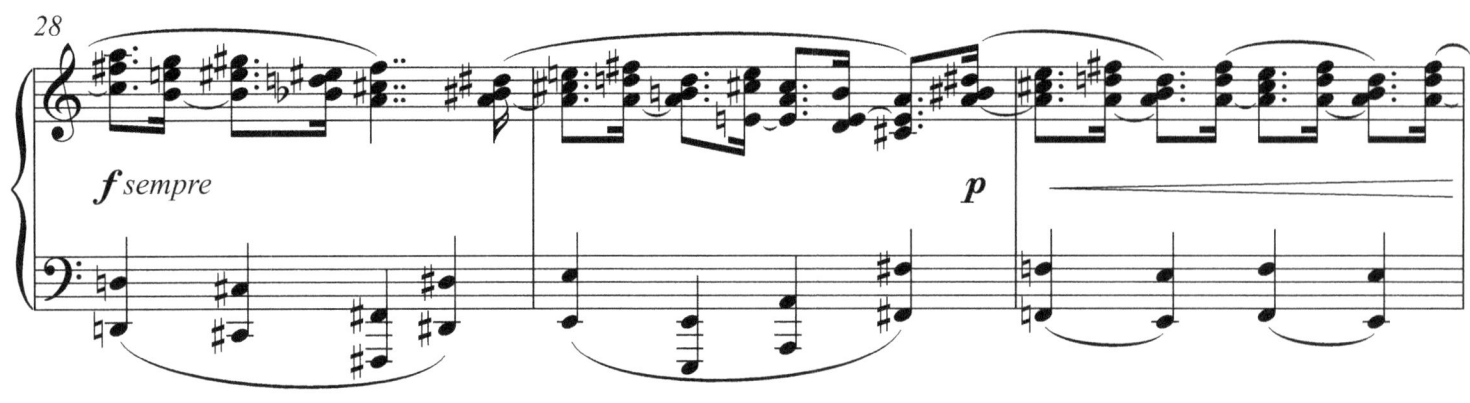
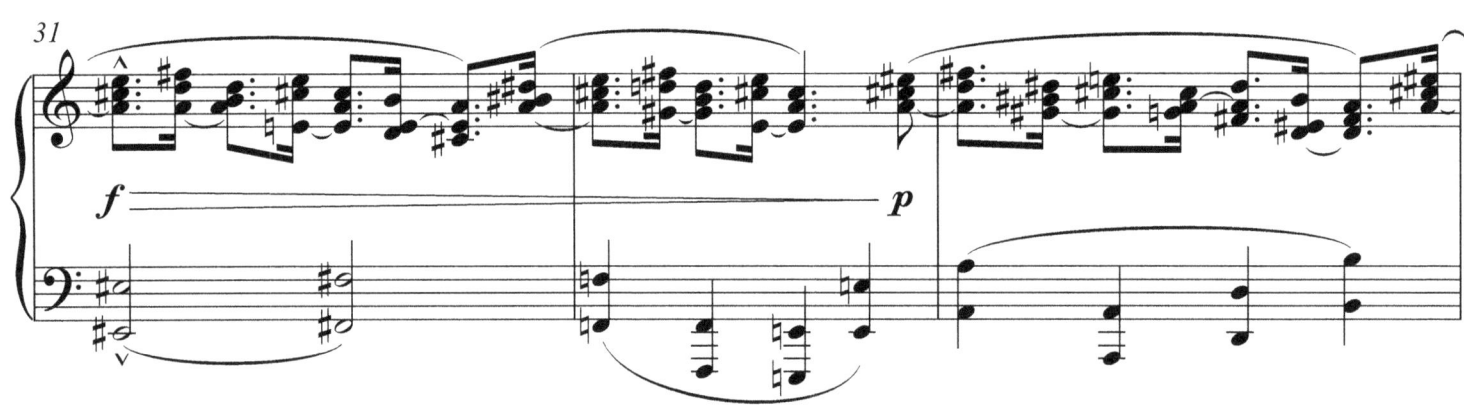

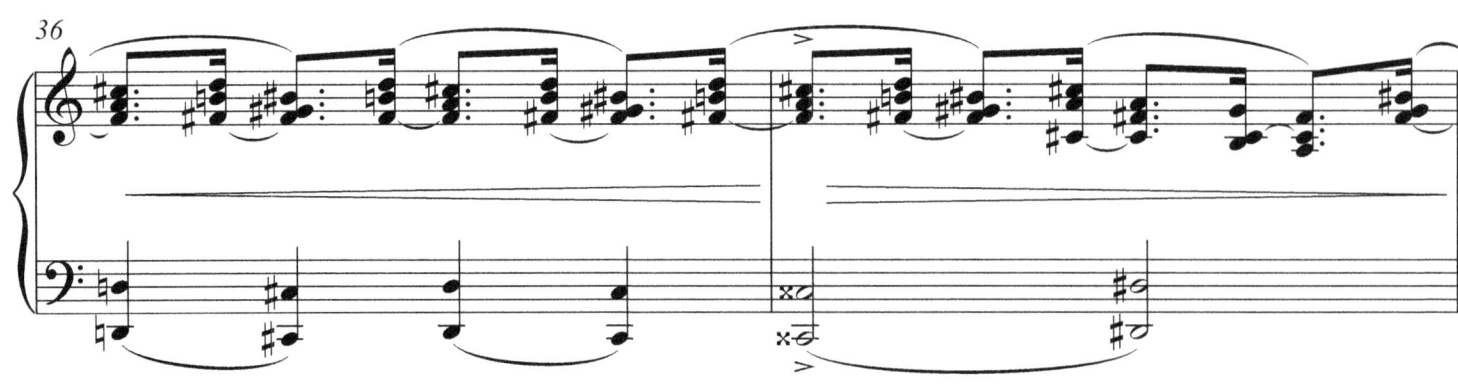

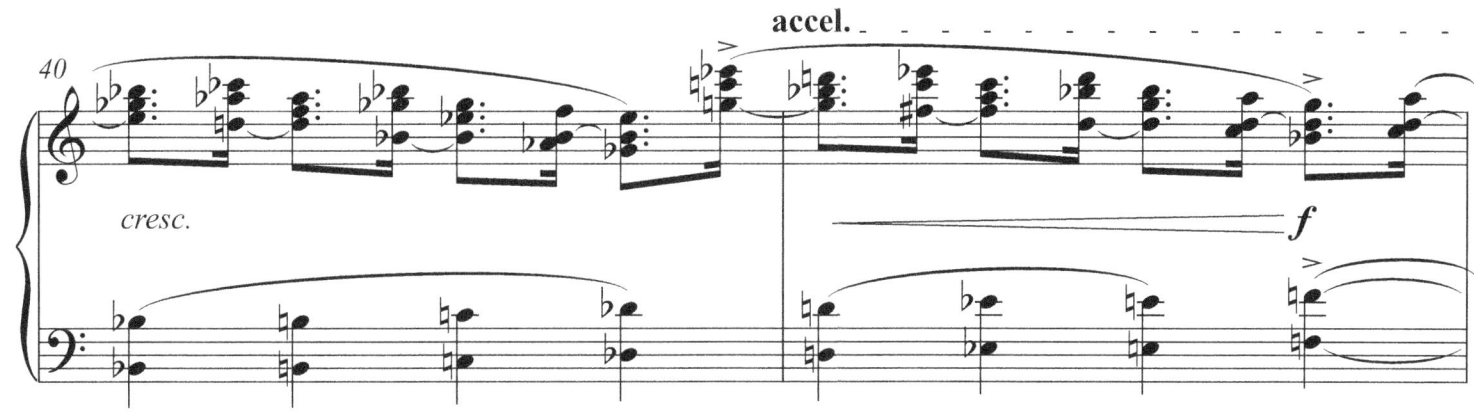
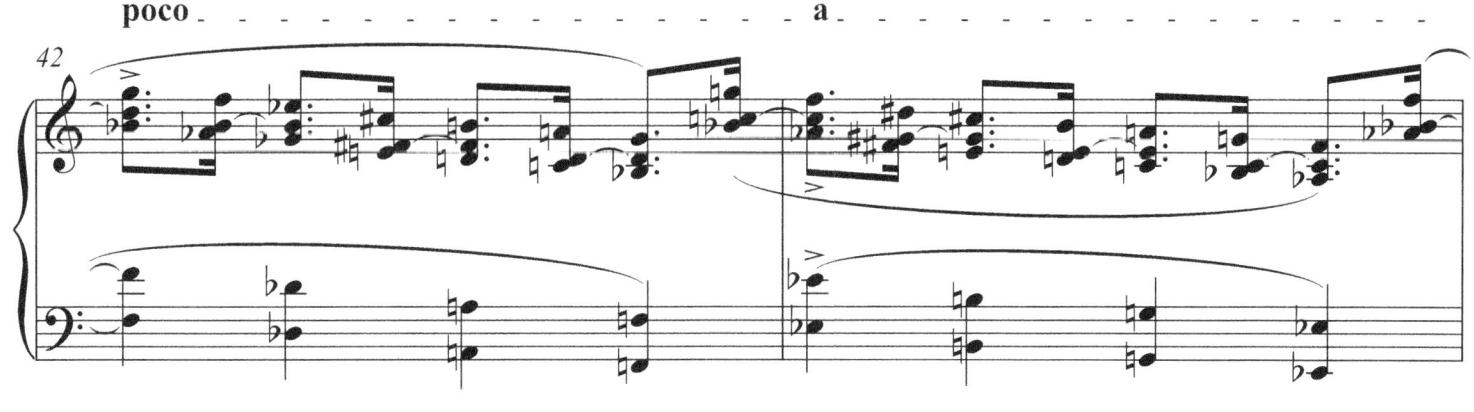

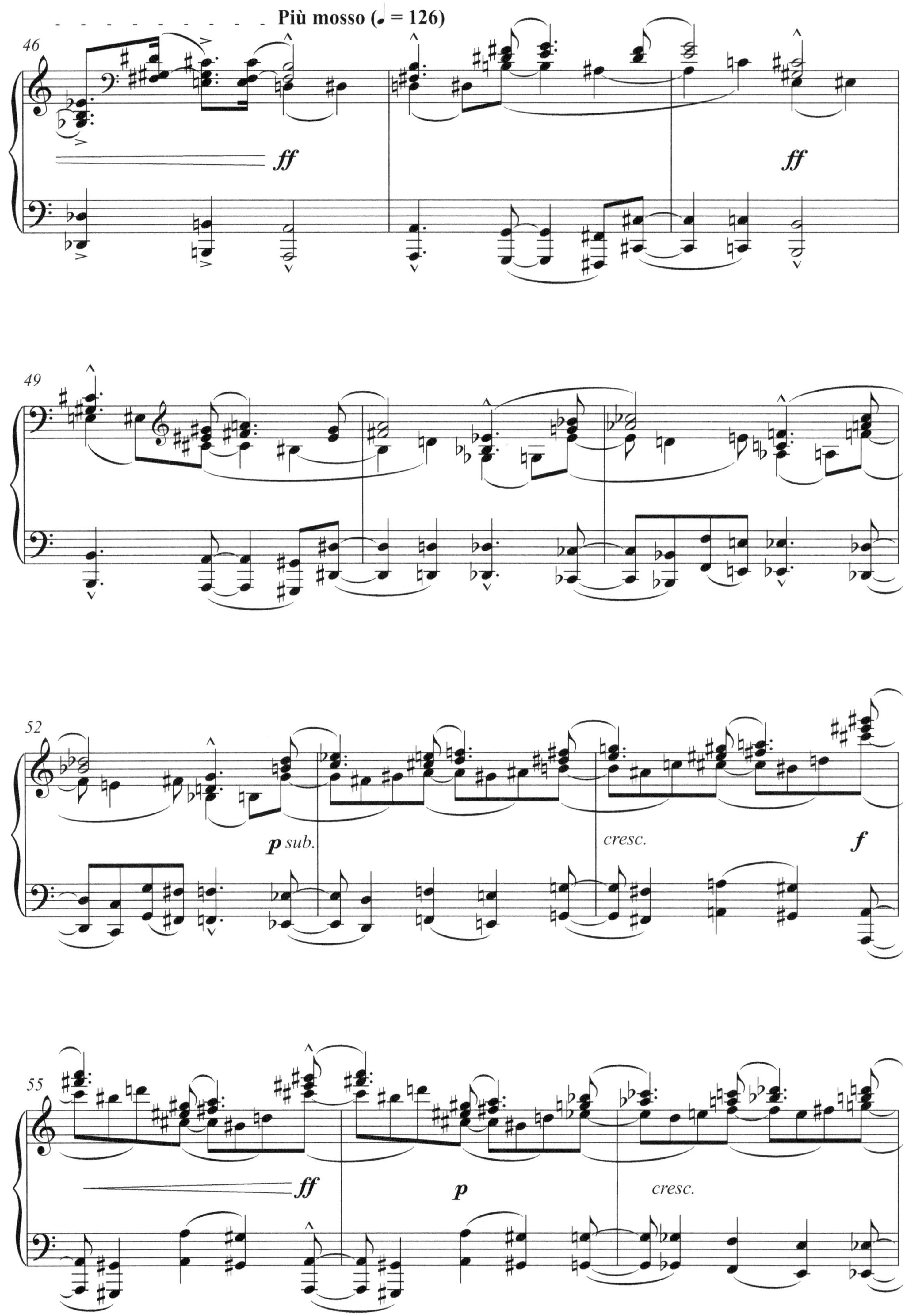
Più mosso (♩ = 126)
46
ff
ff
49
52
p sub.
cresc.
f
55
ff
p
cresc.

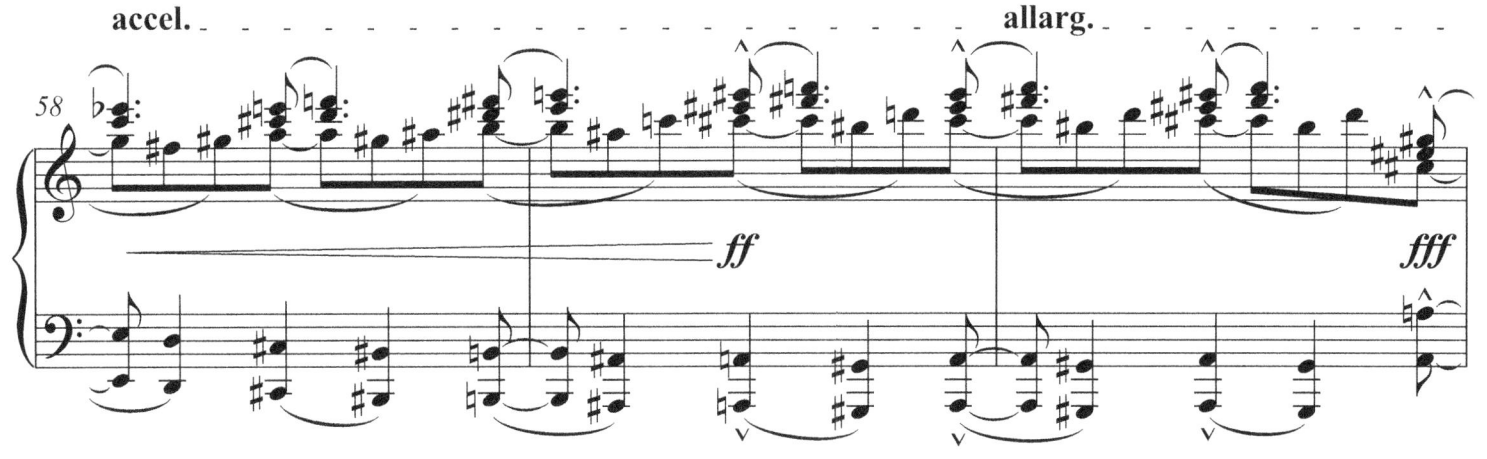

Late in the Game

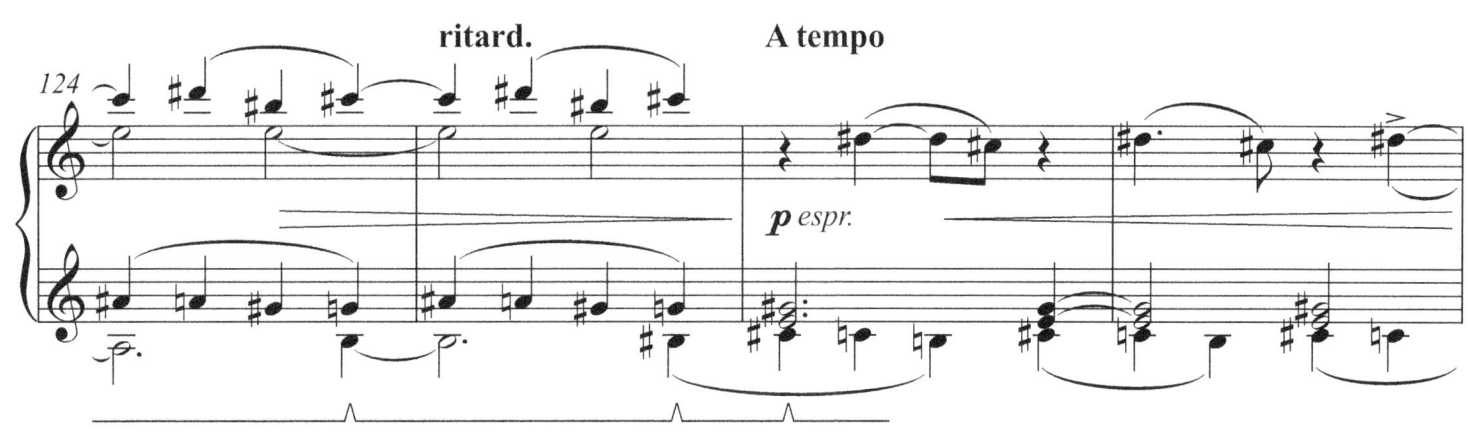

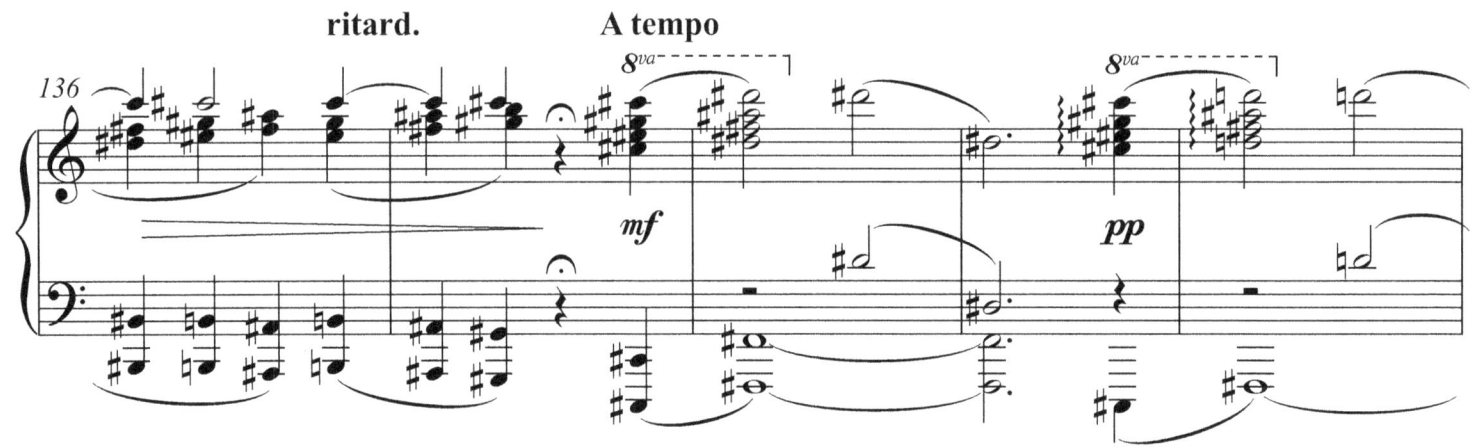
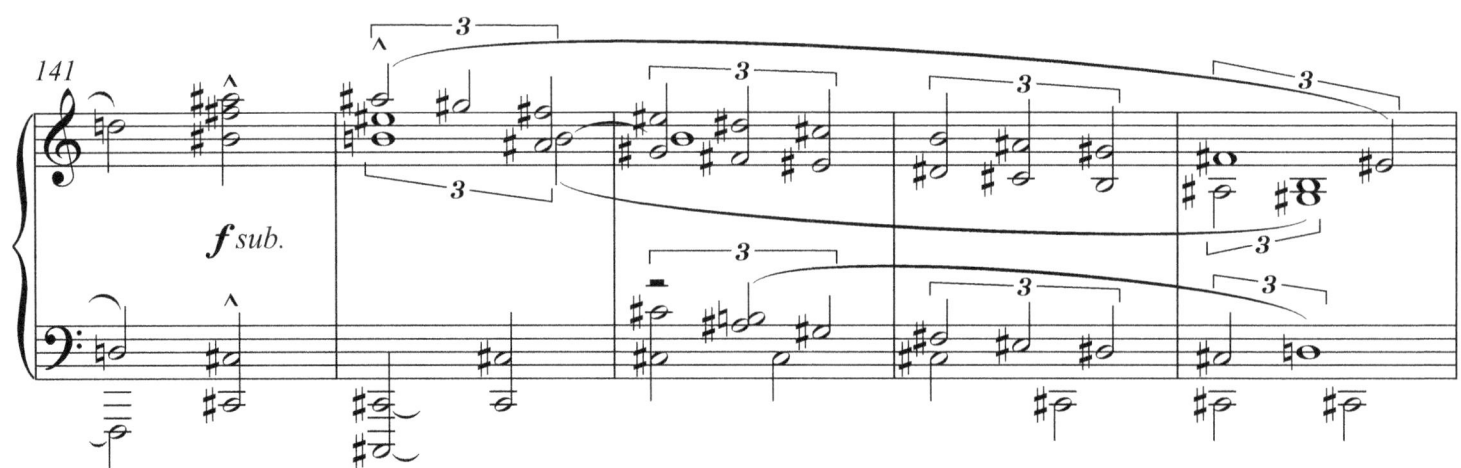

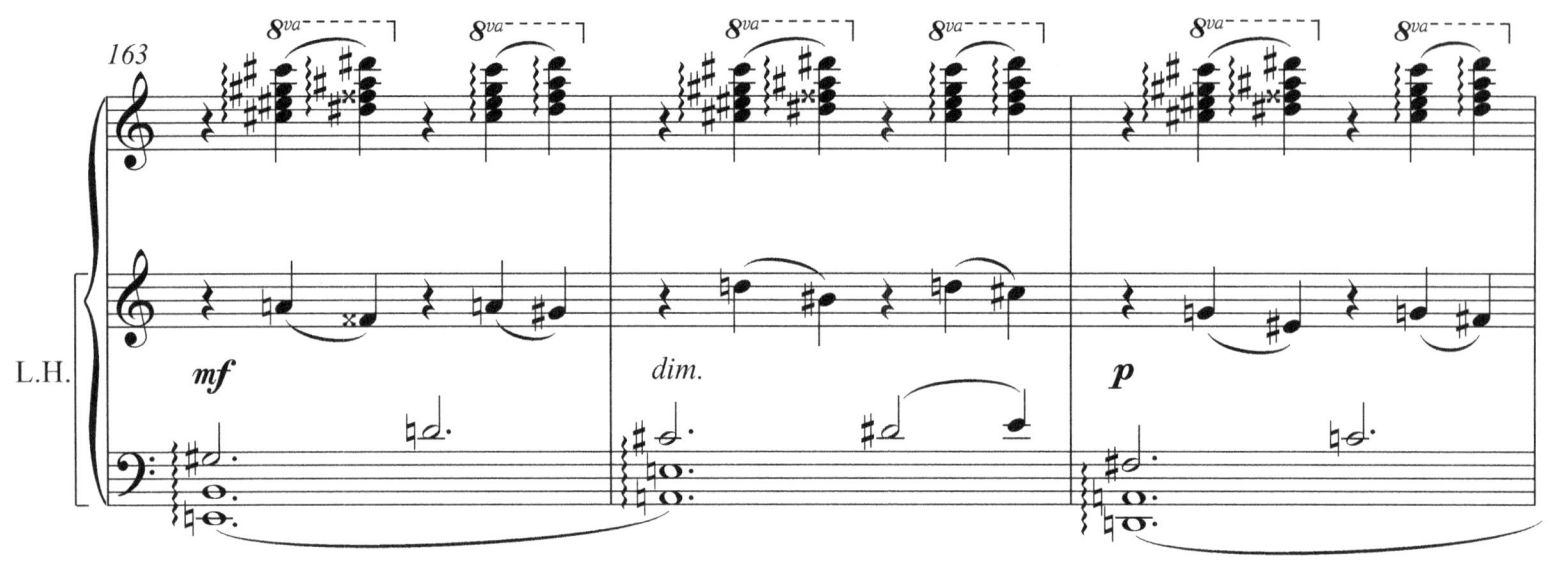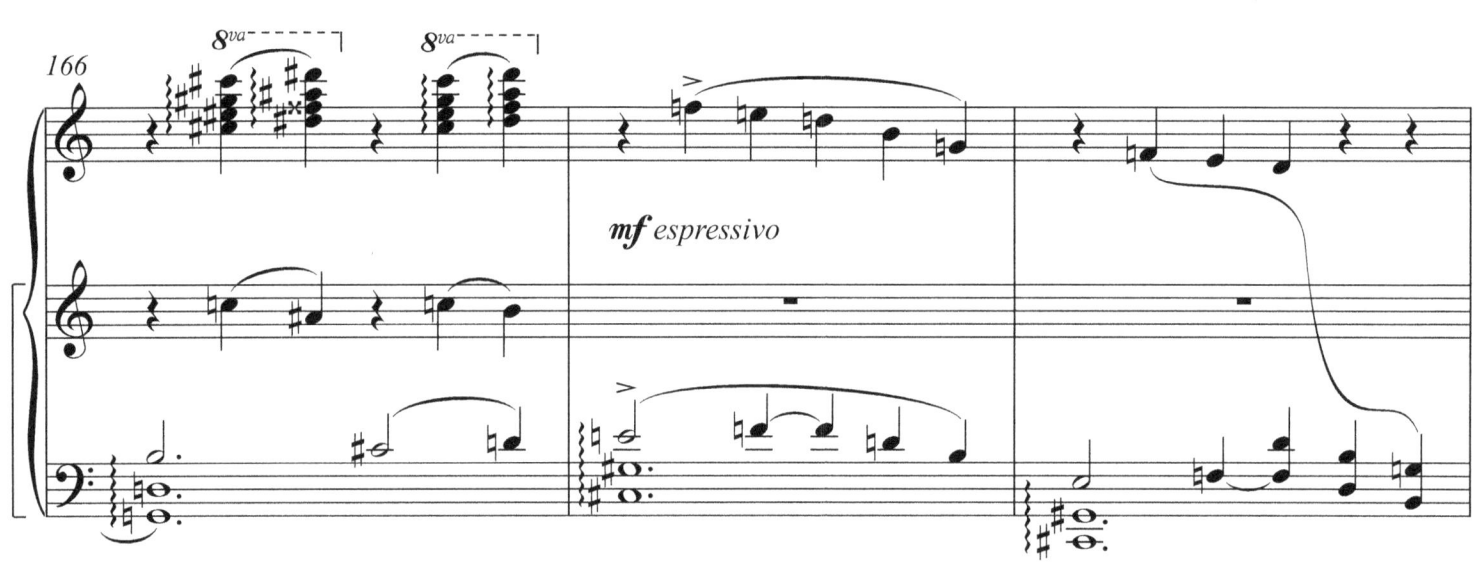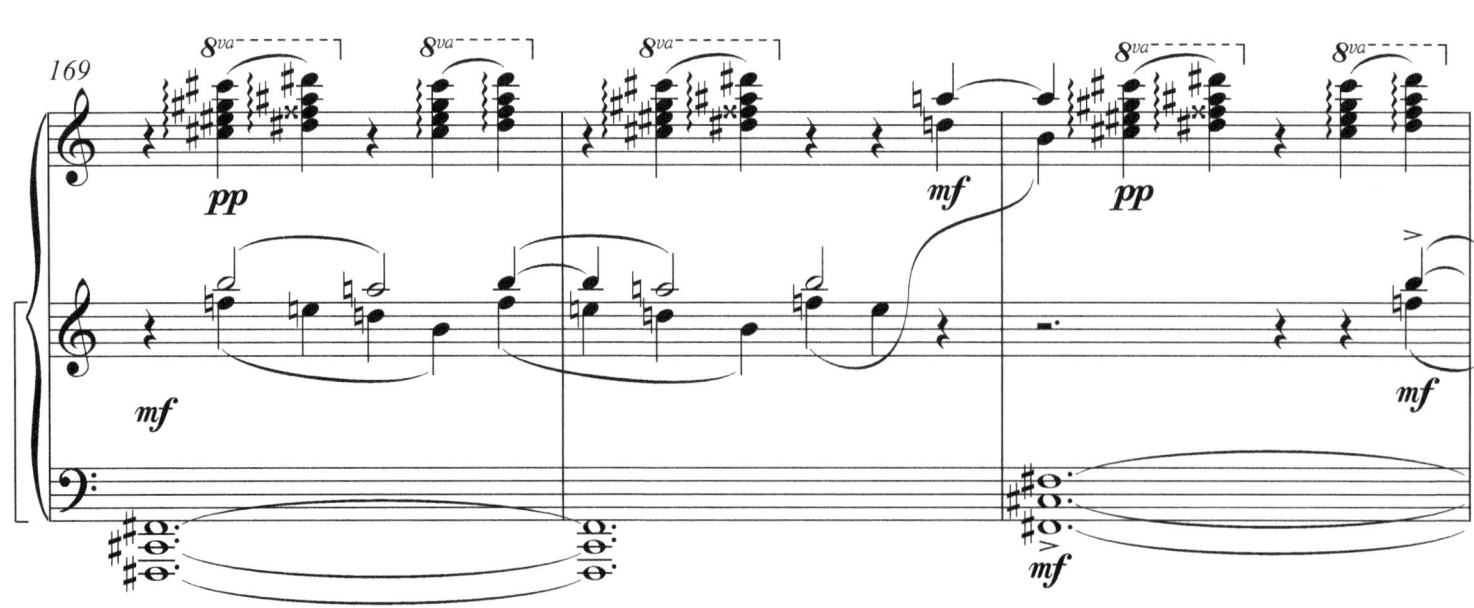

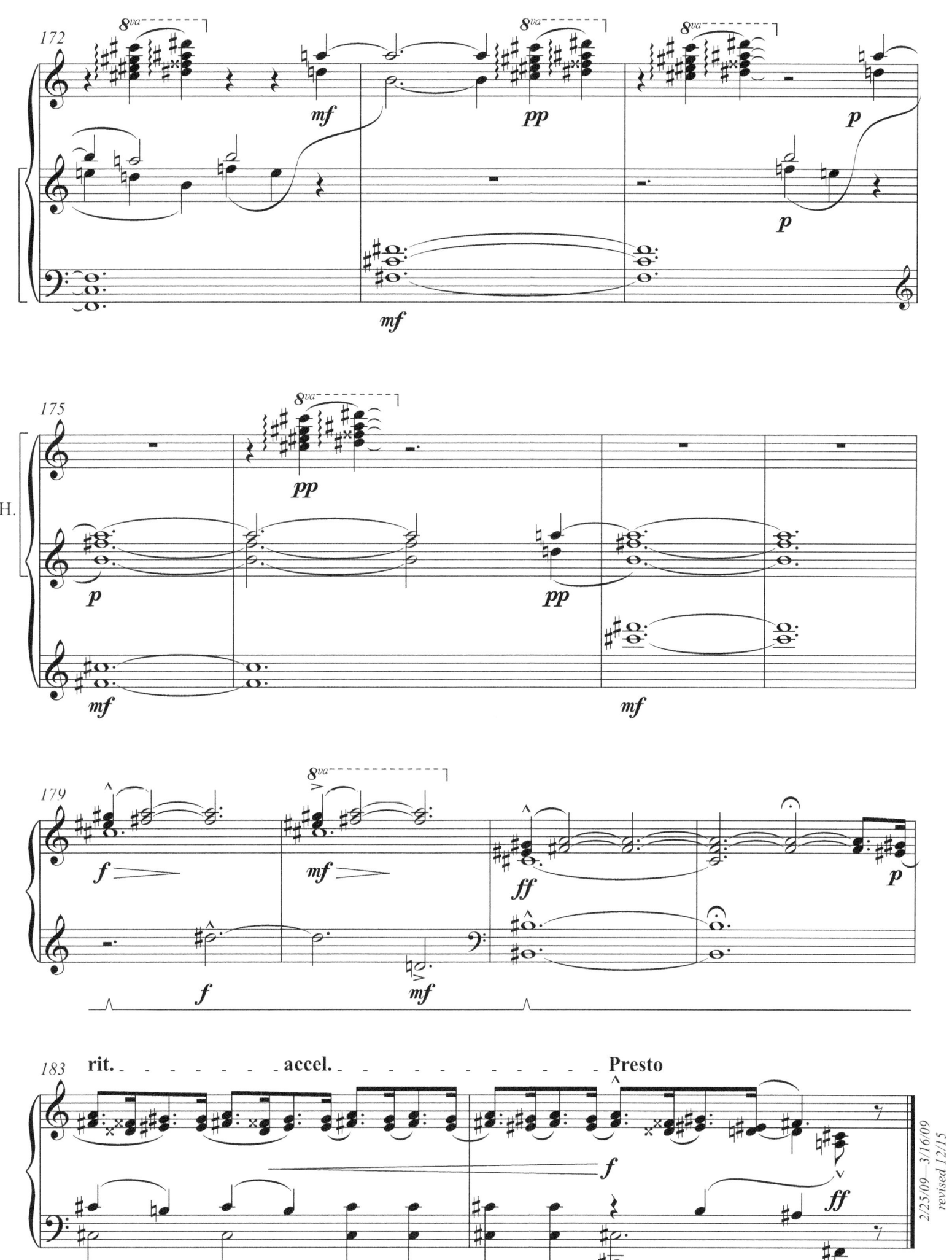

In memoriam: Suzanne Nahalka

IV. Monk

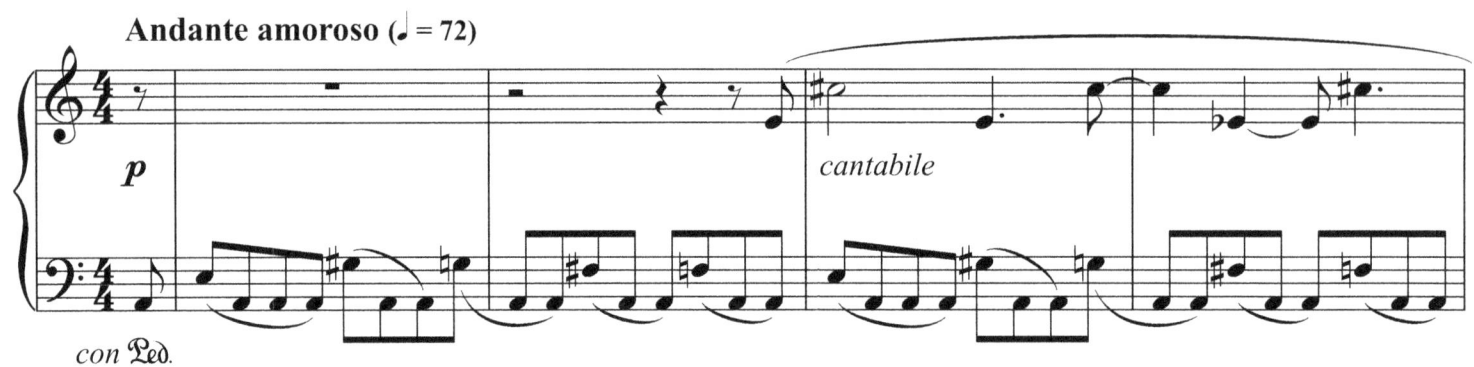

Late in the Game

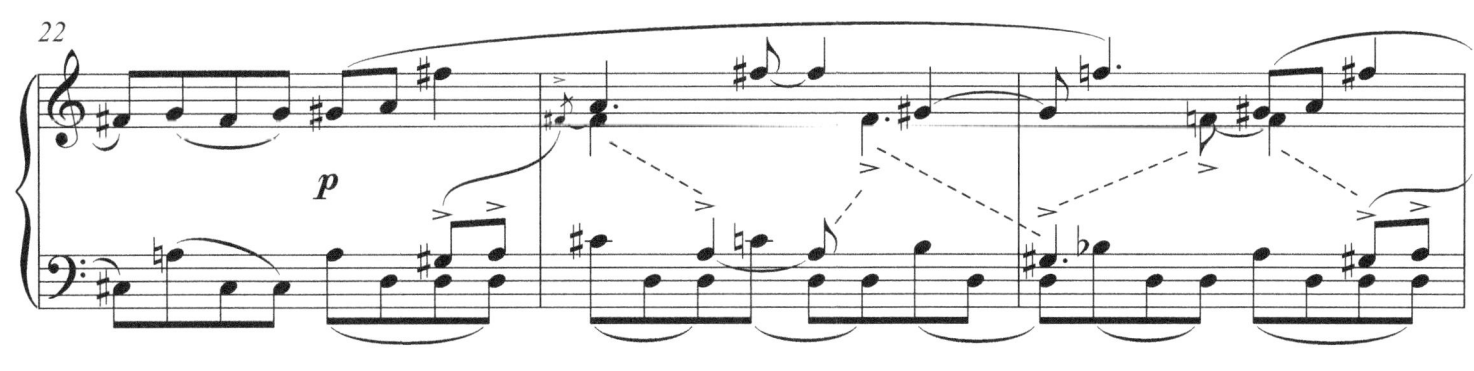
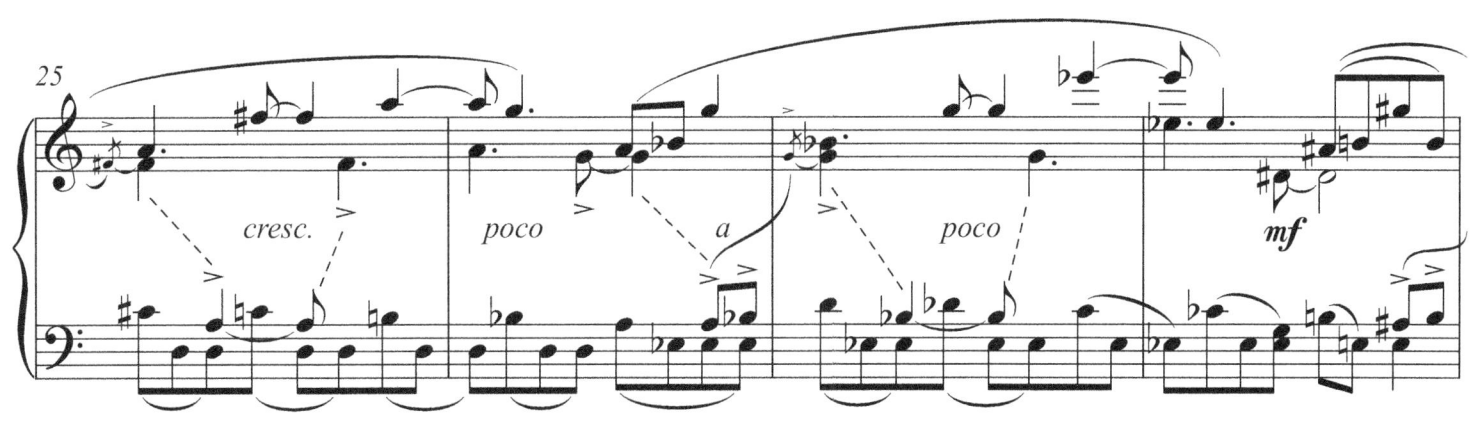

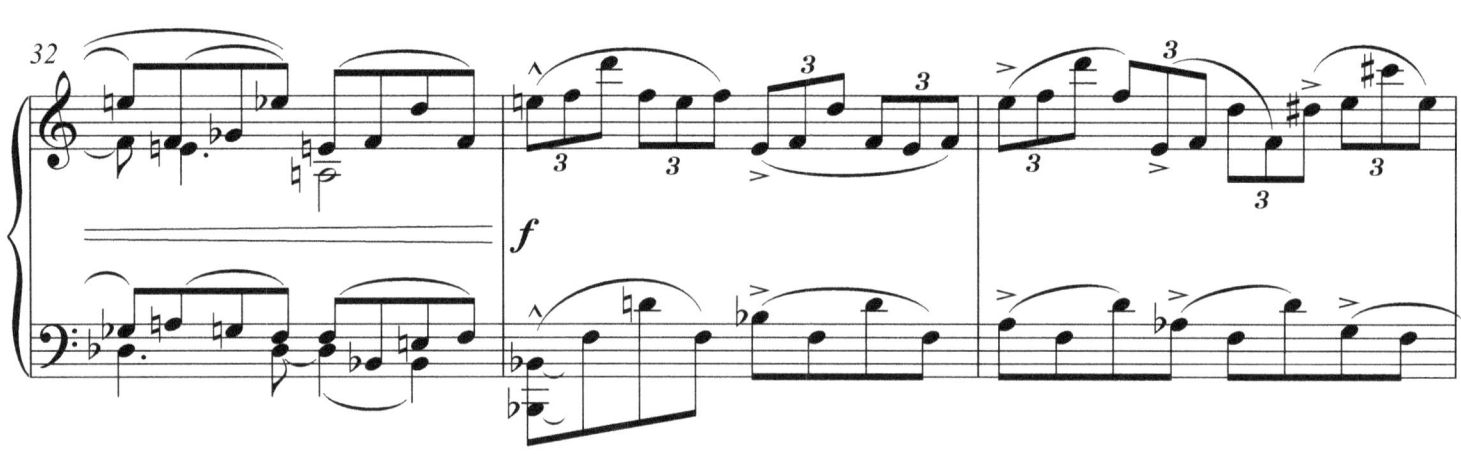
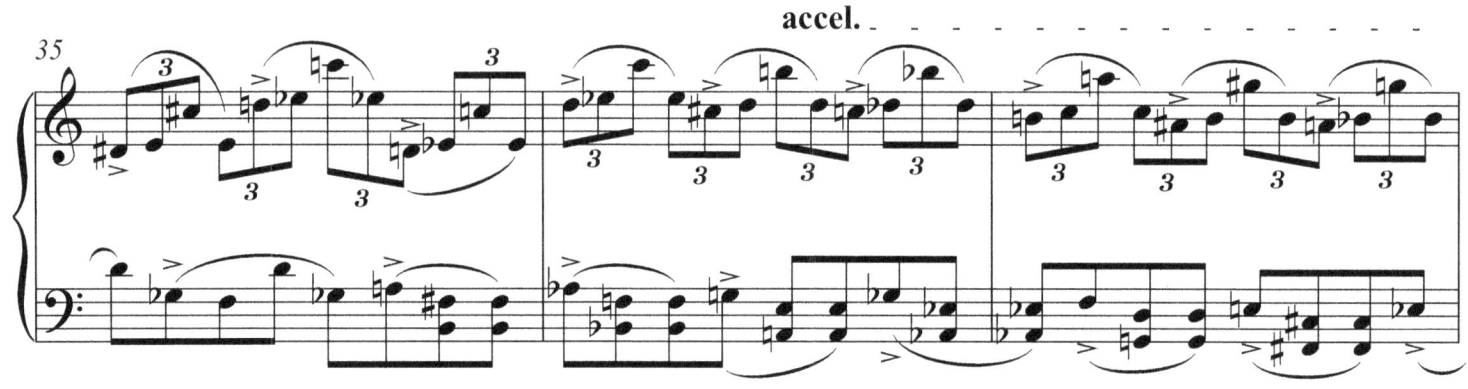

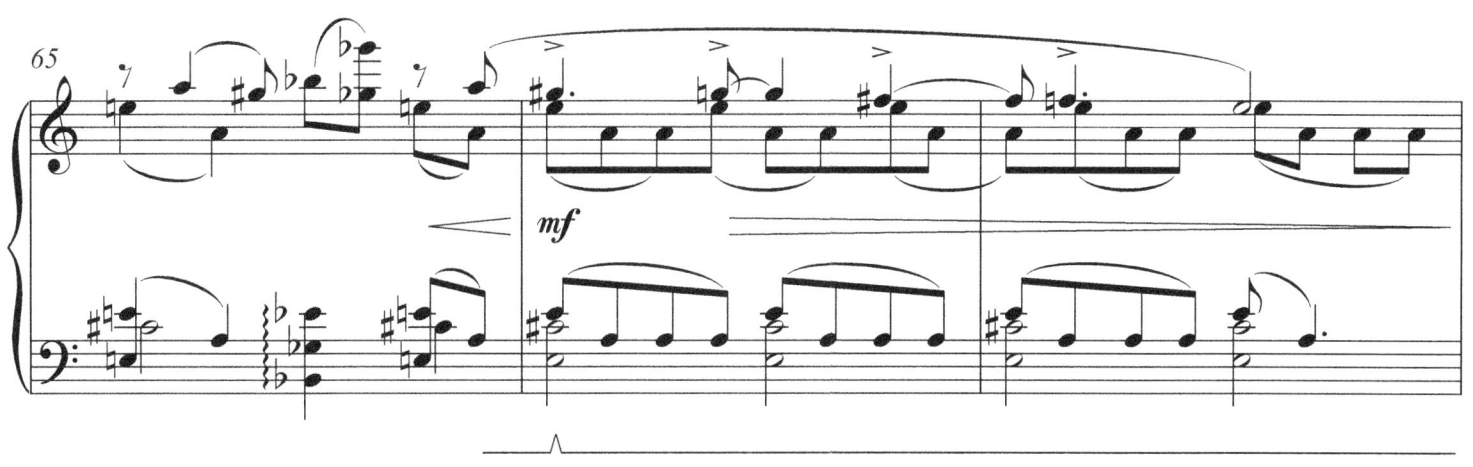

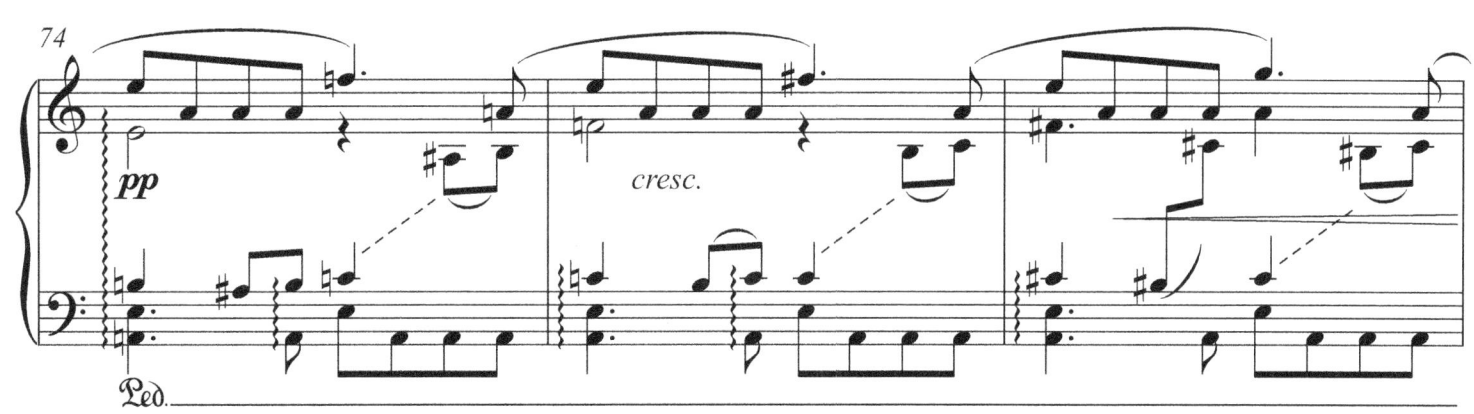

Late in the Game

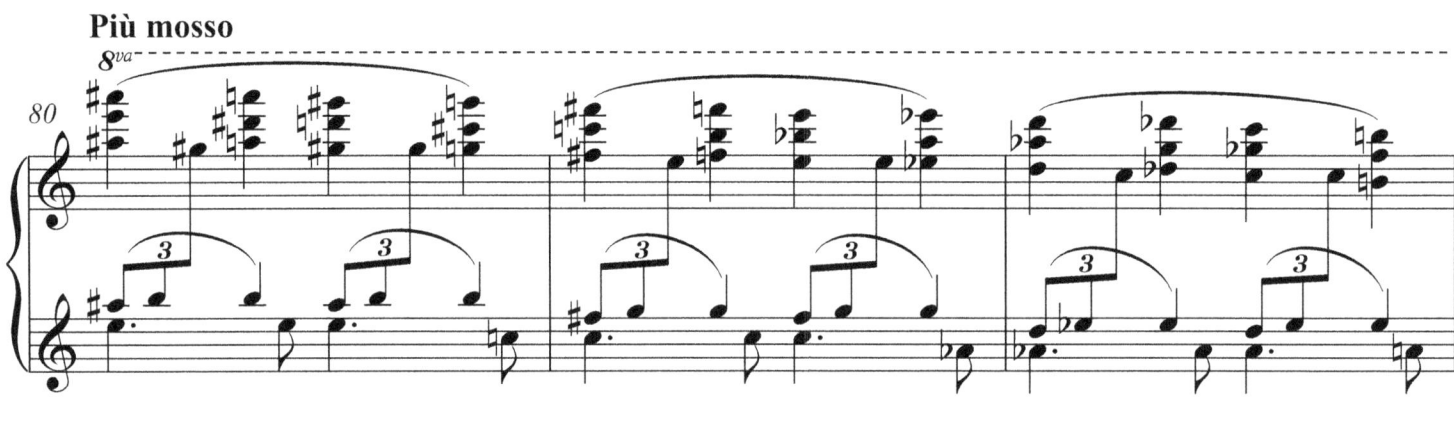

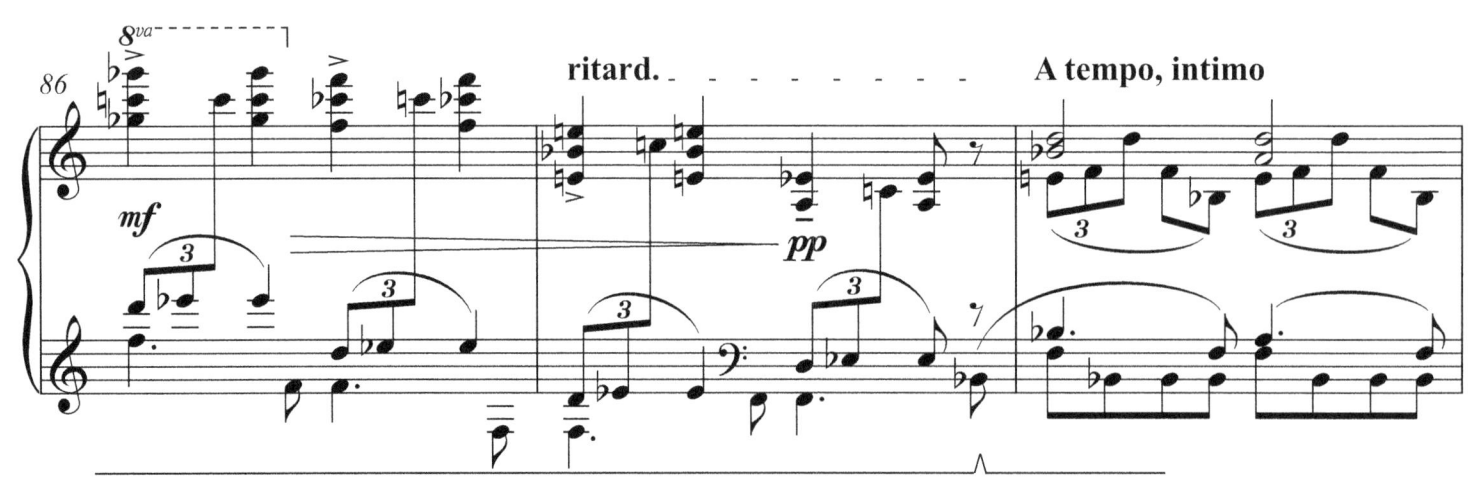

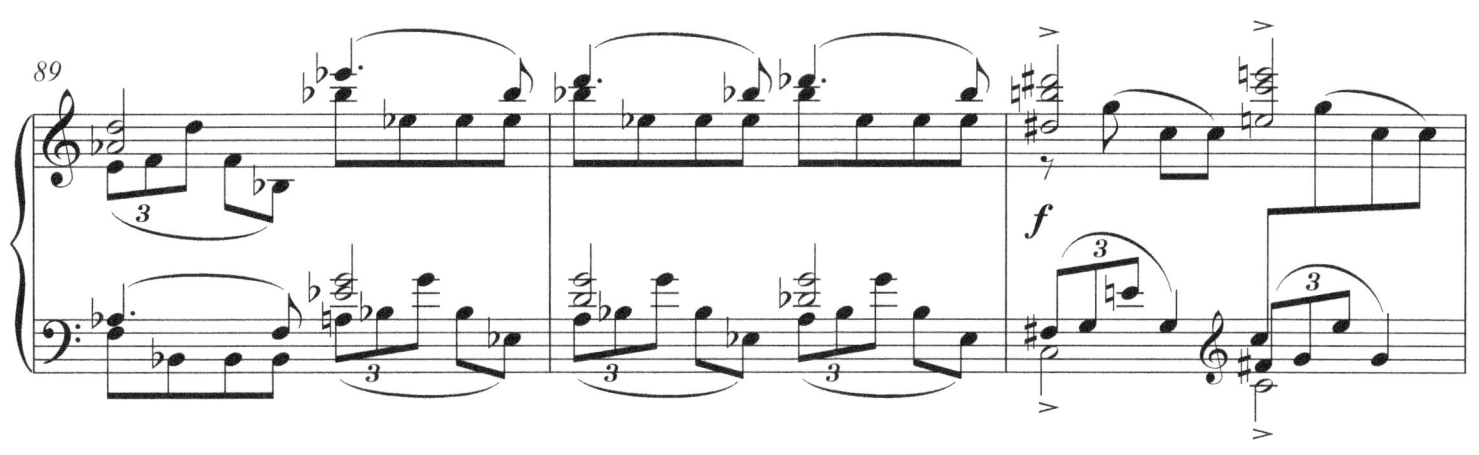

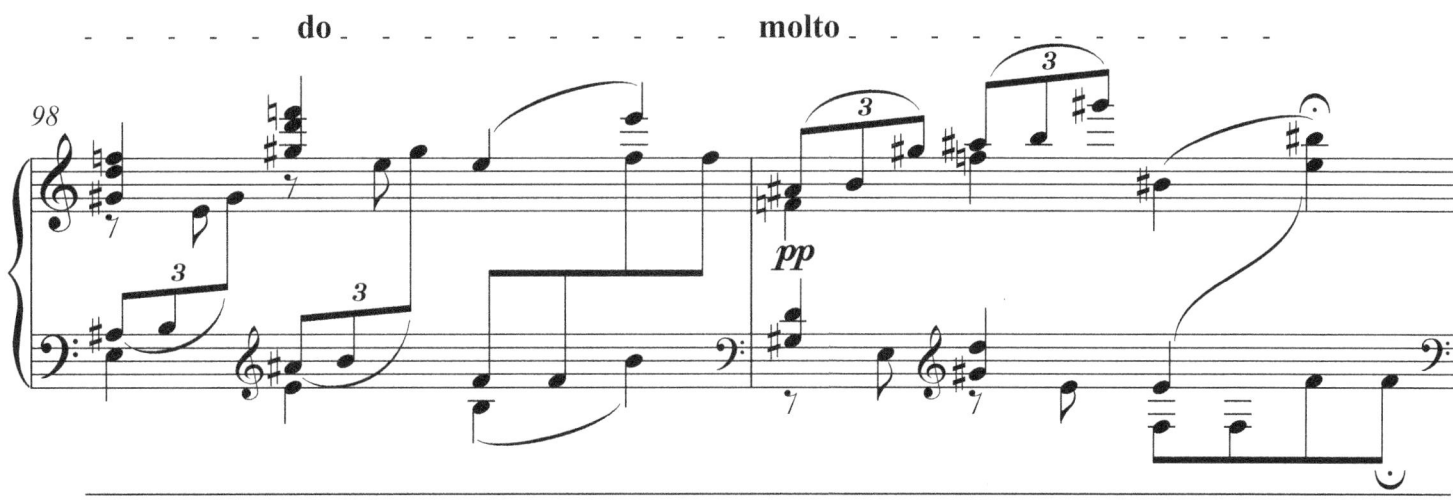

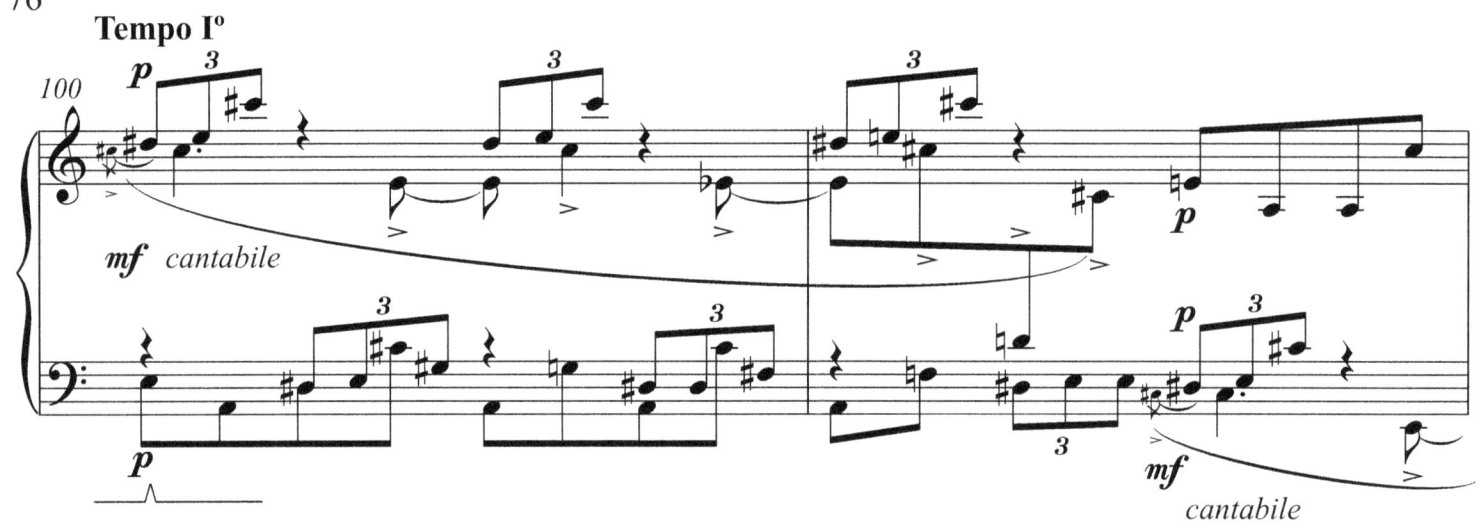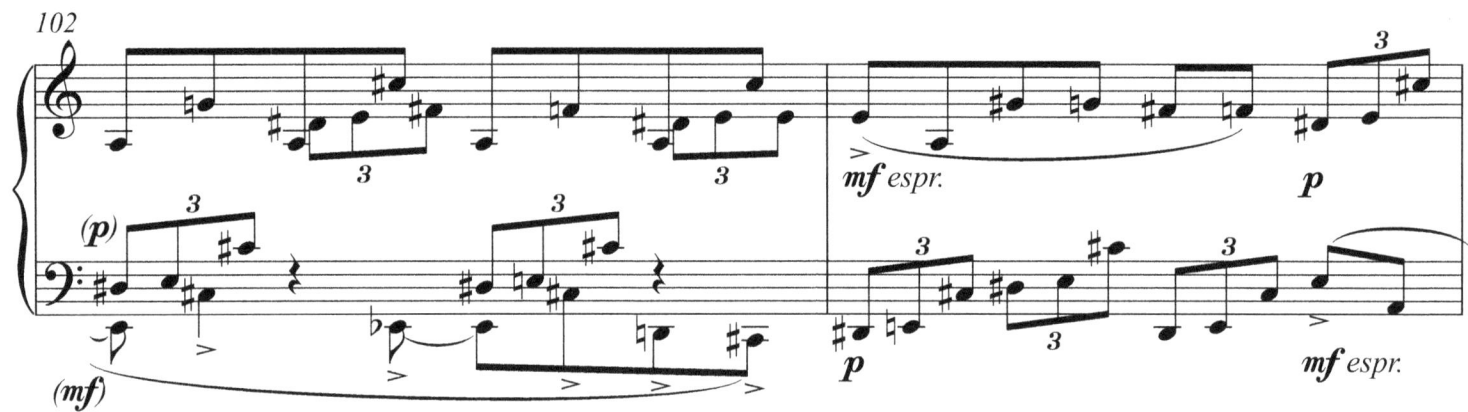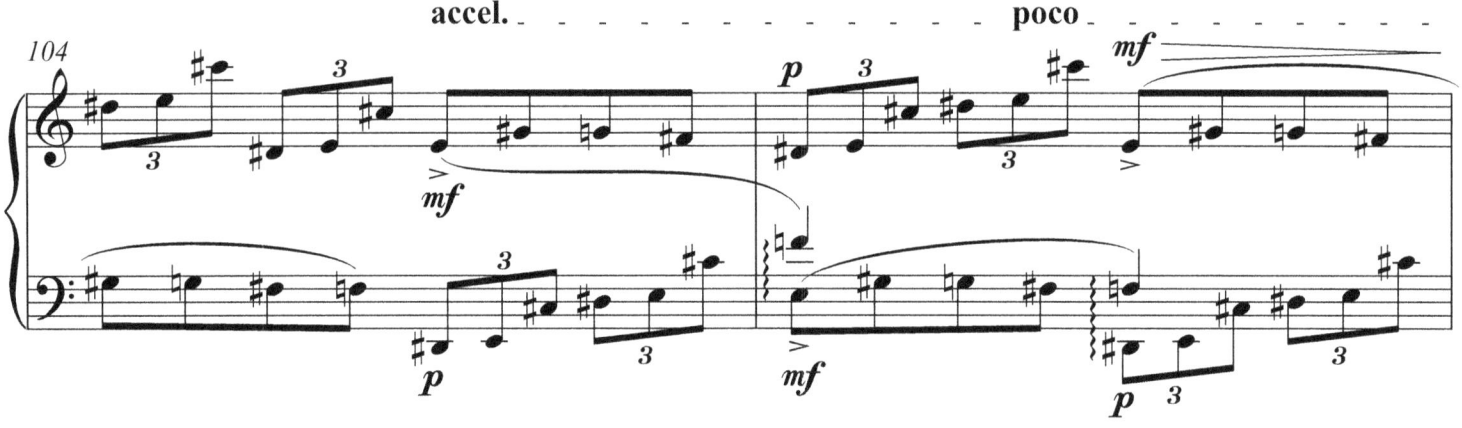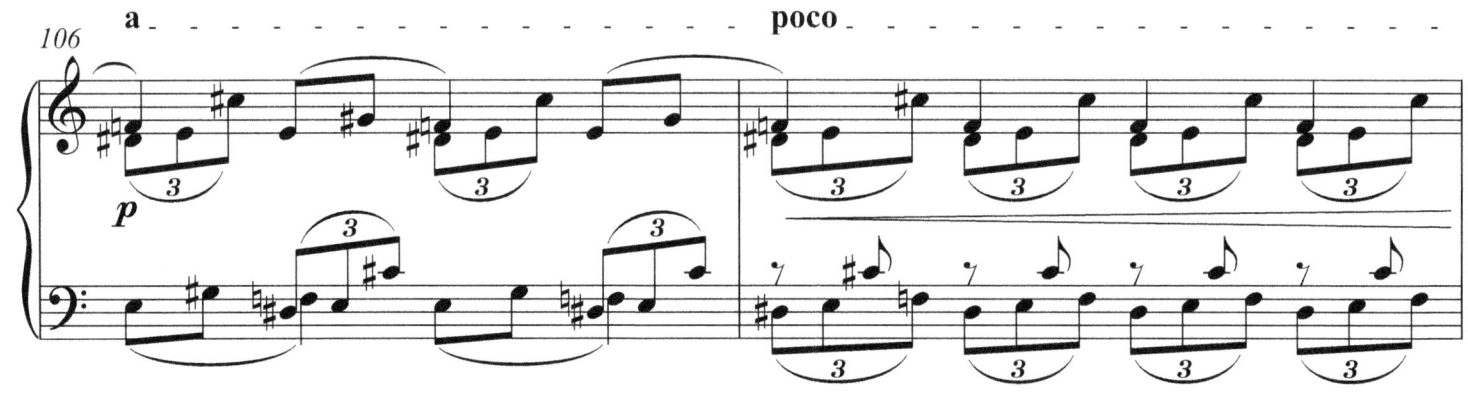

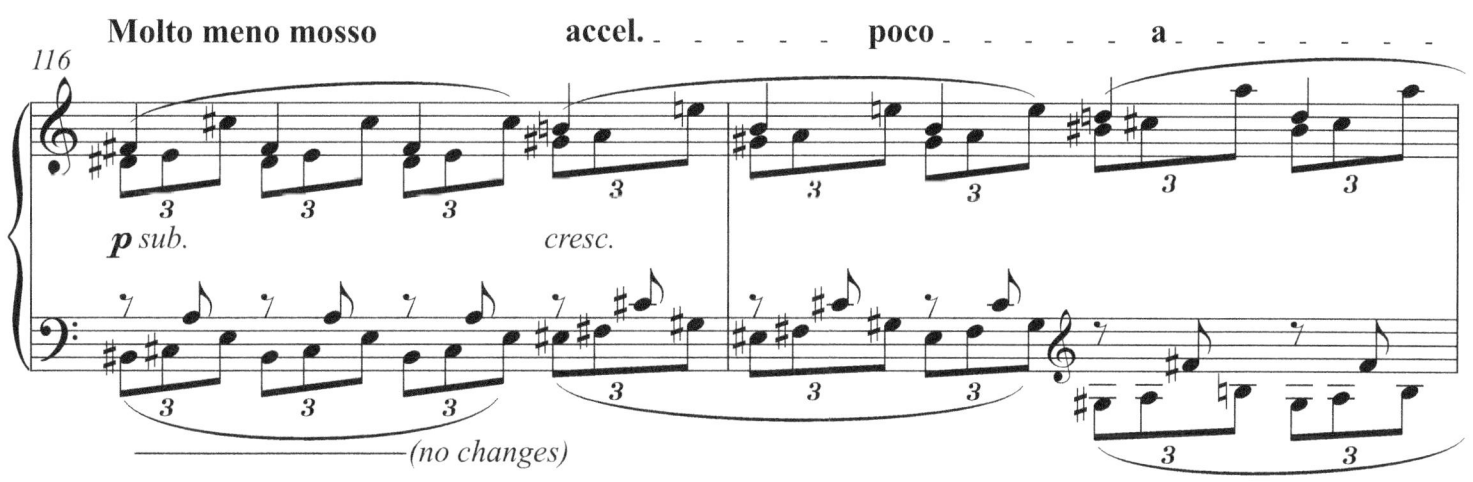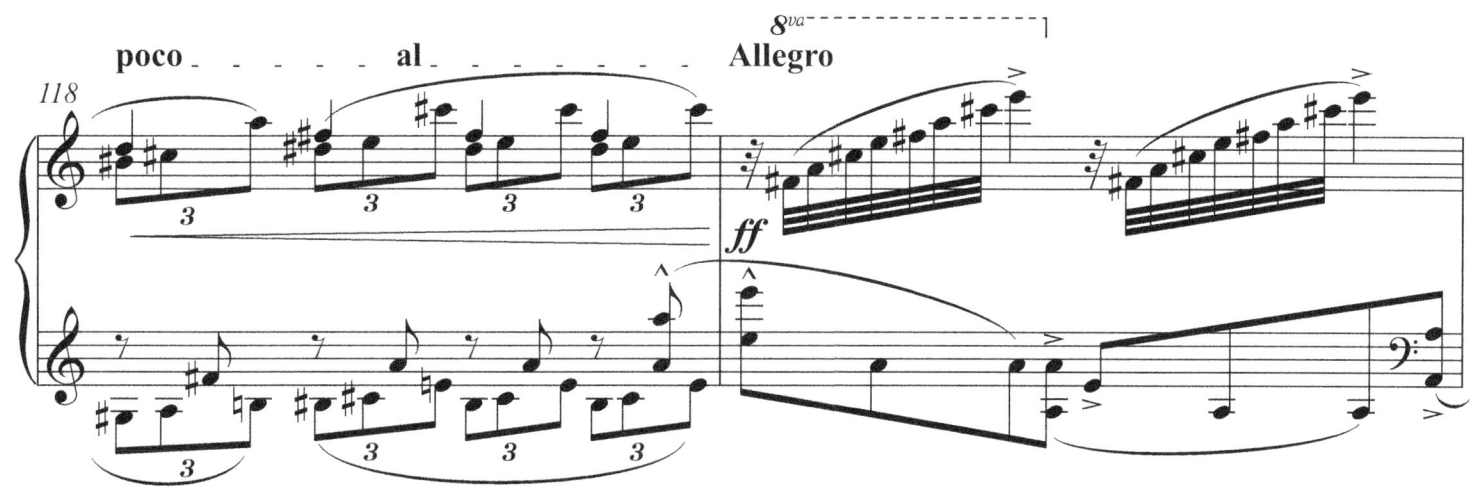

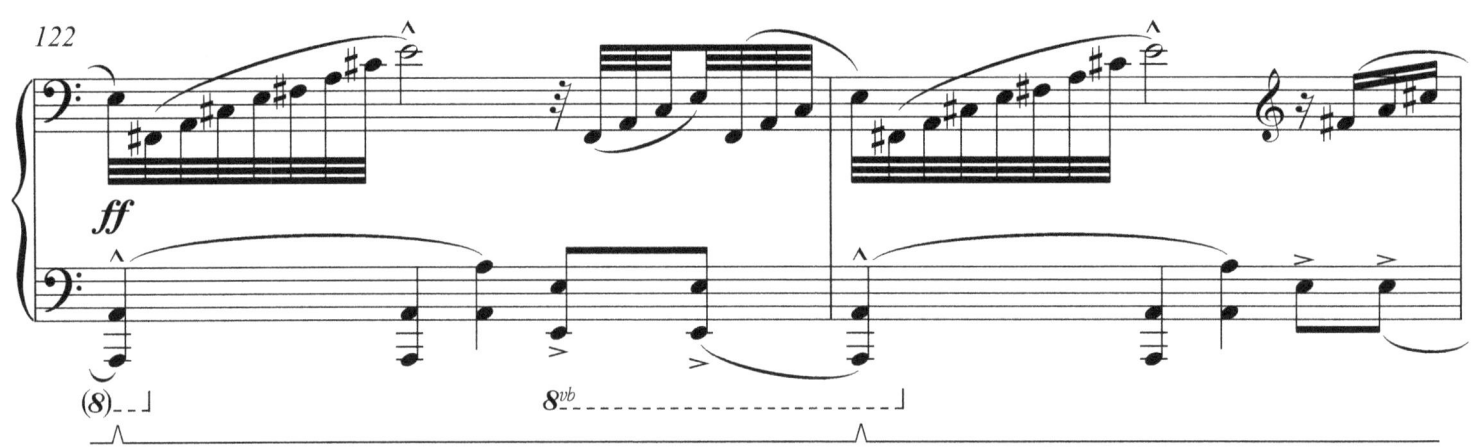

for Marc Peloquin

MANY HANDS

I. For The Left Hand

DAVID DEL TREDICI

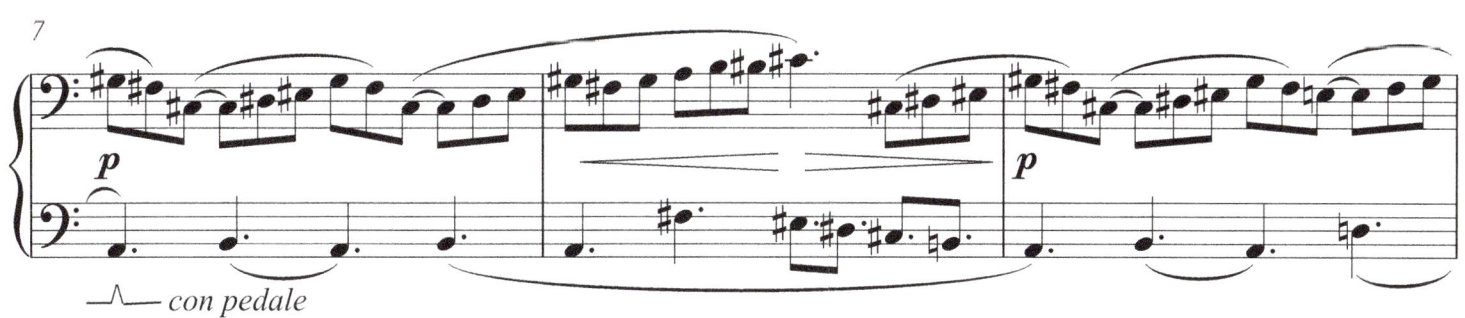

© Copyright 2009 by Boosey & Hawkes, Inc.
International copyright secured. All rights reserved.

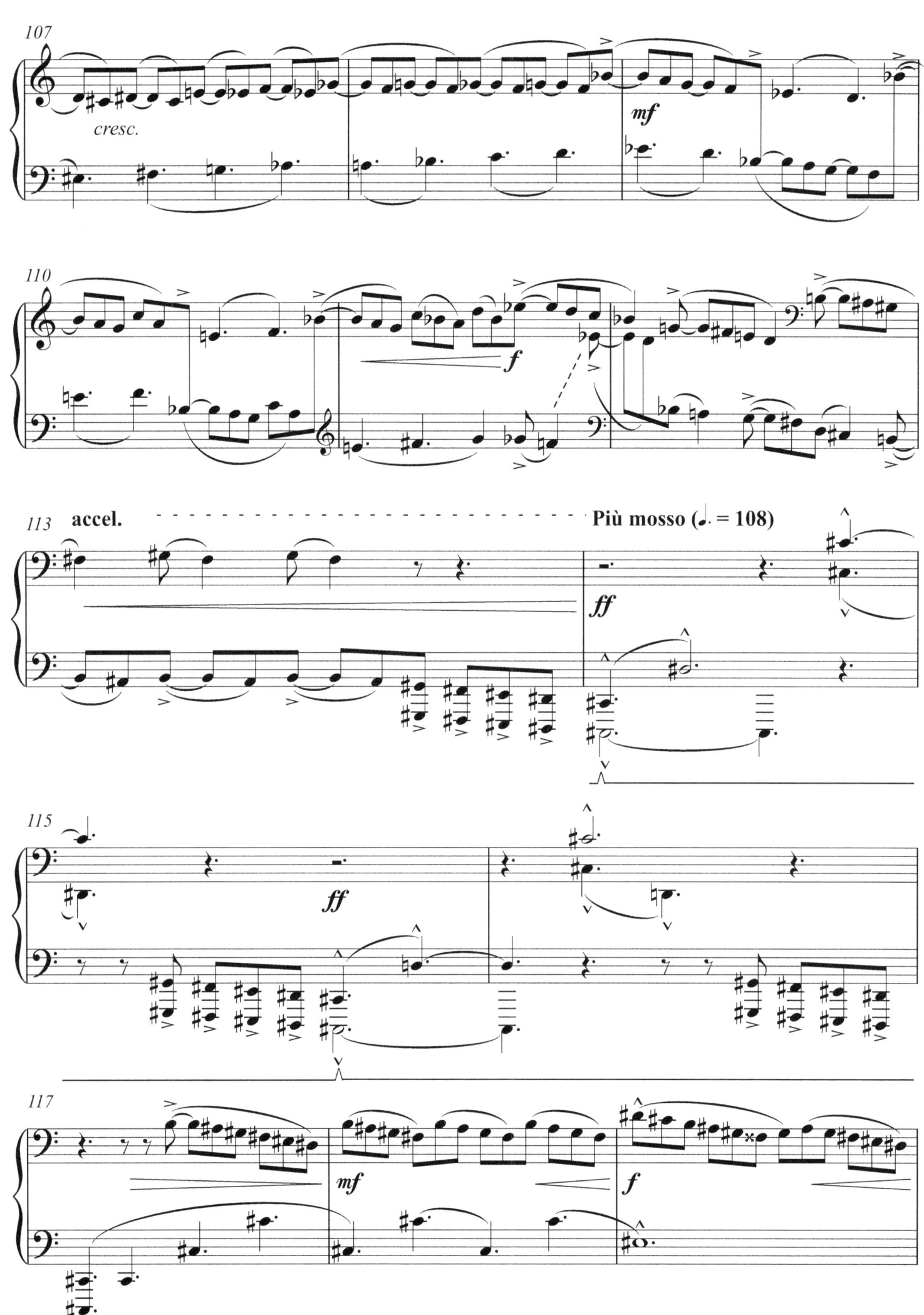

Poco più mosso

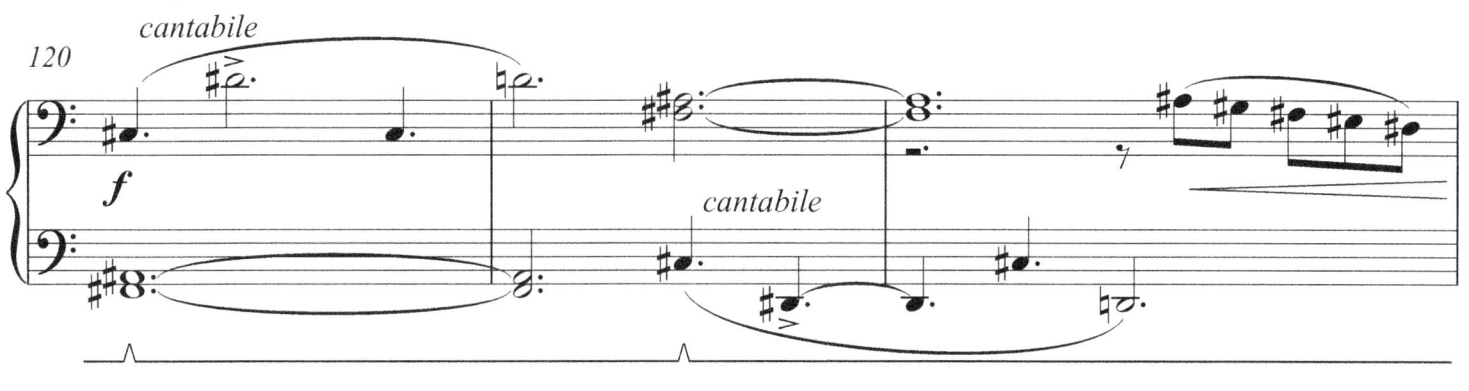
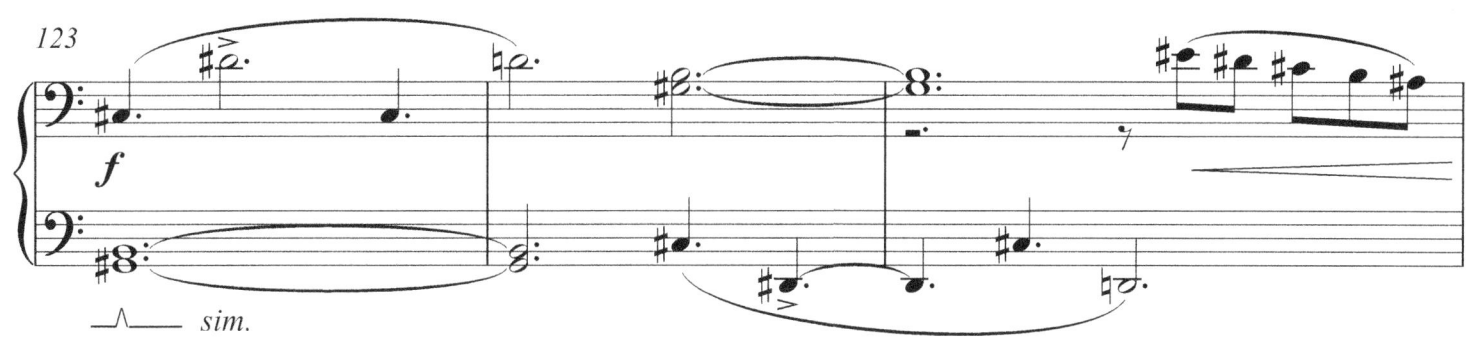
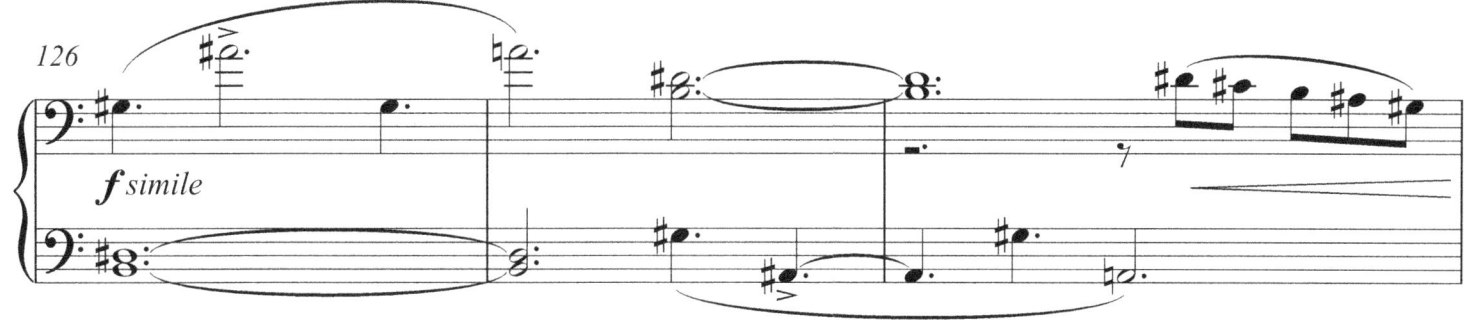
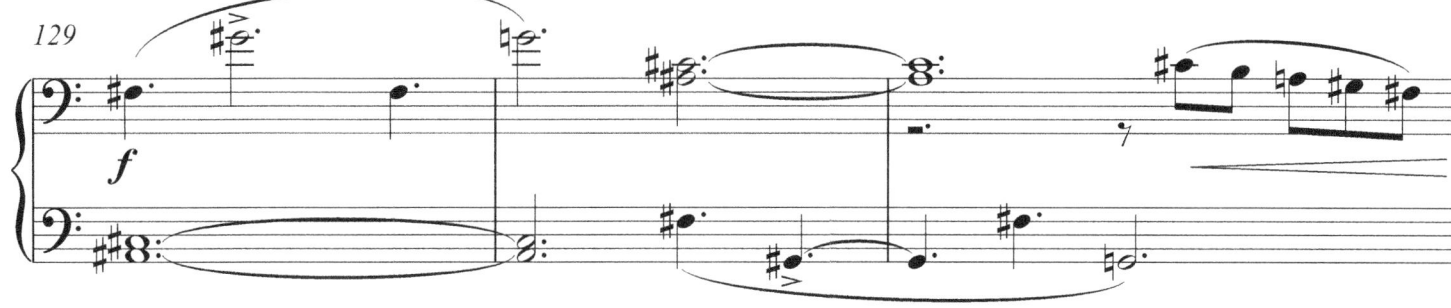

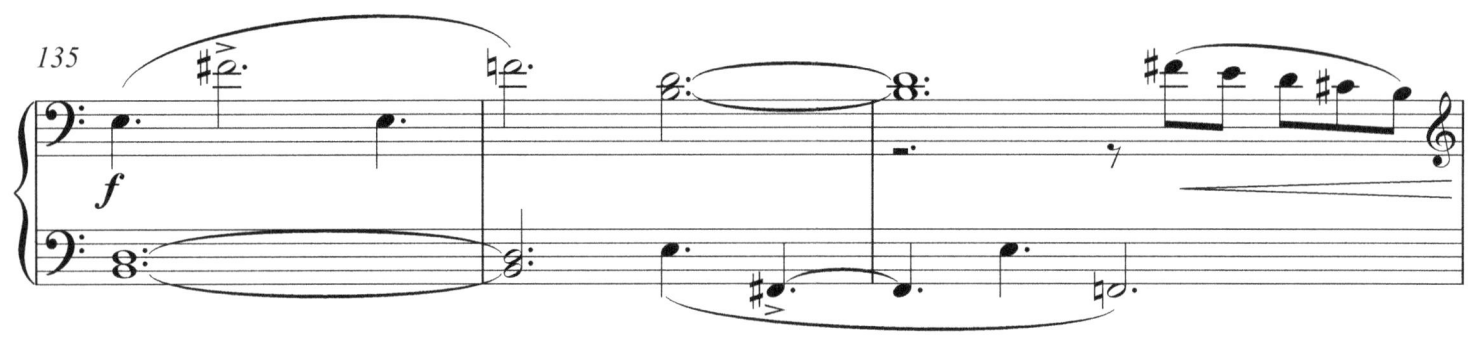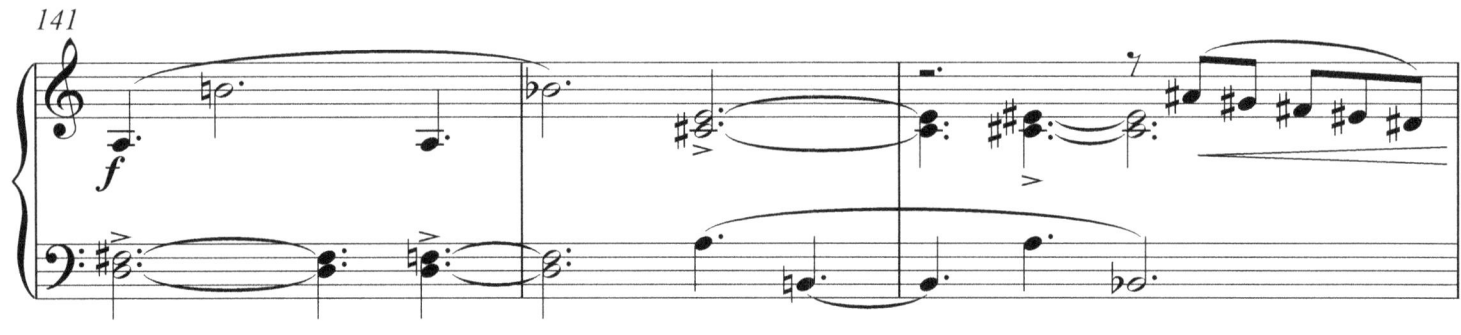

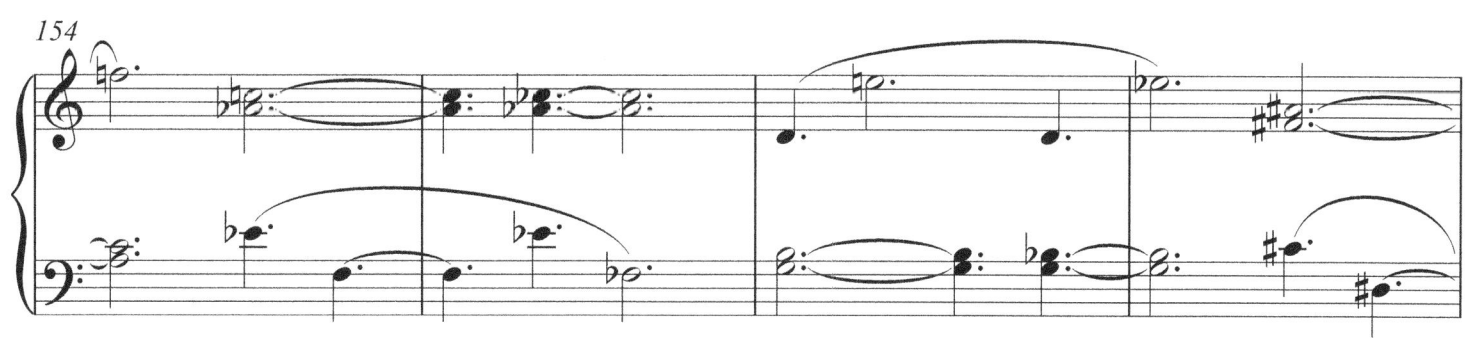

for Bob Peterson

II. Bank Street Prelude

DAVID DEL TREDICI

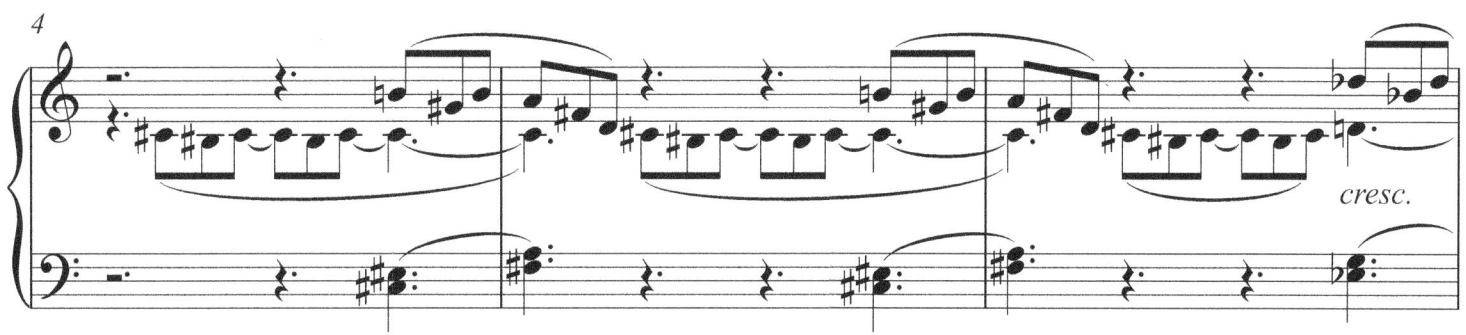

92

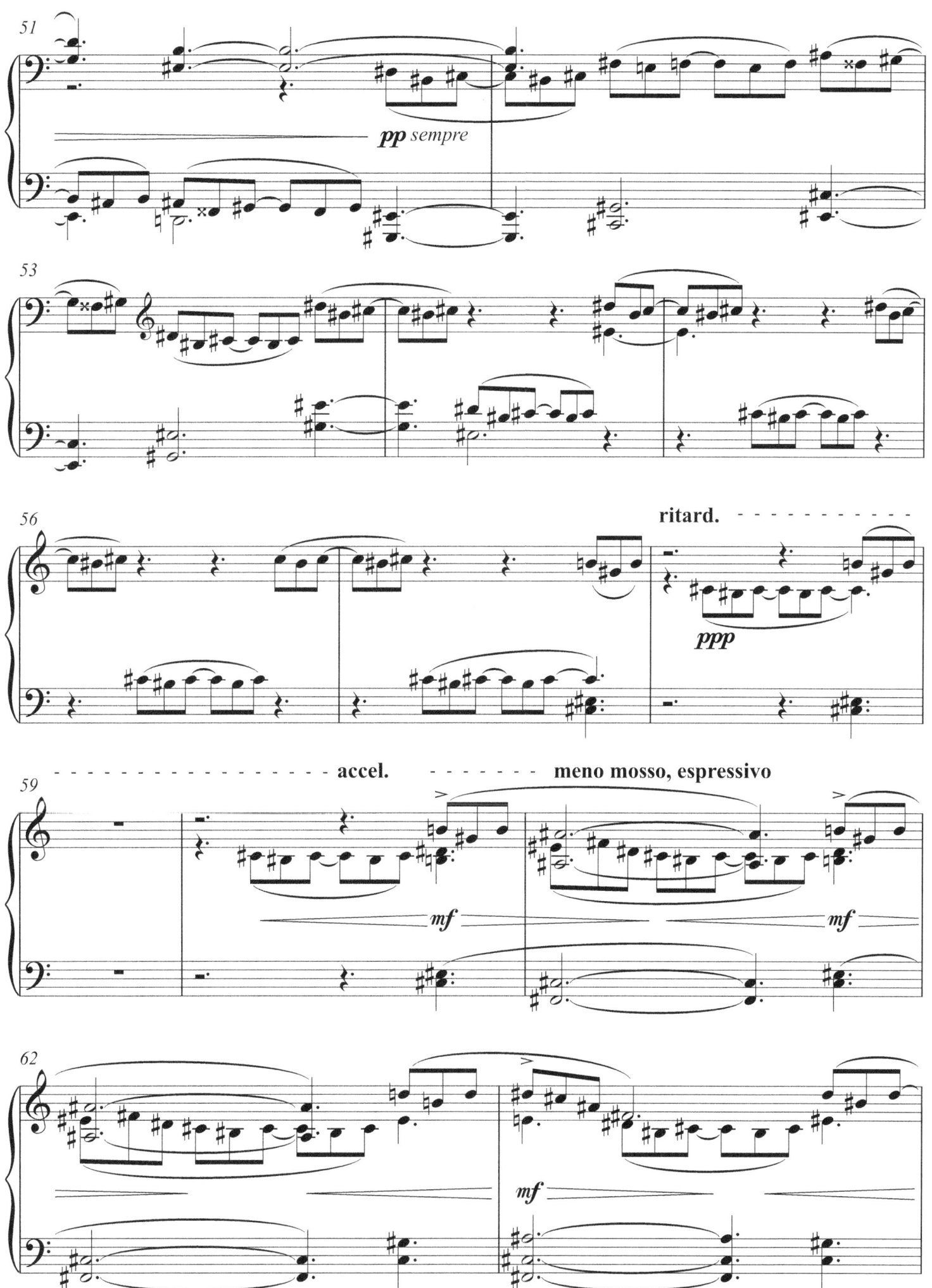

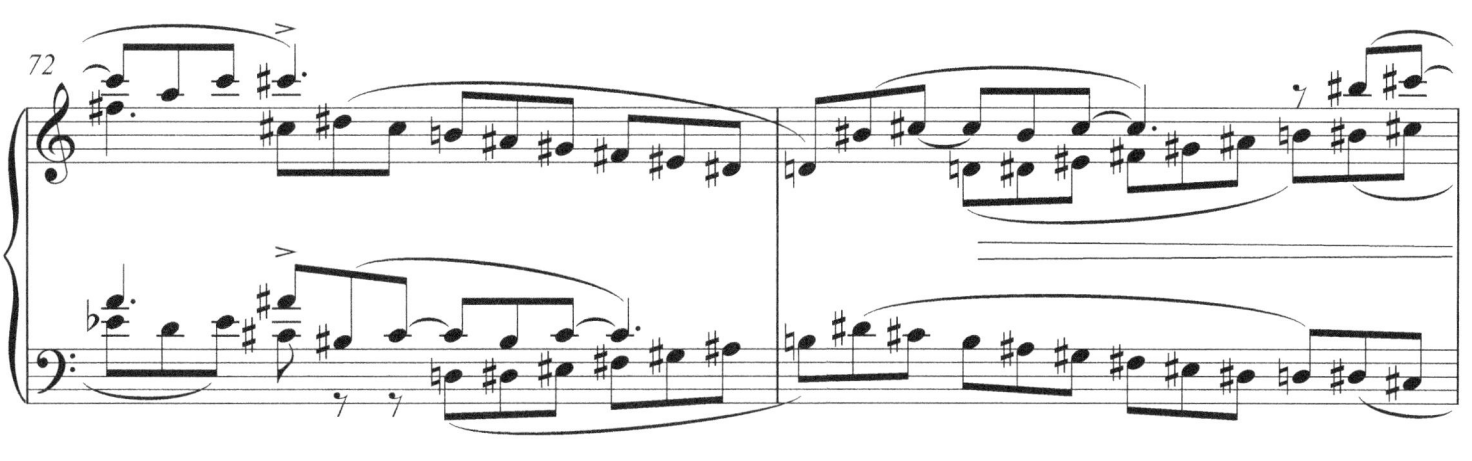

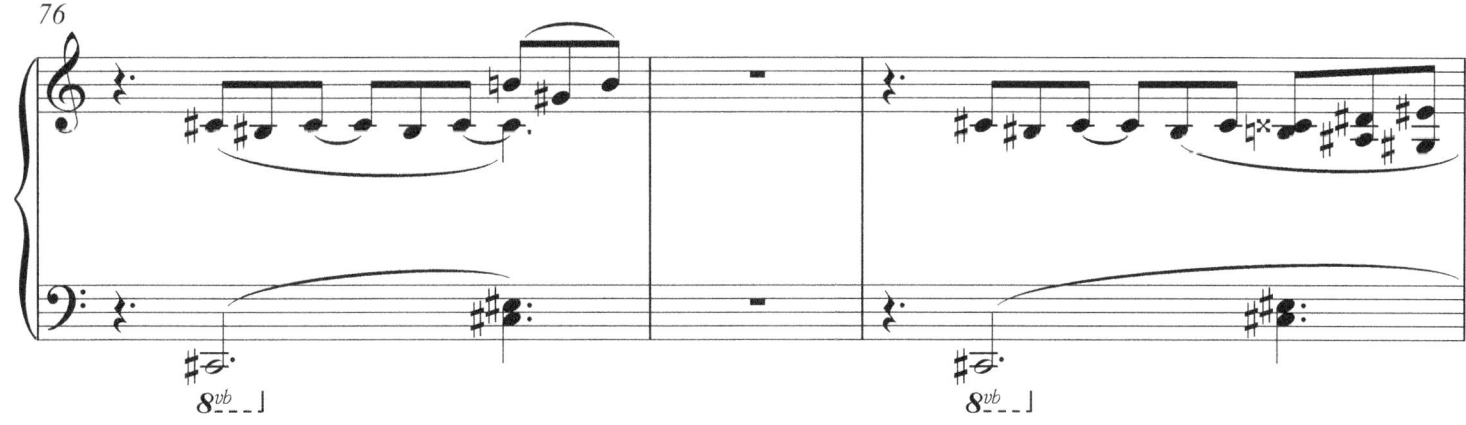
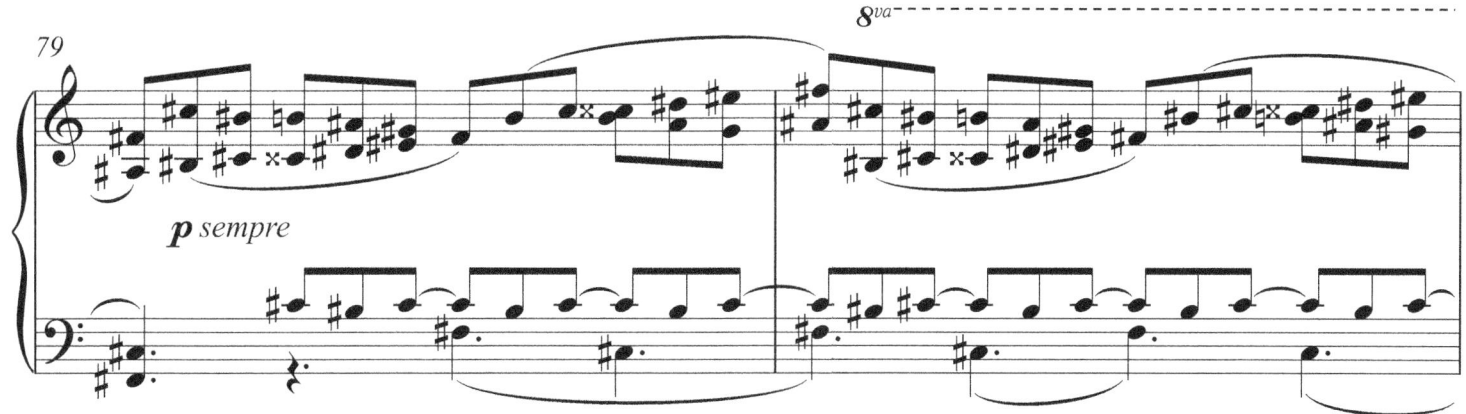

MANY HANDS

for Stephen Gosling

III. Perry Street Fugue

DAVID DEL TREDICI

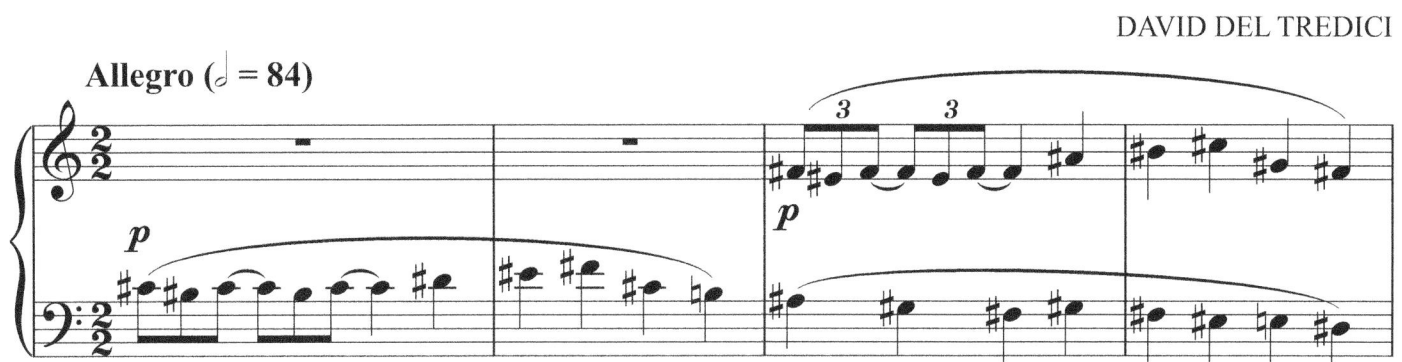

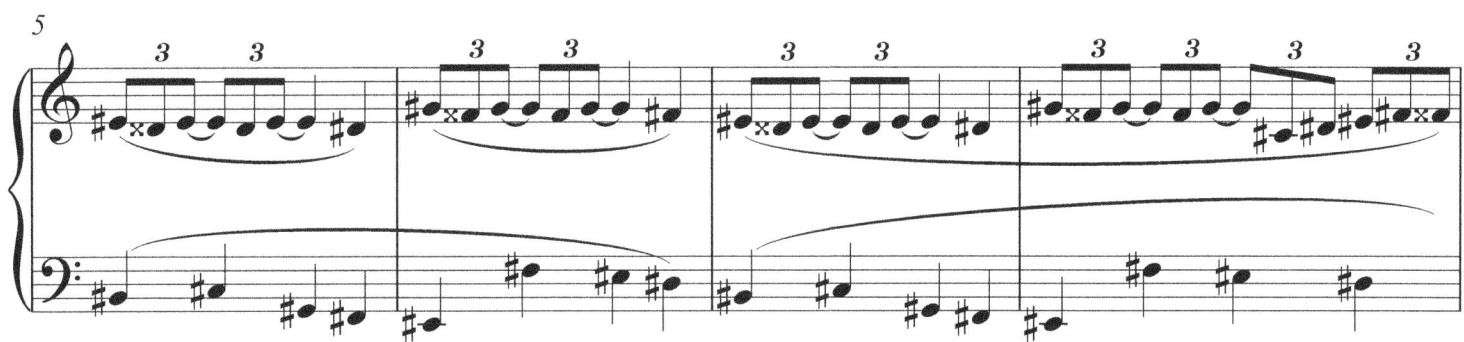

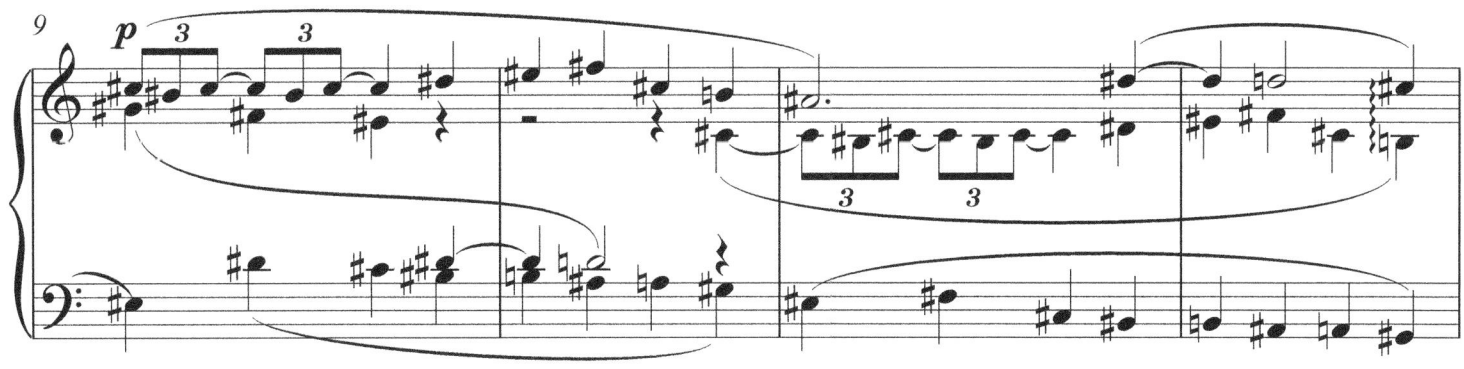

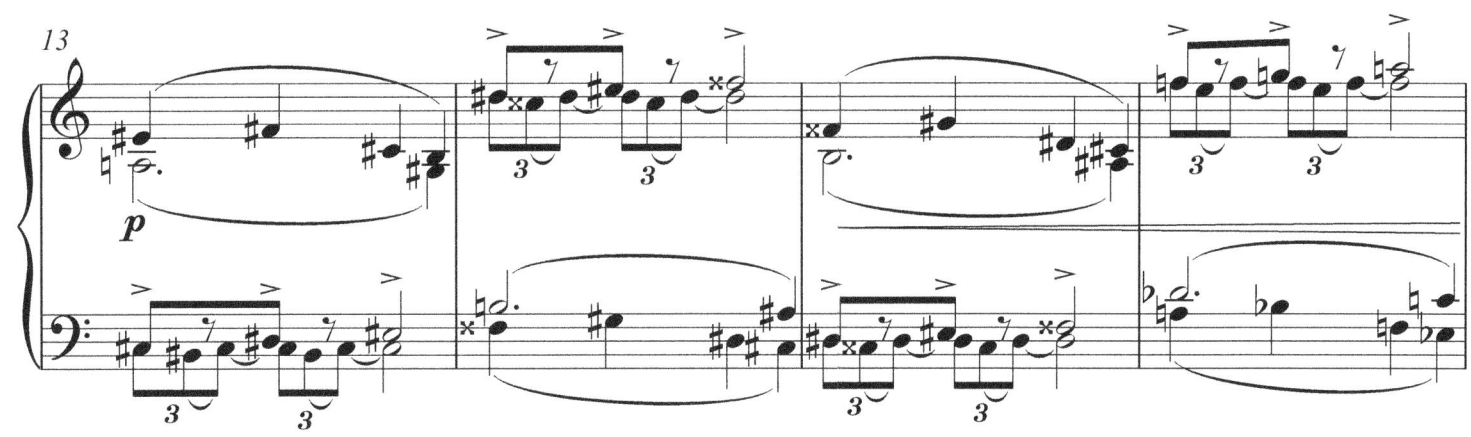

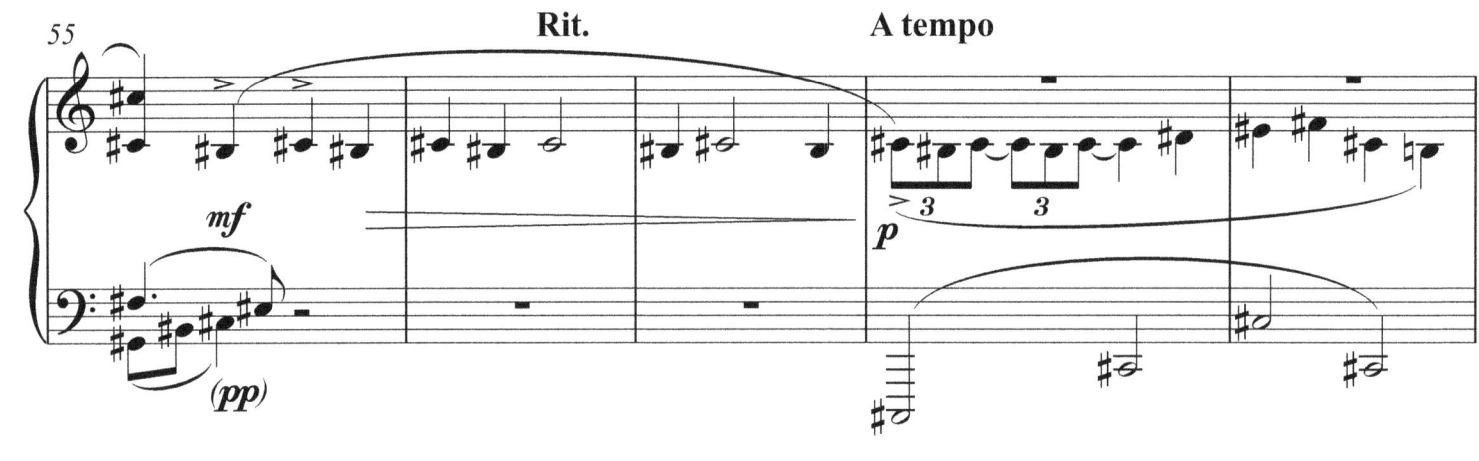
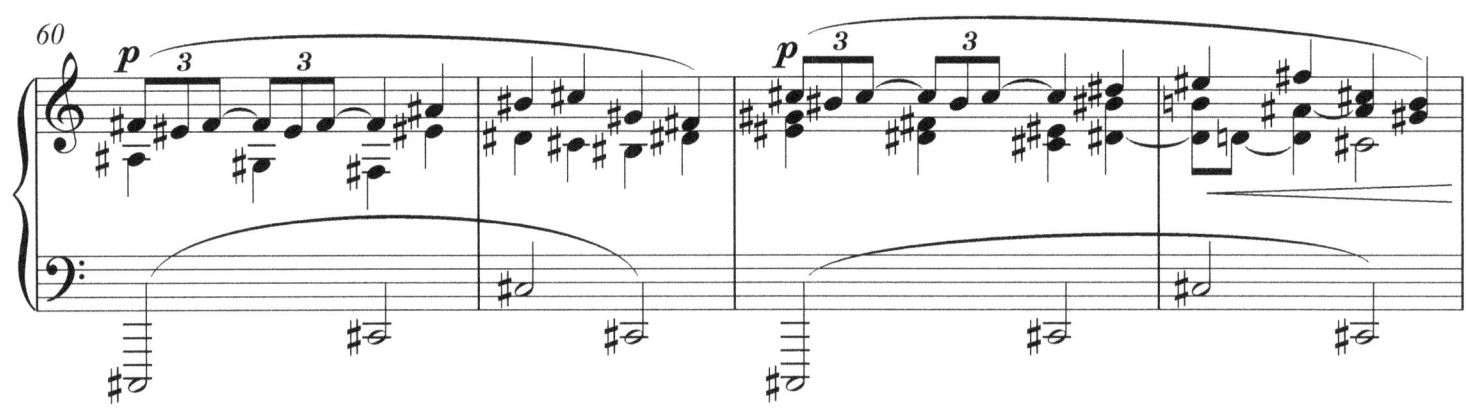

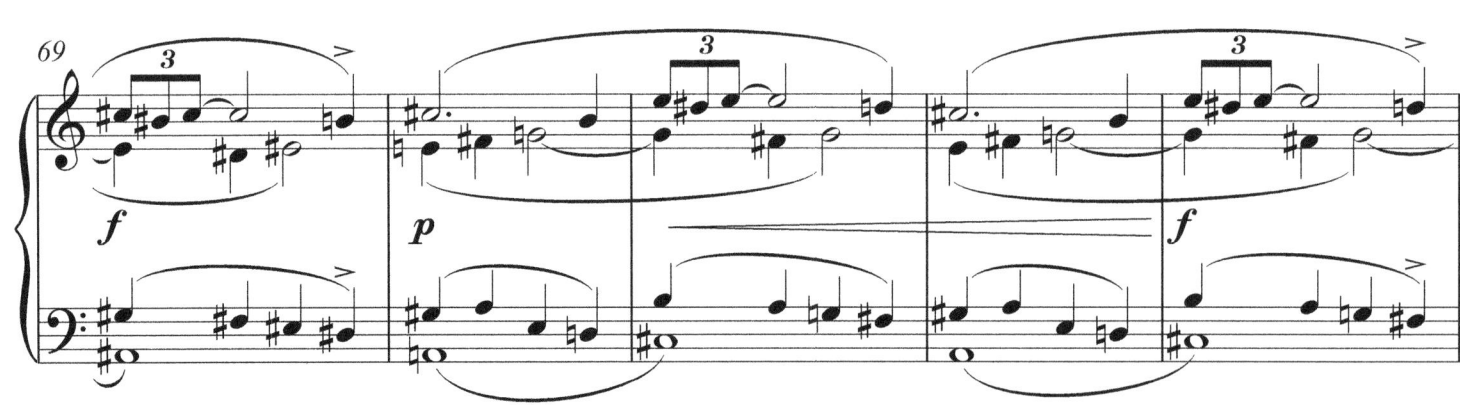

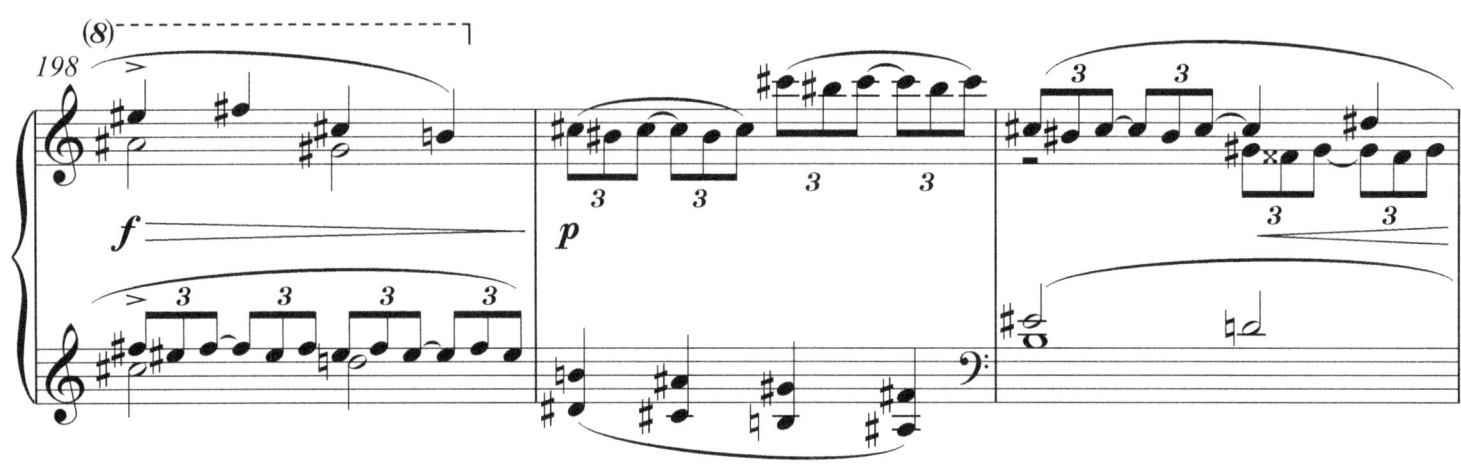

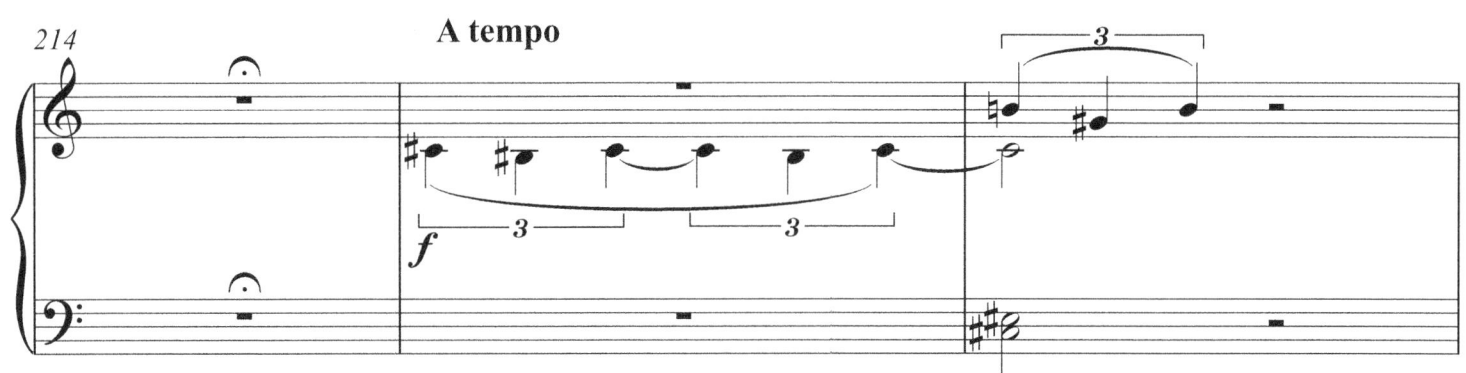

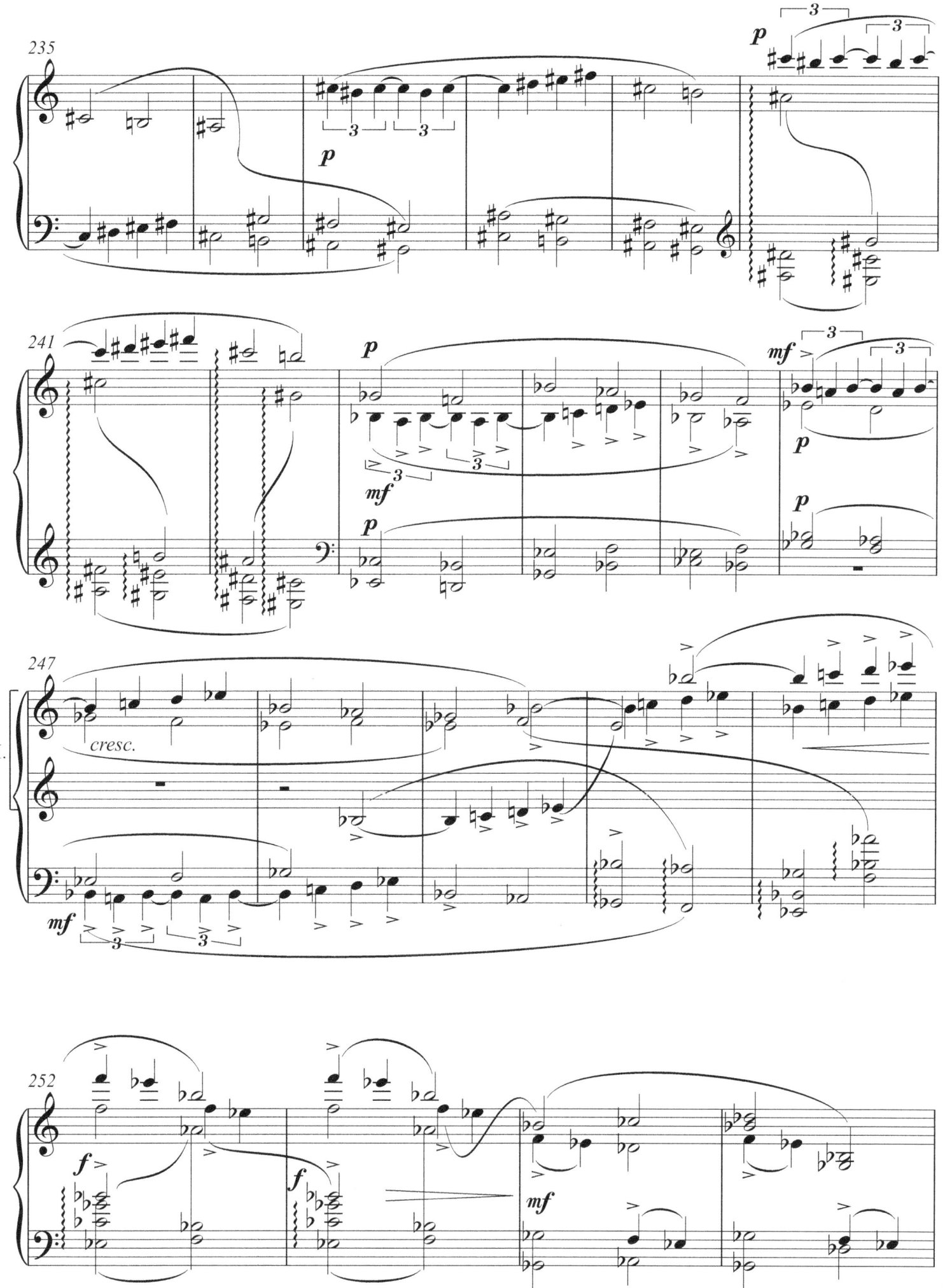

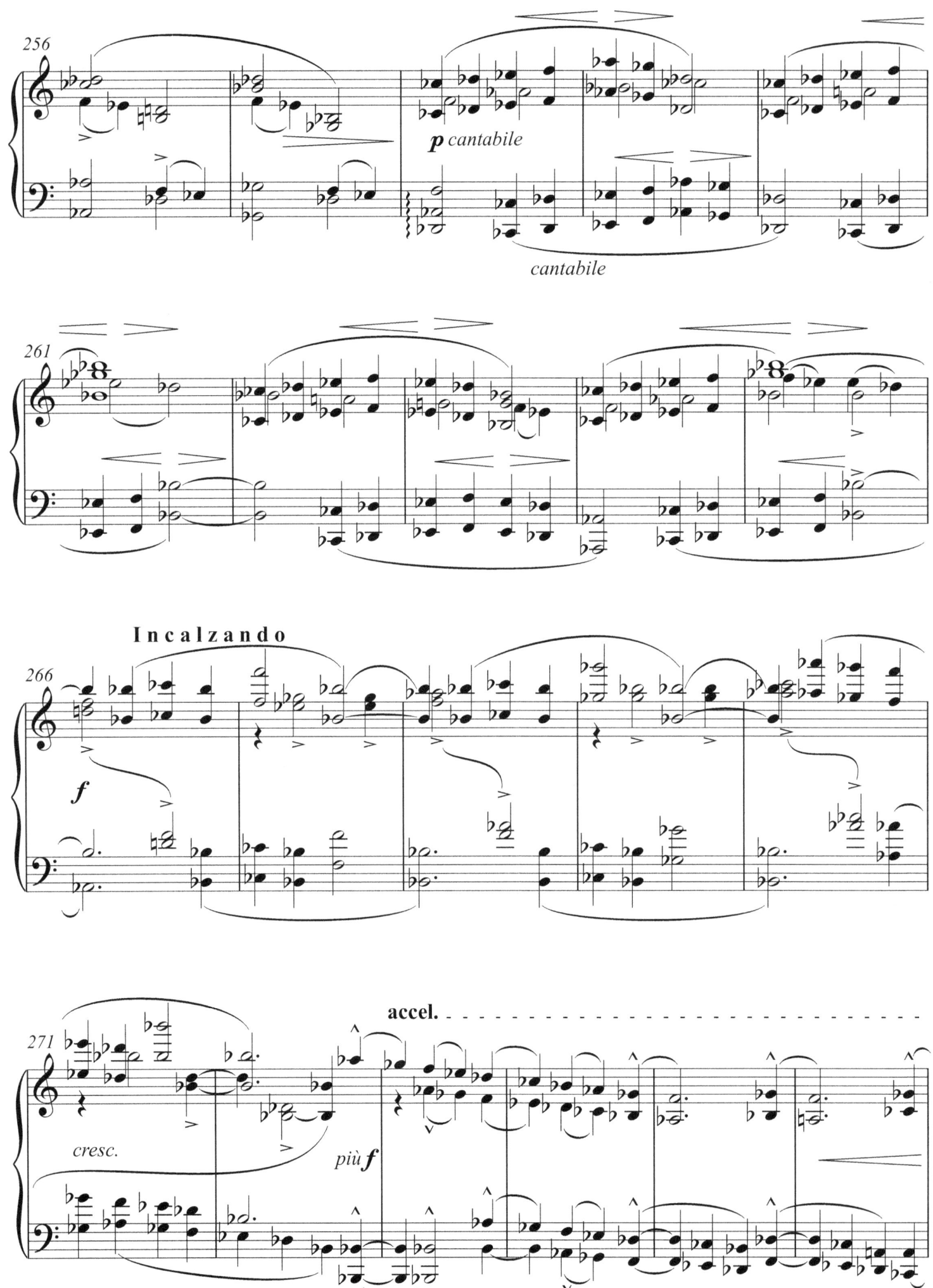

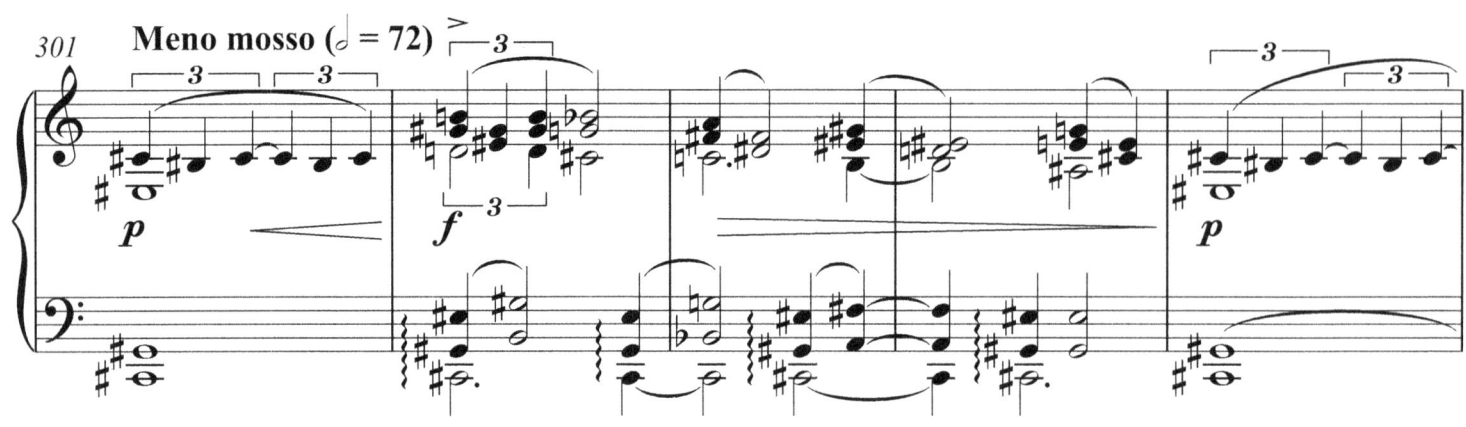

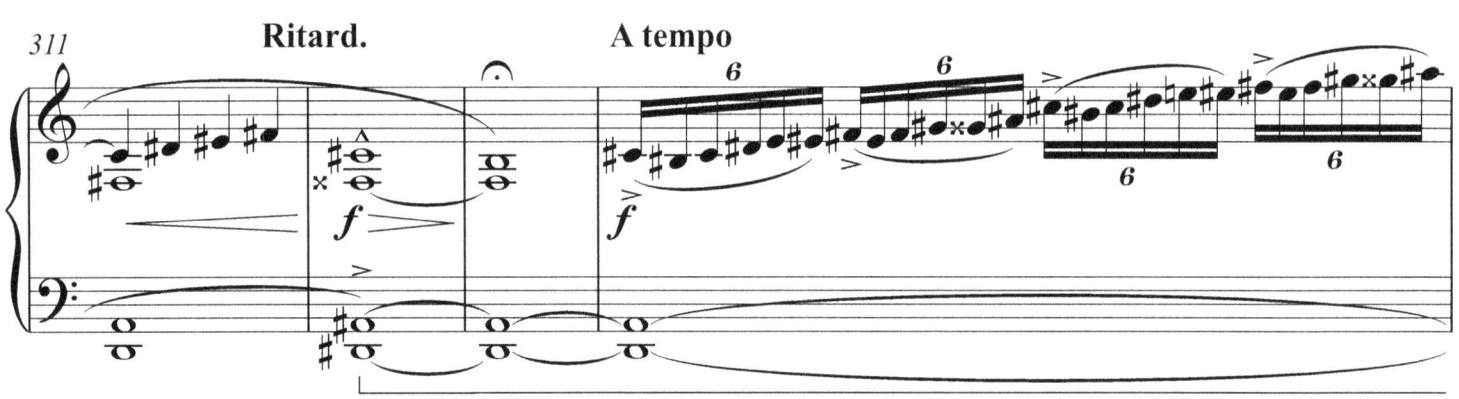
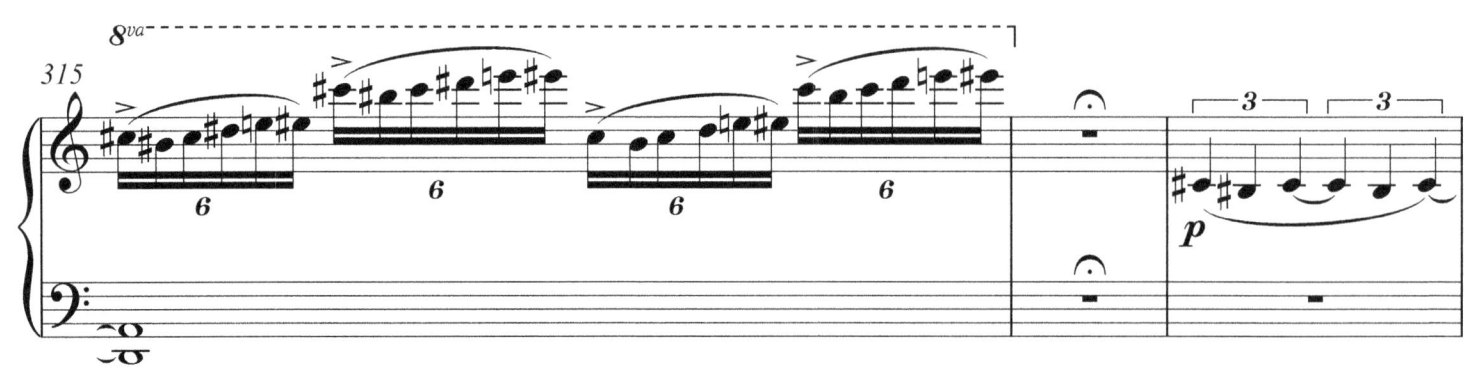

318
sub
f
Ritard.
A tempo
320
pp (echo)
sub
f
323
Andante (♩. = 92)
pp
325
pp sempre
mf
L.H.
(Ped.)

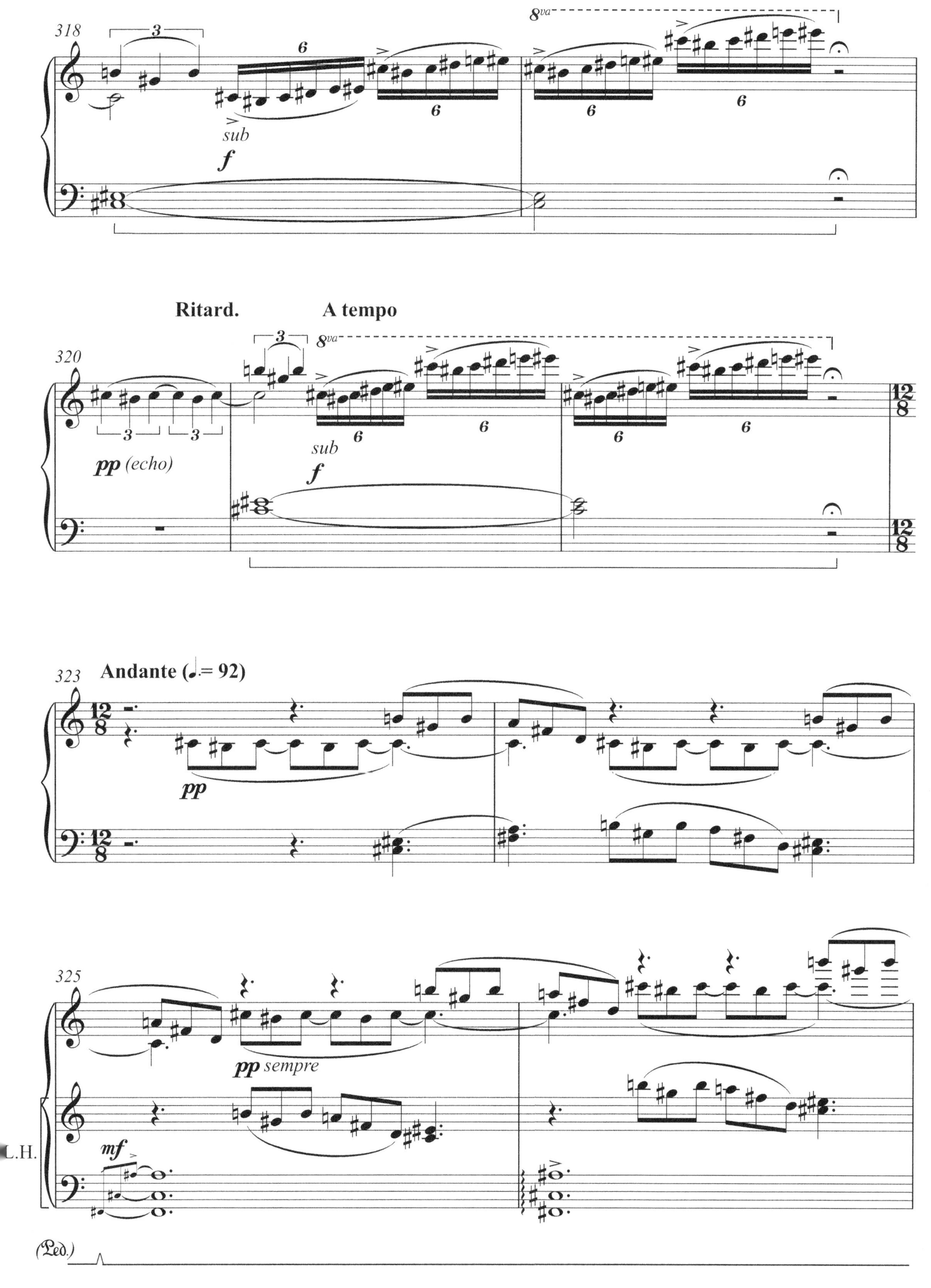

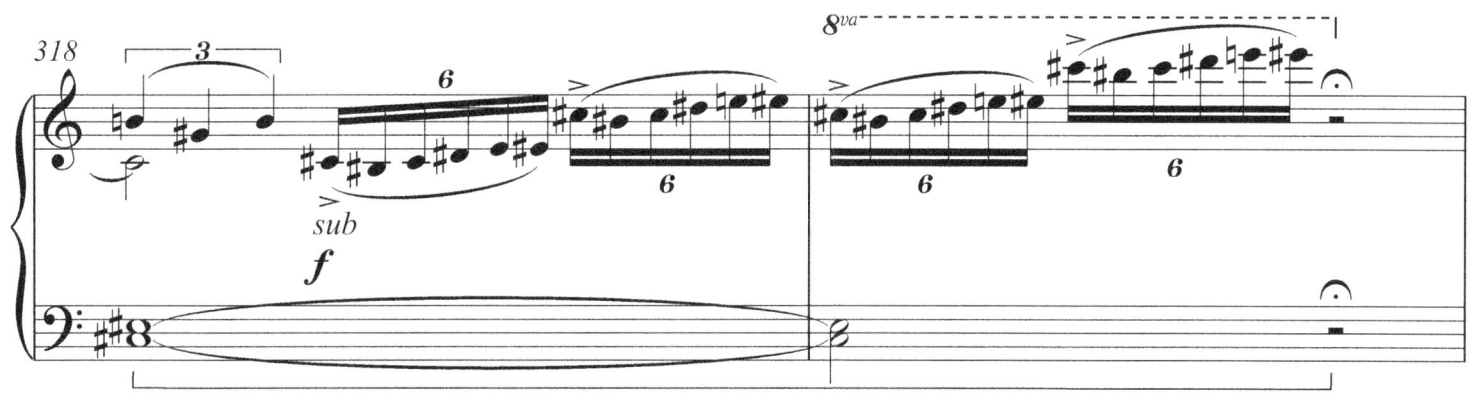

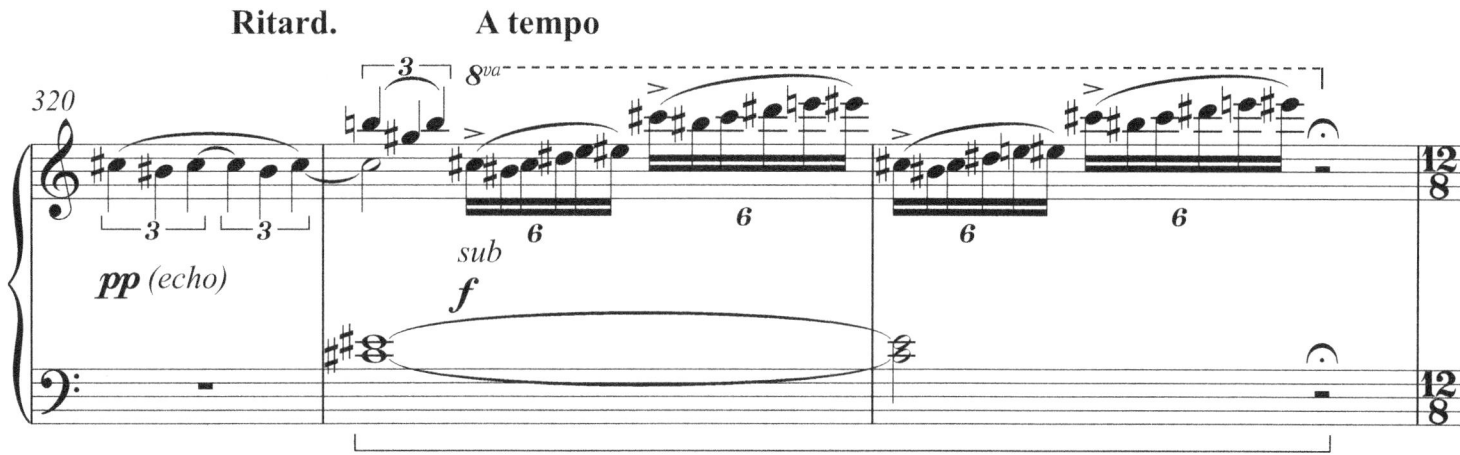

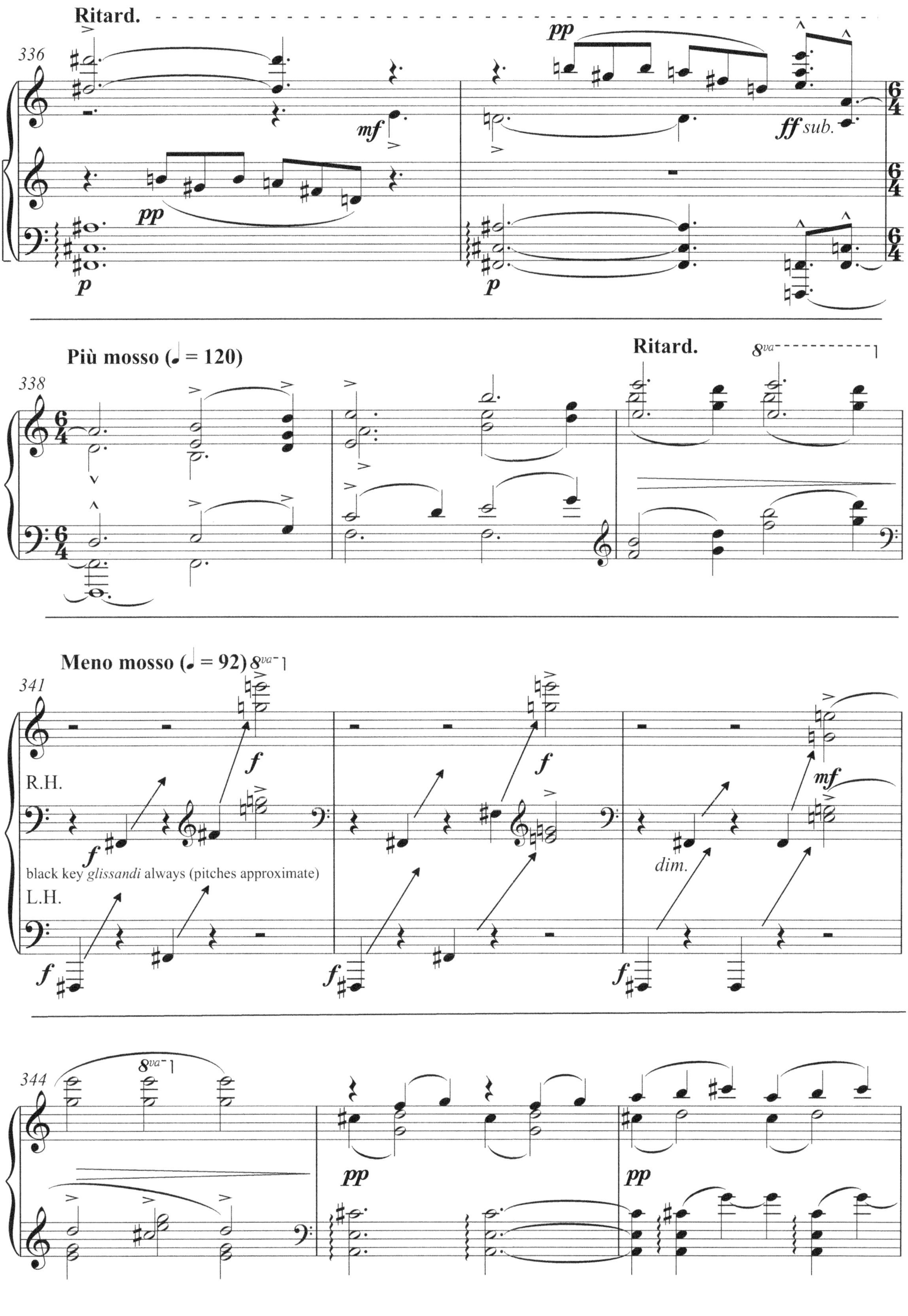
Ritard.
336
pp
mf
ff sub.
p
Più mosso (♩ = 120)
Ritard.
8va
338
Meno mosso (♩ = 92)
341
R.H.
f
black key glissandi always (pitches approximate)
L.H.
dim.
mf
344

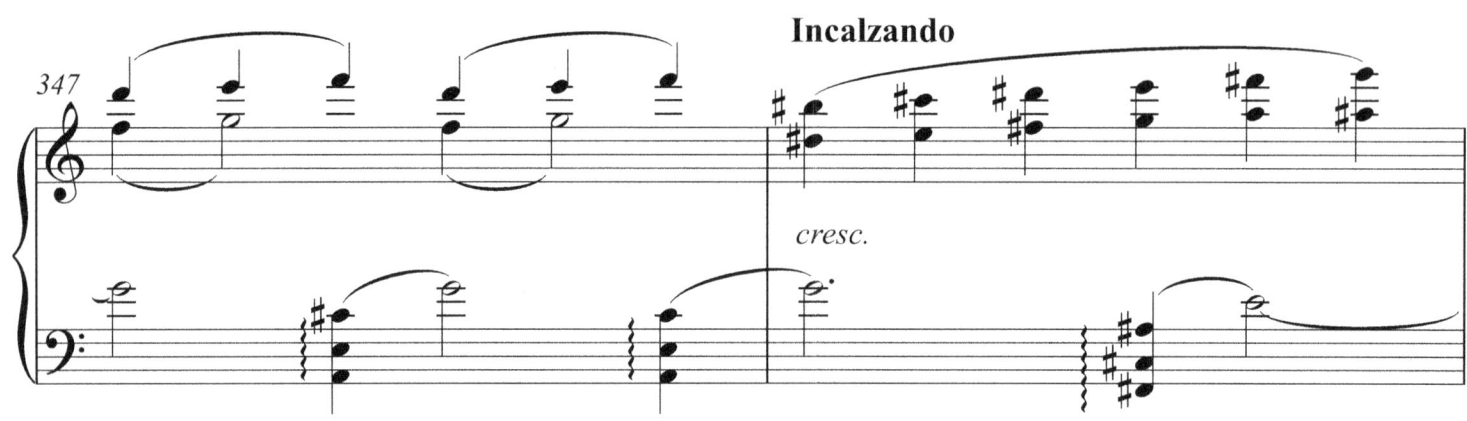

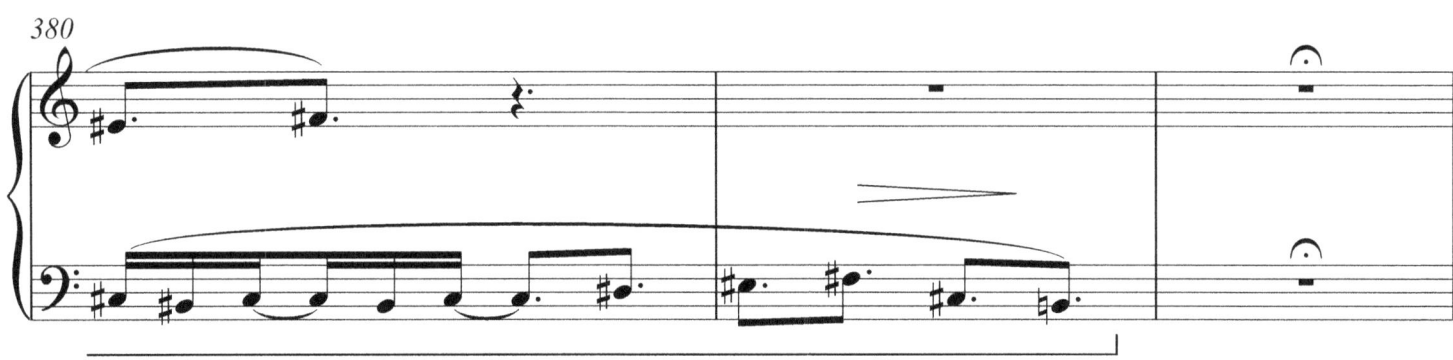

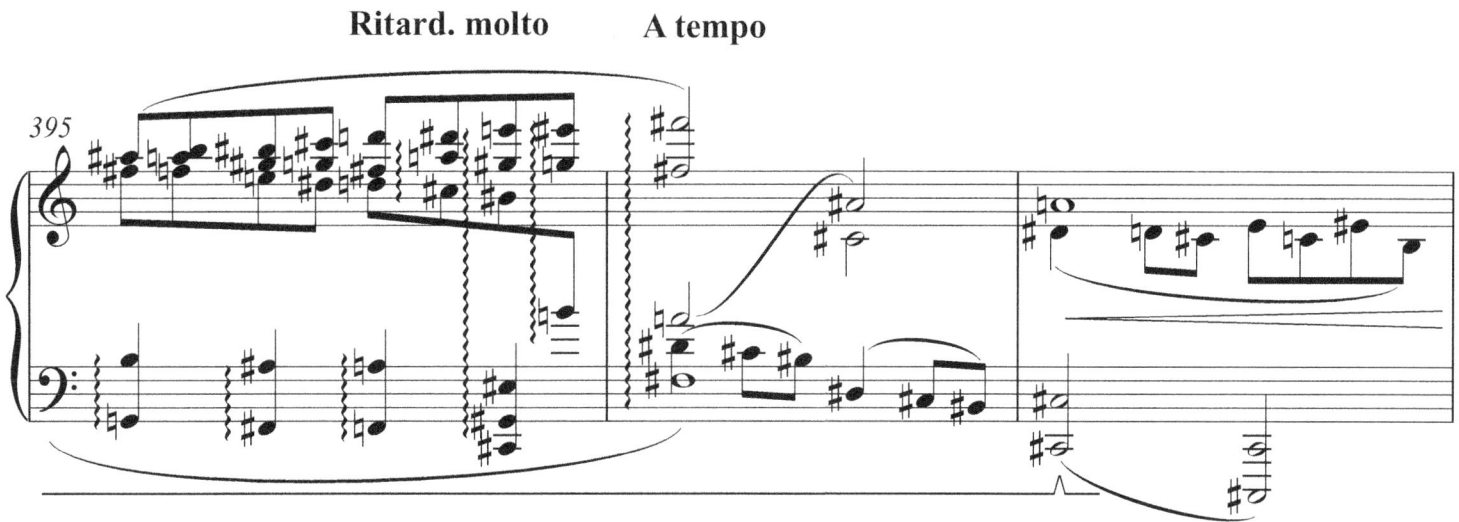

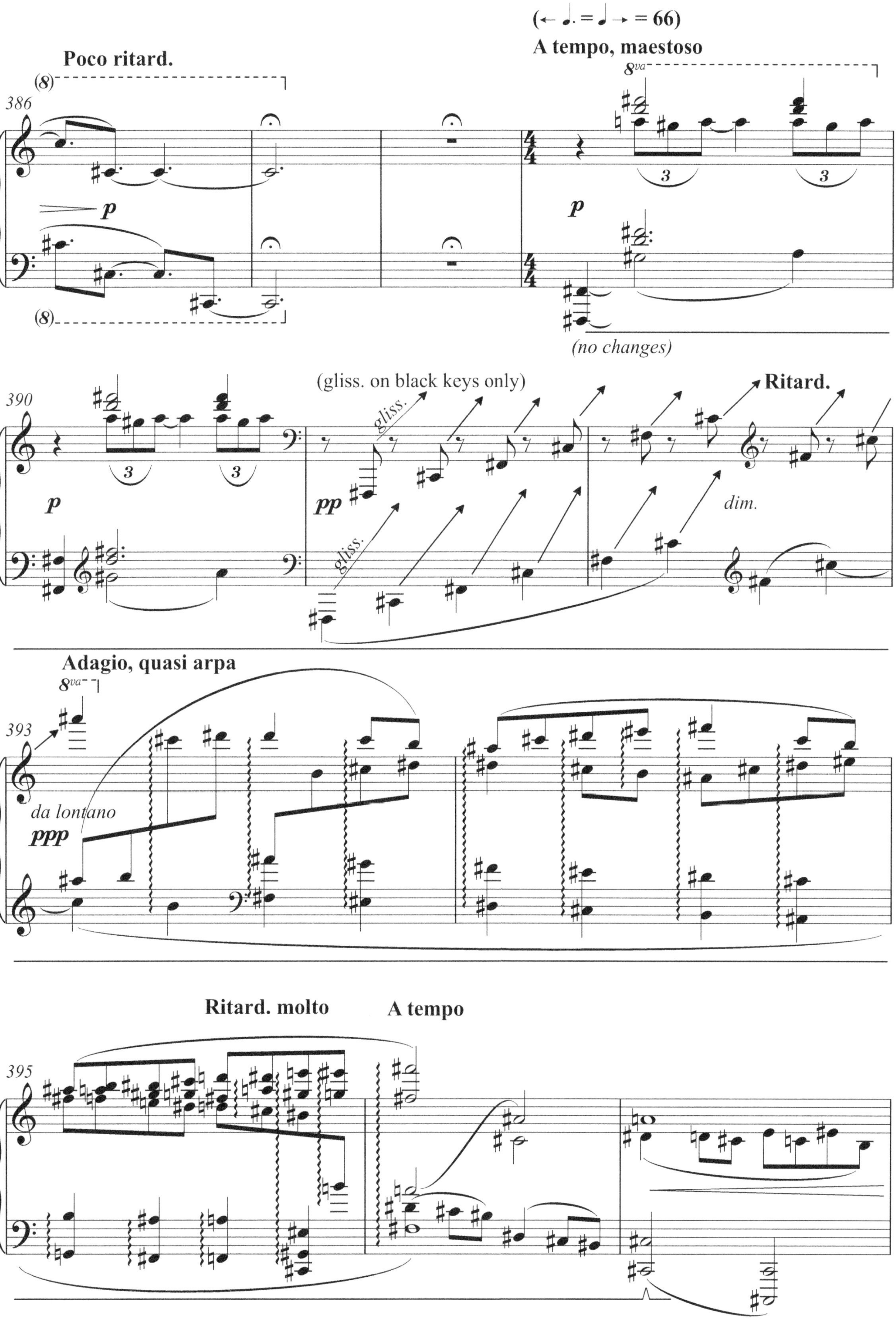
(← ♩. = ♩ → = 66)
A tempo, maestoso
Poco ritard.
386
(8)
8va
p
(no changes)
390
(gliss. on black keys only)
gliss.
Ritard.
pp
dim.
Adagio, quasi arpa
8va
393
da lontano
ppp
395
Ritard. molto
A tempo

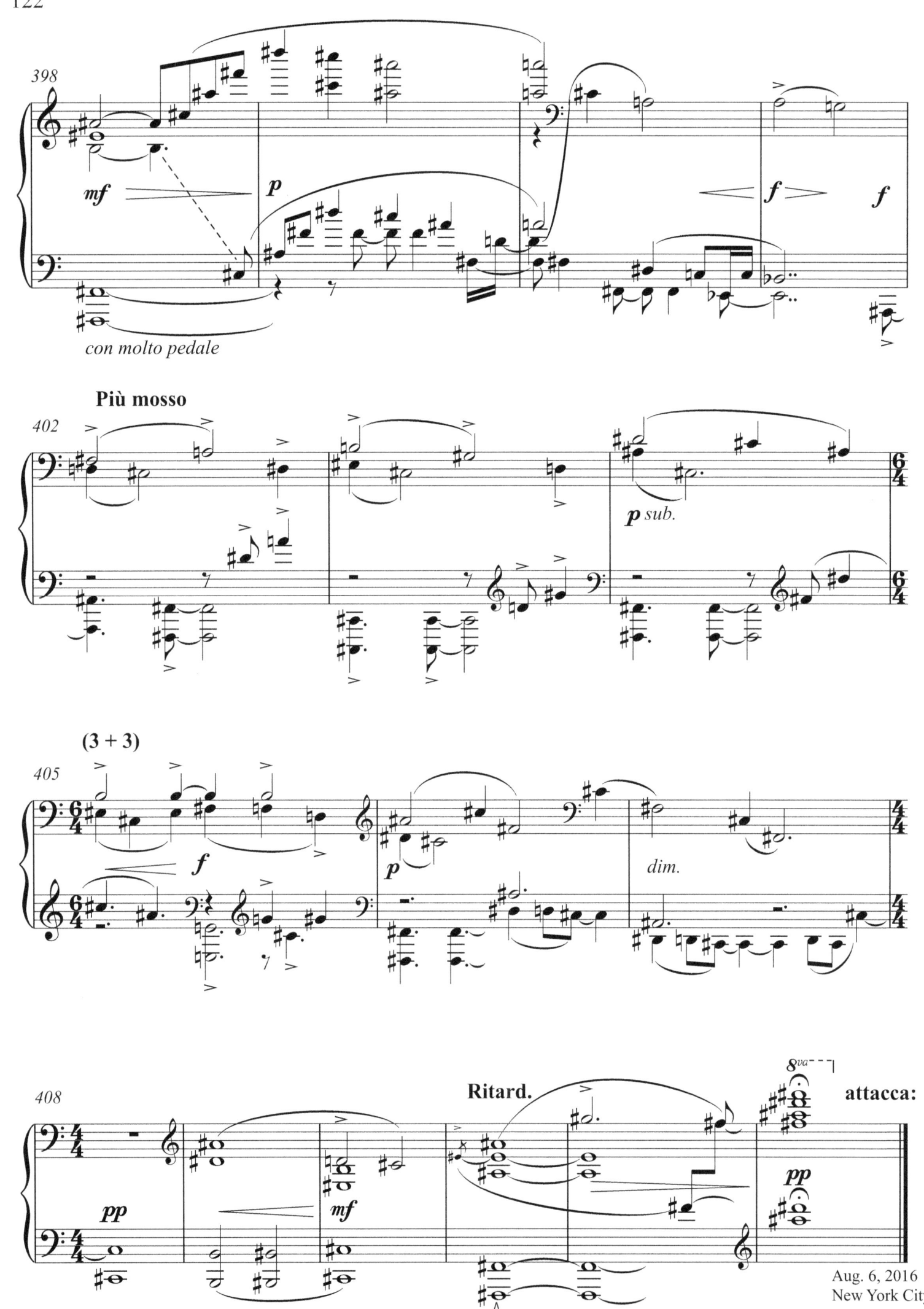

123

for Steven Beck

IV. For the Right Hand
(Theme and 6 Variations)

DAVID DEL TREDICI

attacca:

© Copyright by Boosey & Hawkes, Inc.
International copyright secured. All rights reserved.

Var. 3
Più mosso, marziale (♩ = 96)

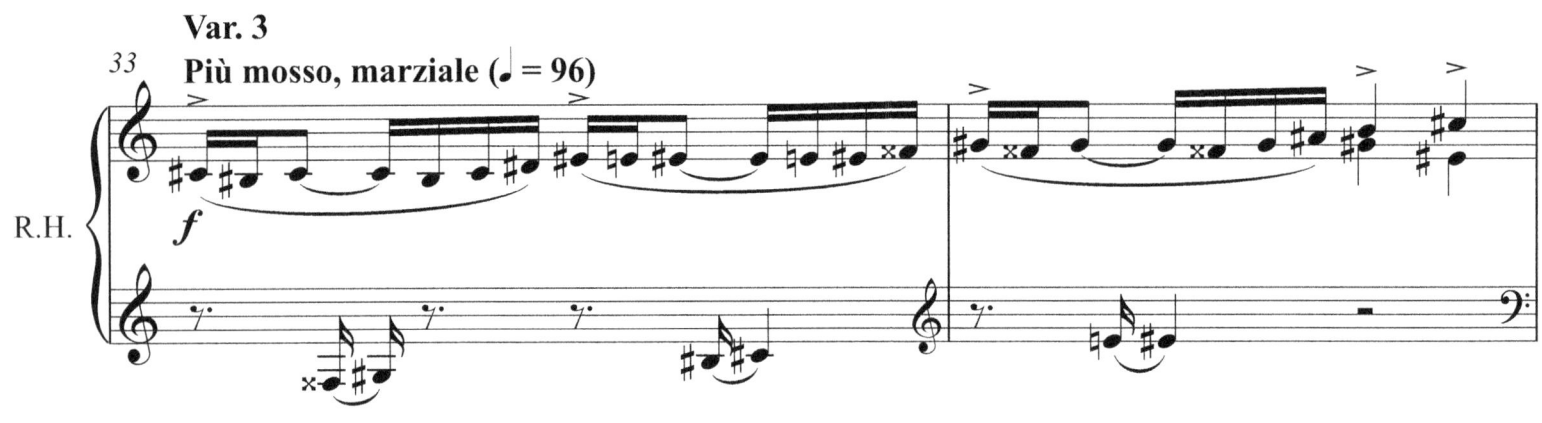

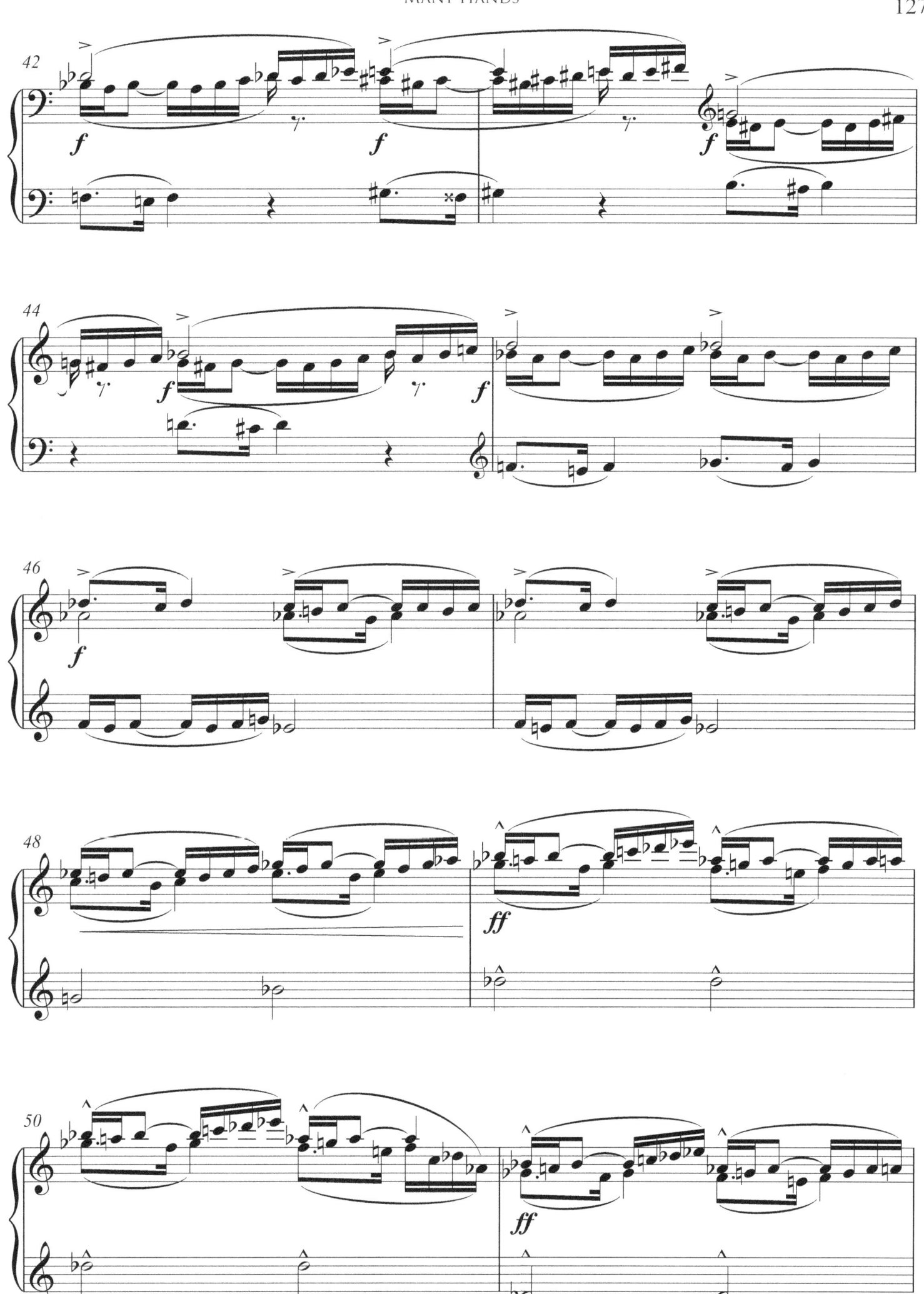

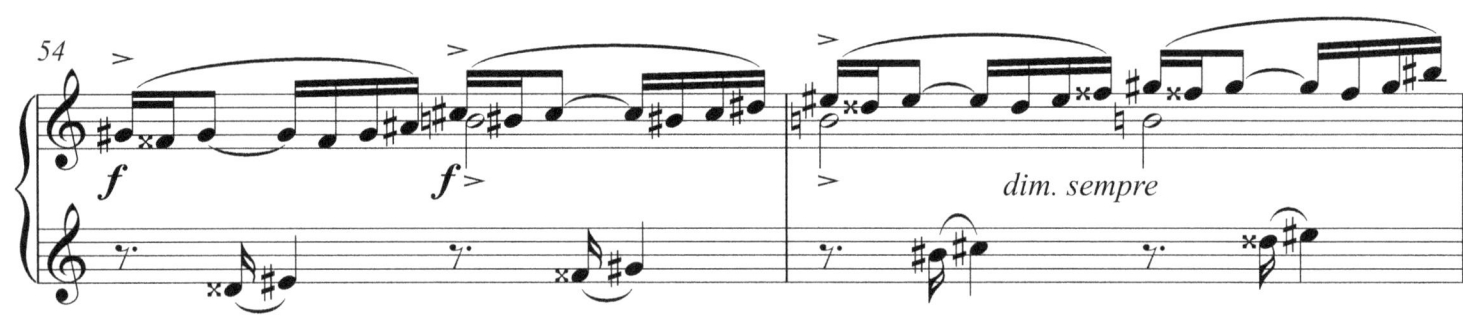

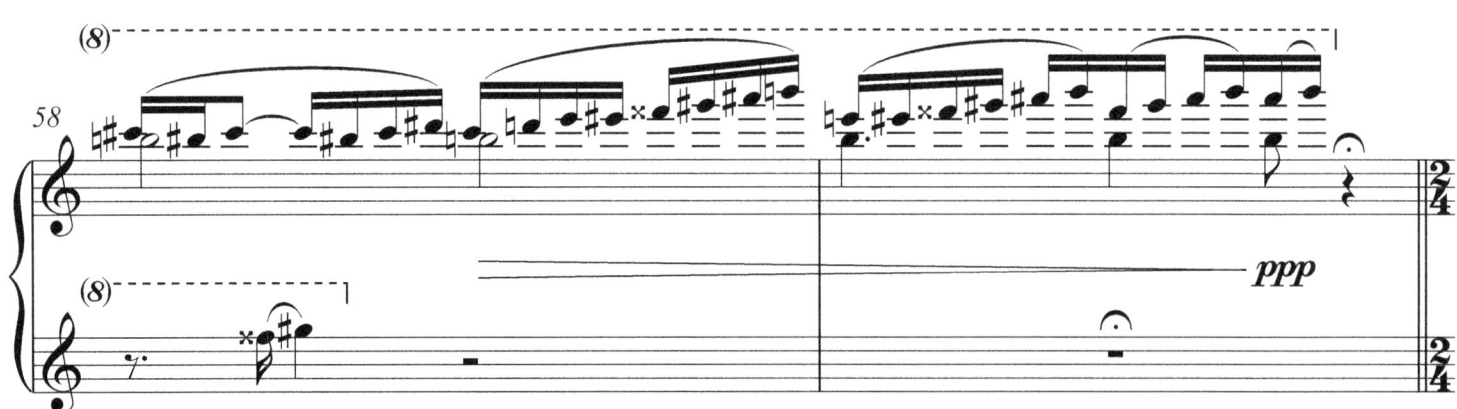

Var. 4
Canon at the octave and at the quarter note
Poco meno mosso (♩ = 88)

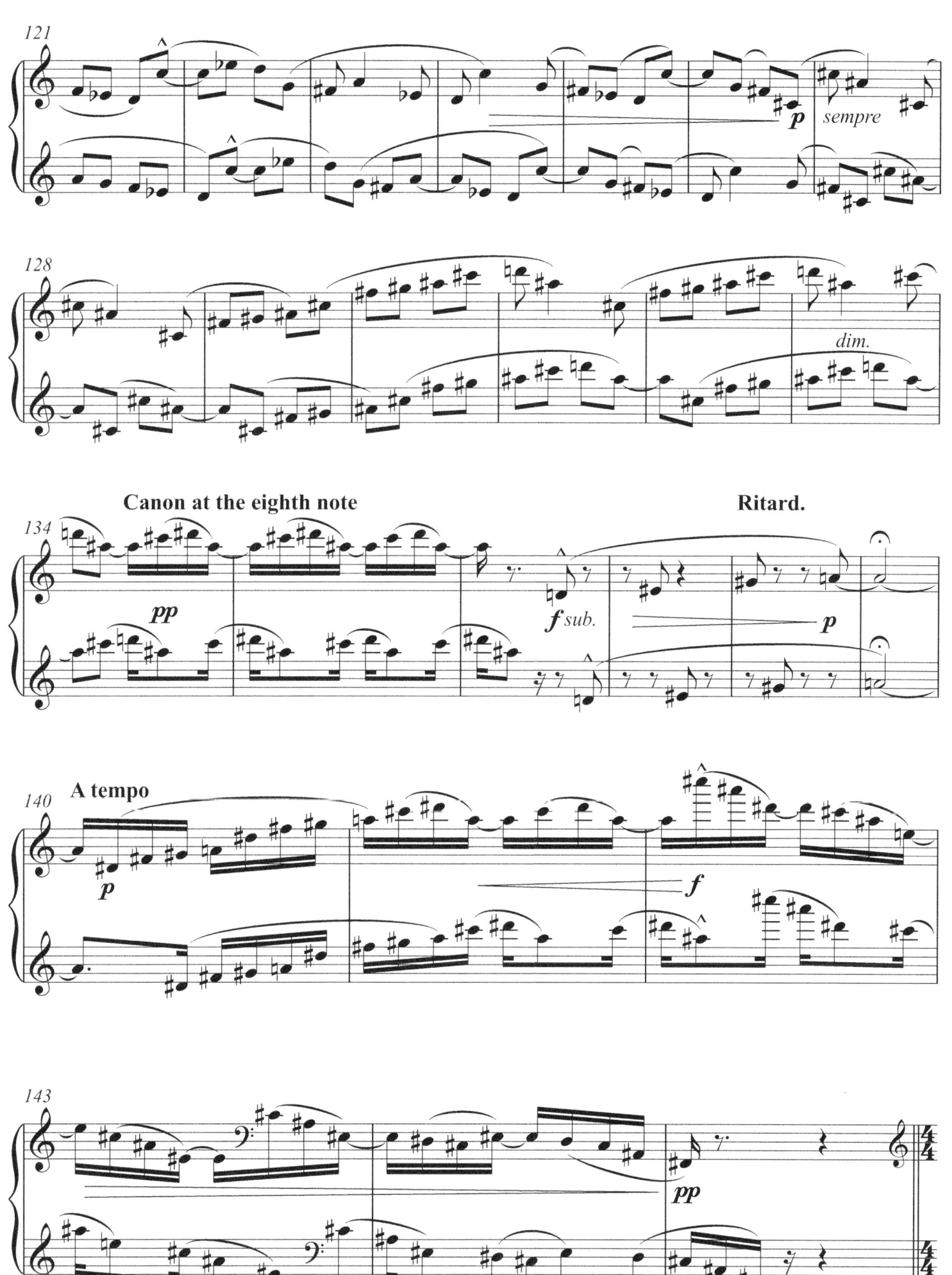

Var. 5
Tempo primo (♩ = 86)

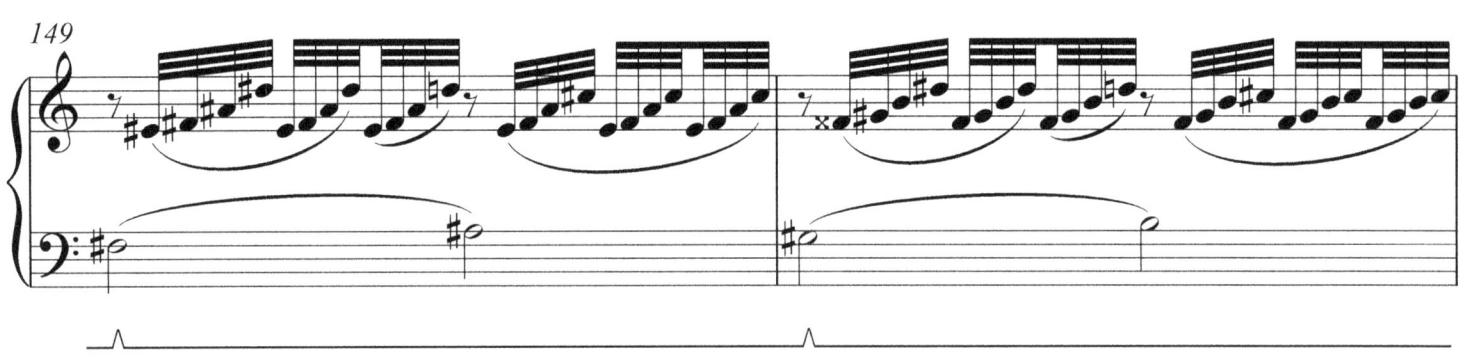

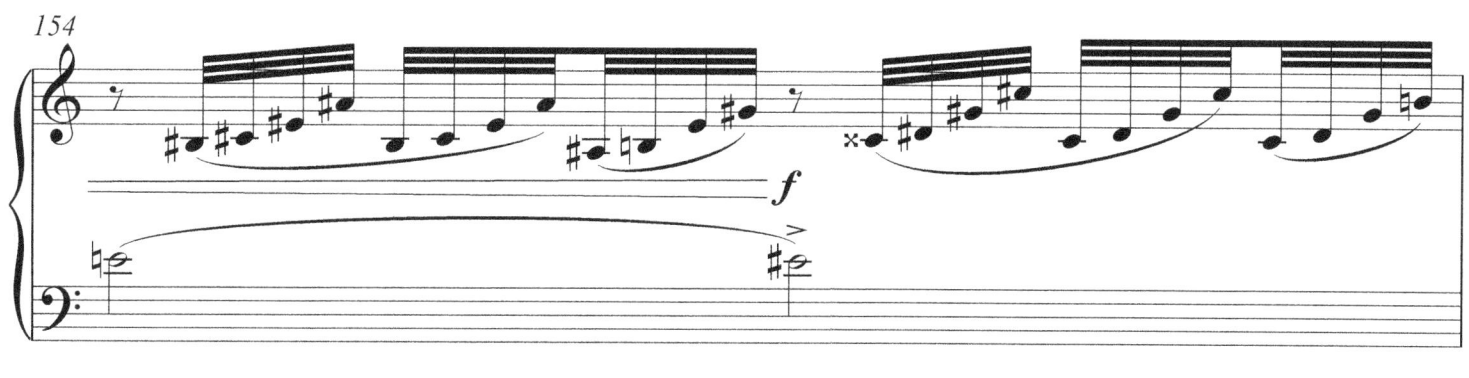
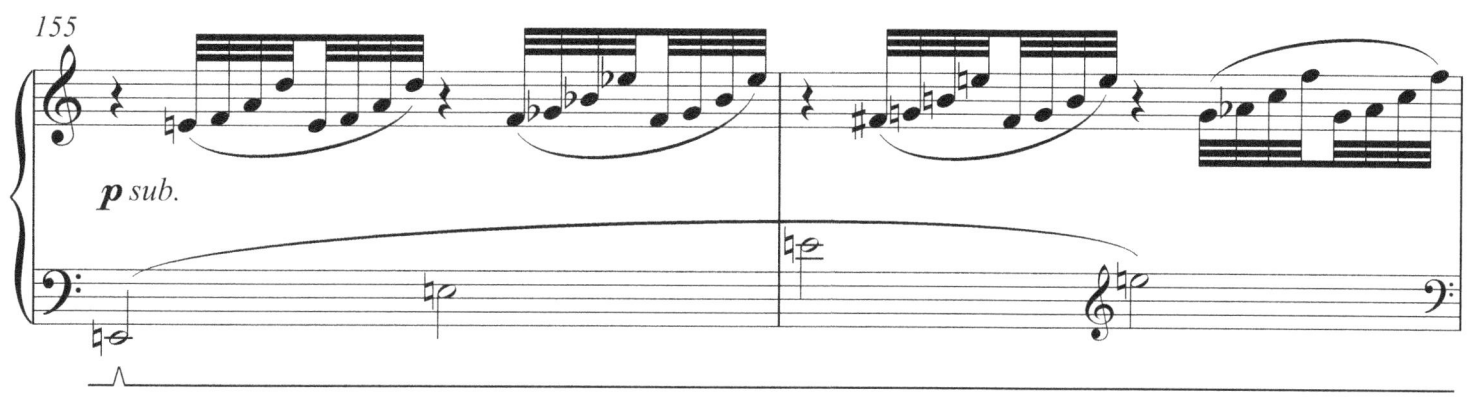

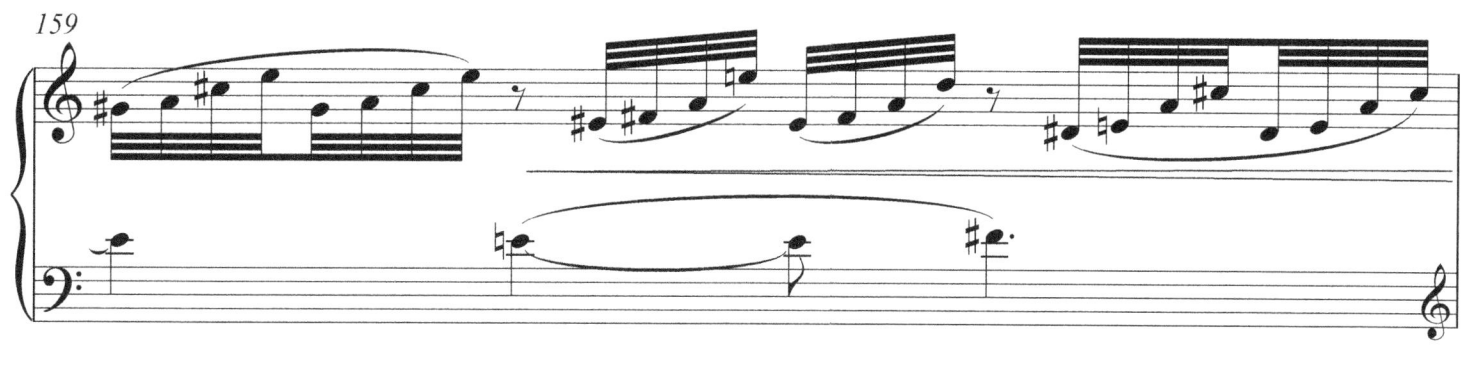

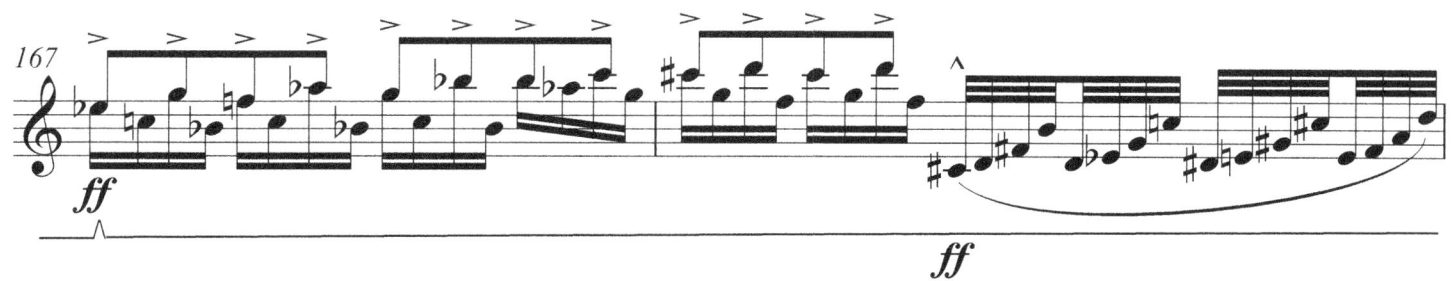

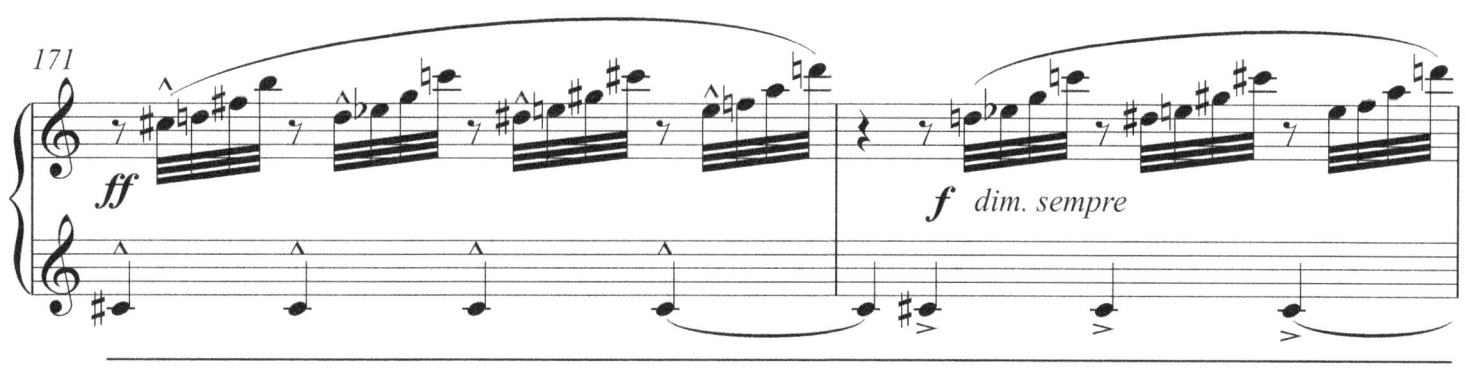
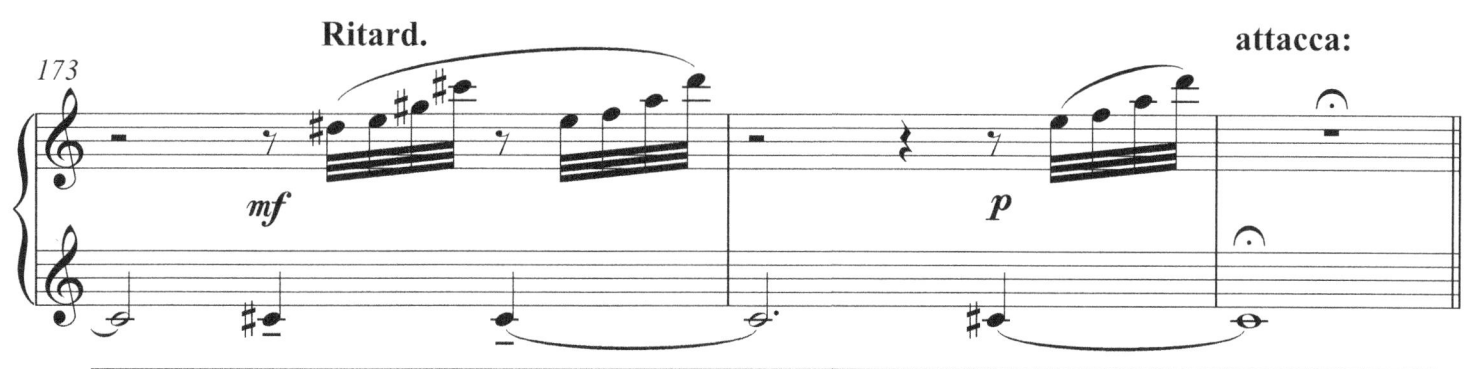

136

Variation 6
Tempo primo (♩ = 86)

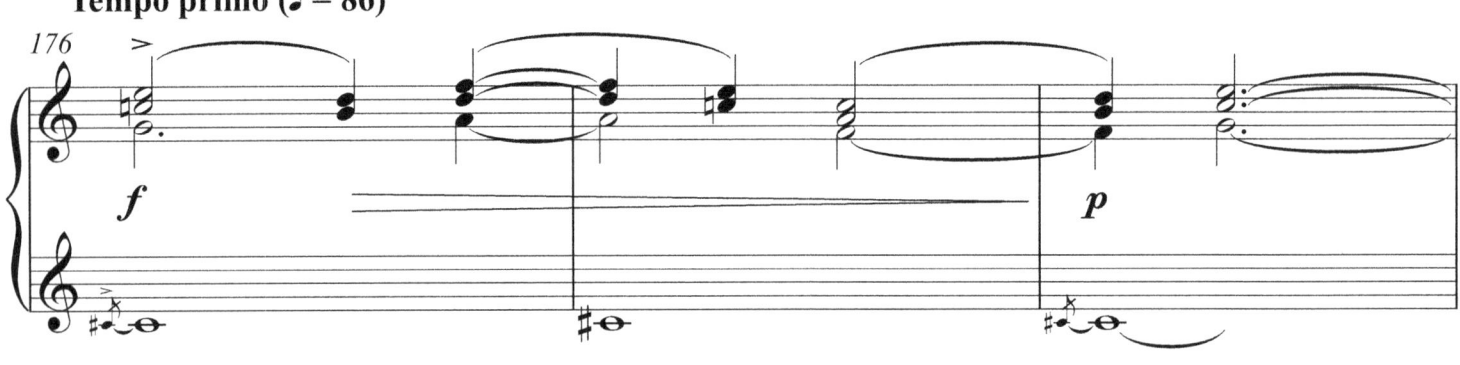

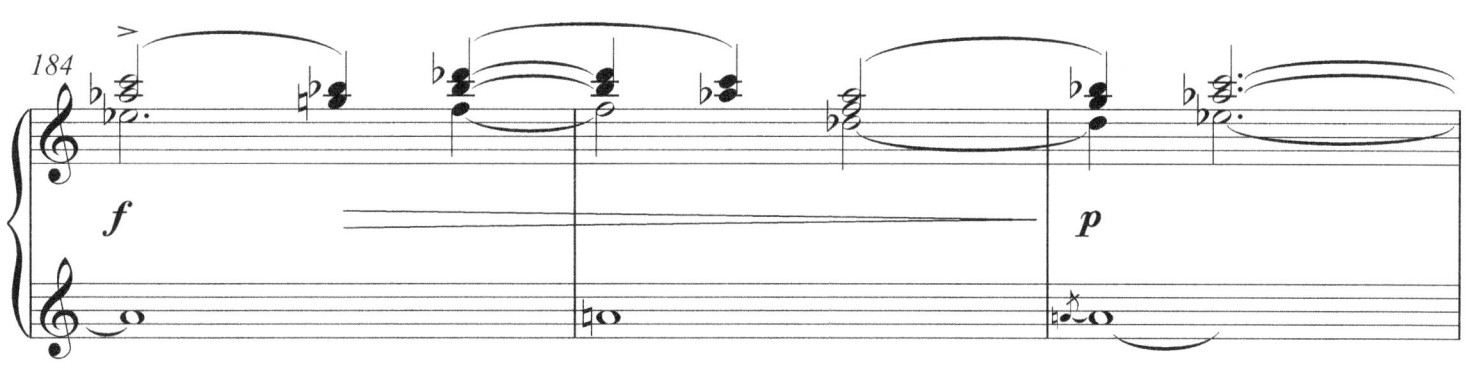

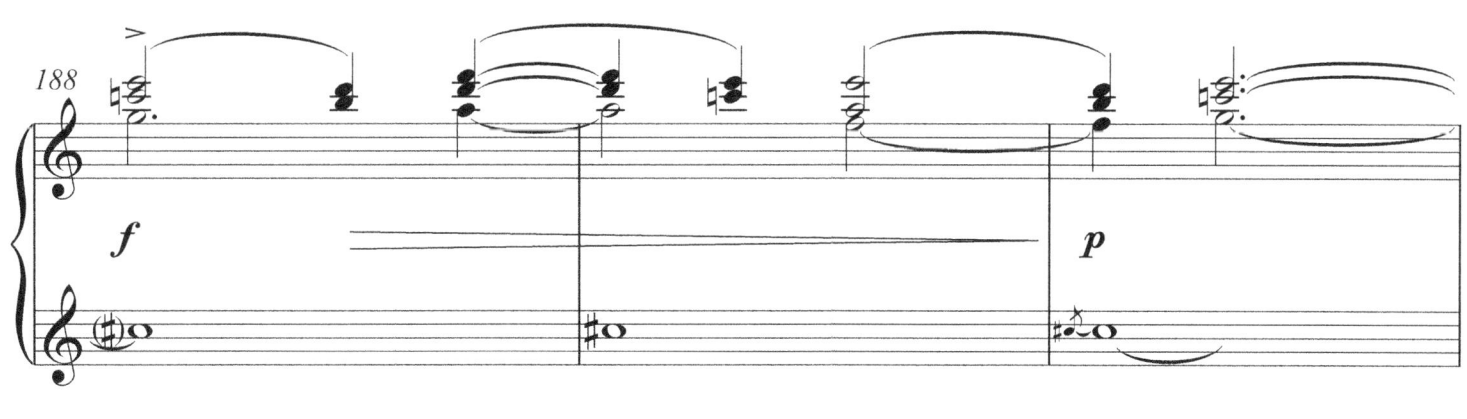
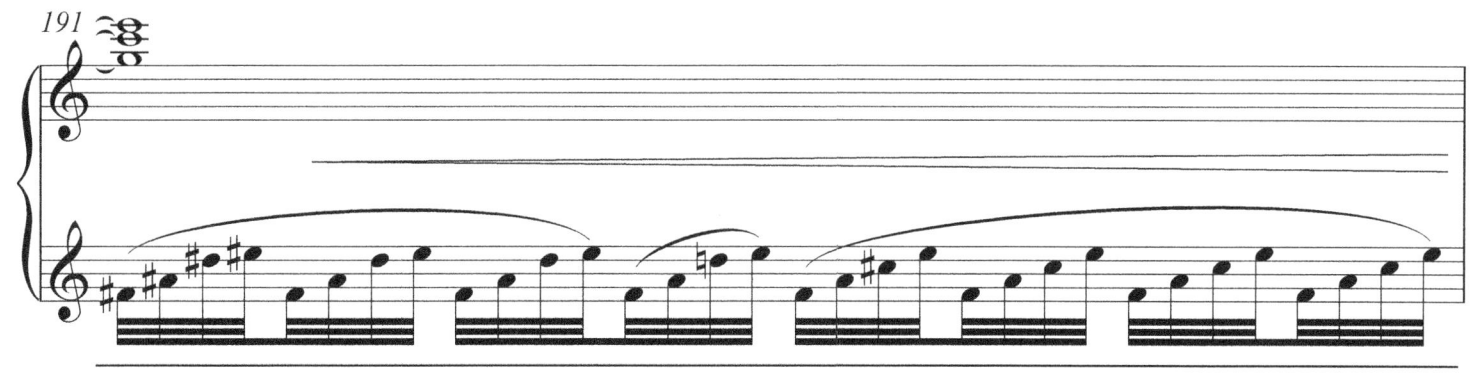

192
f
dim.
tr
(no pedal change)
194
8va
mf
dim.
tr
dim.
196
pp
6
197
(8)
198
cresc. ed accel.
attacca:
199
molto

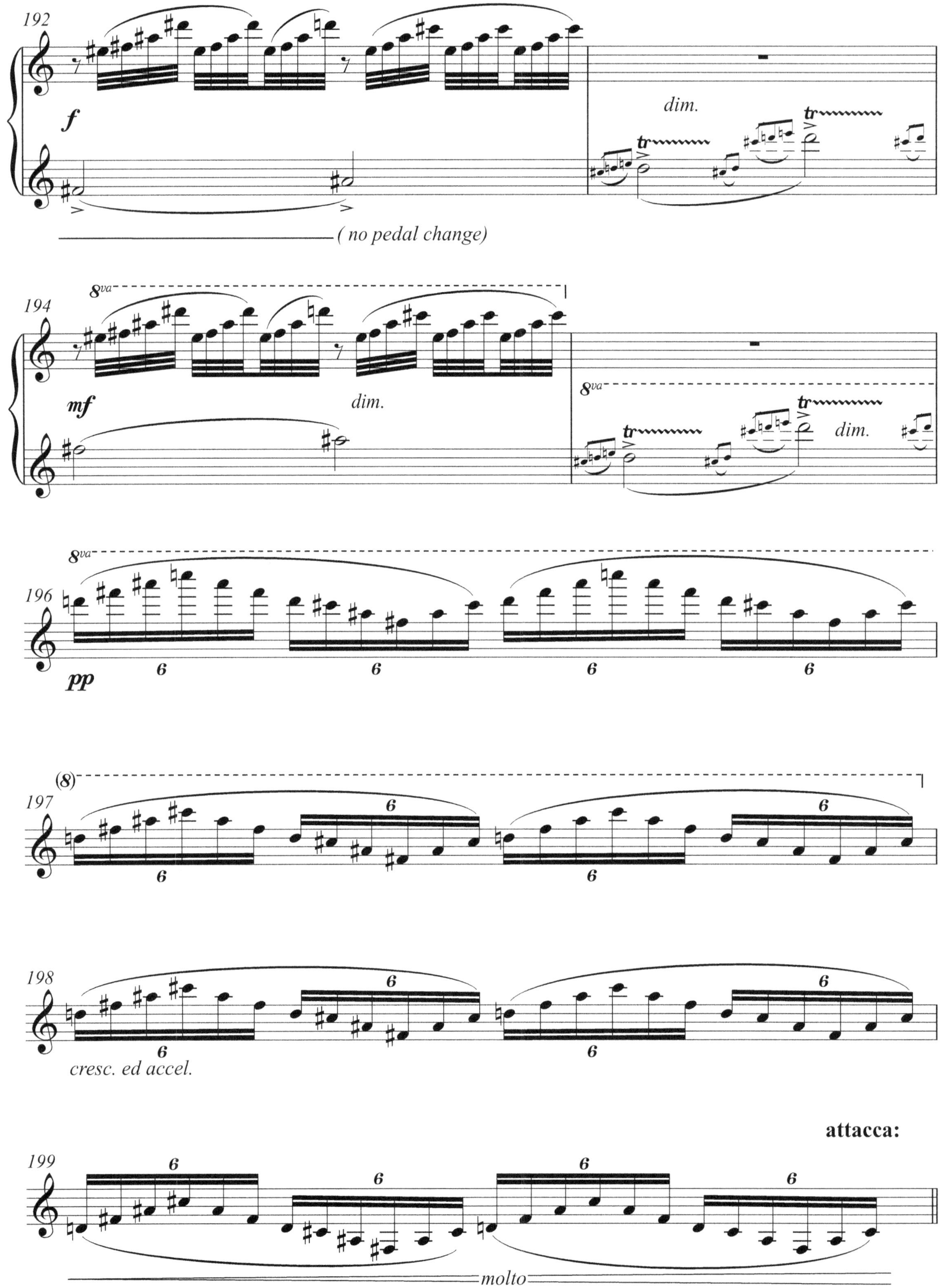

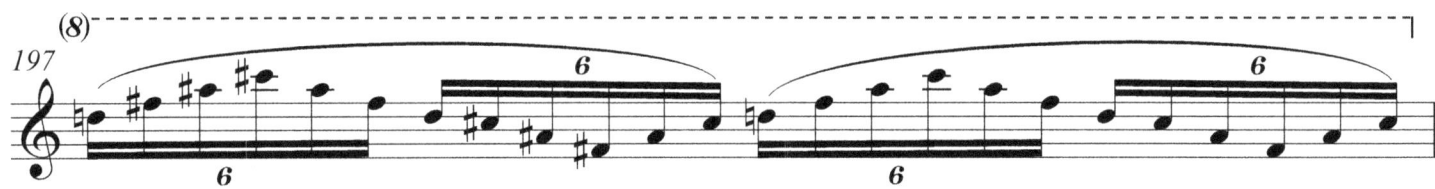

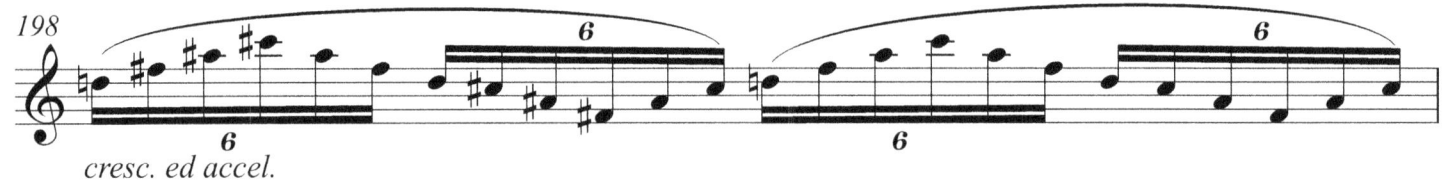

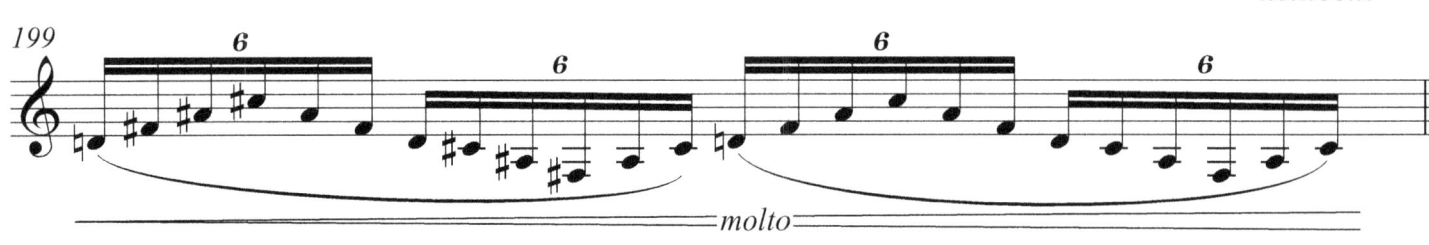

7'30"

V. Quodlibet/Finale

for Orion Weiss

DAVID DEL TREDICI

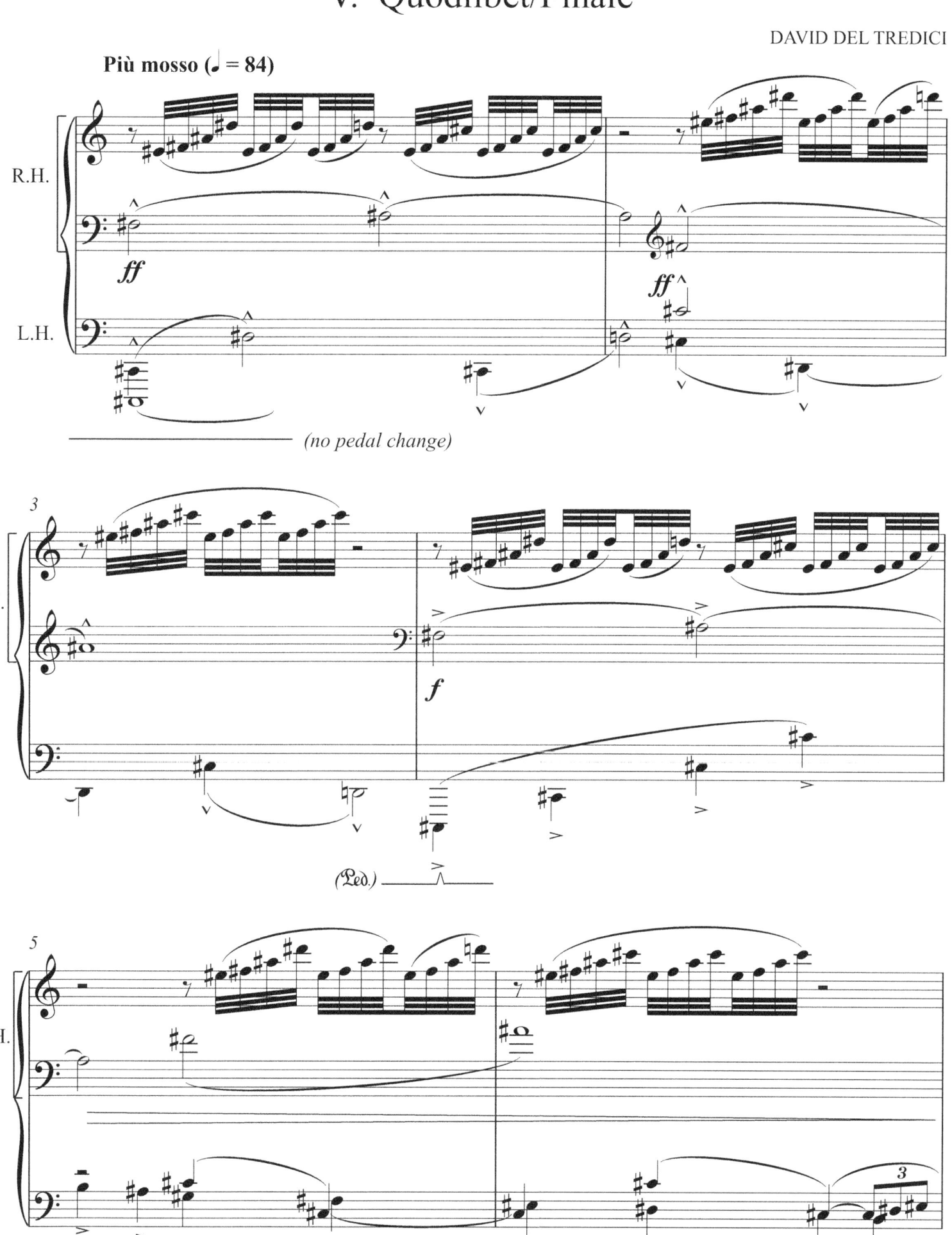

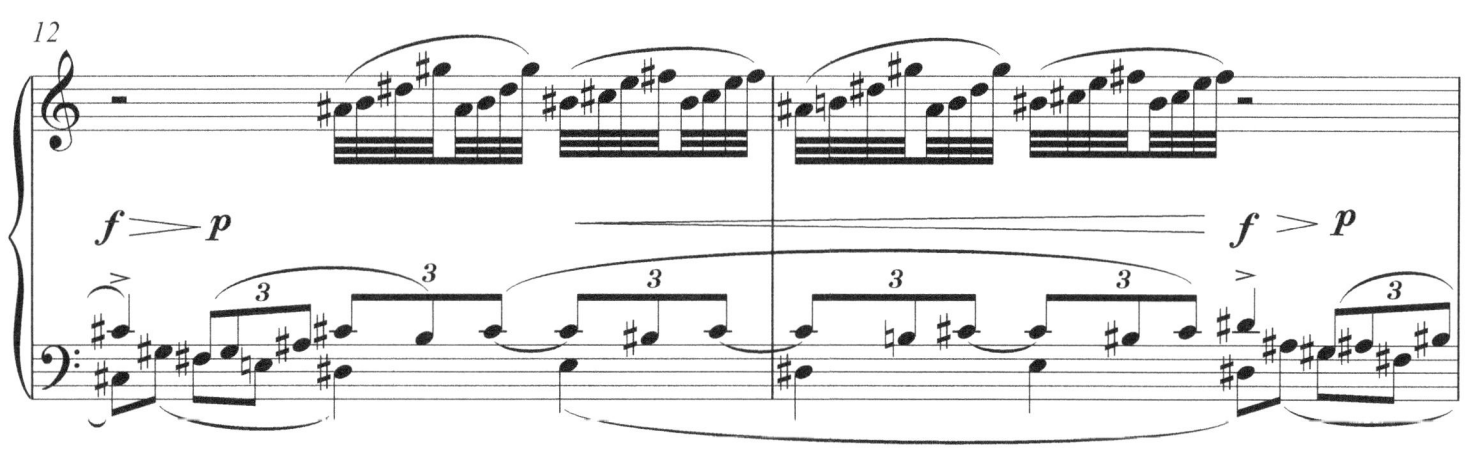

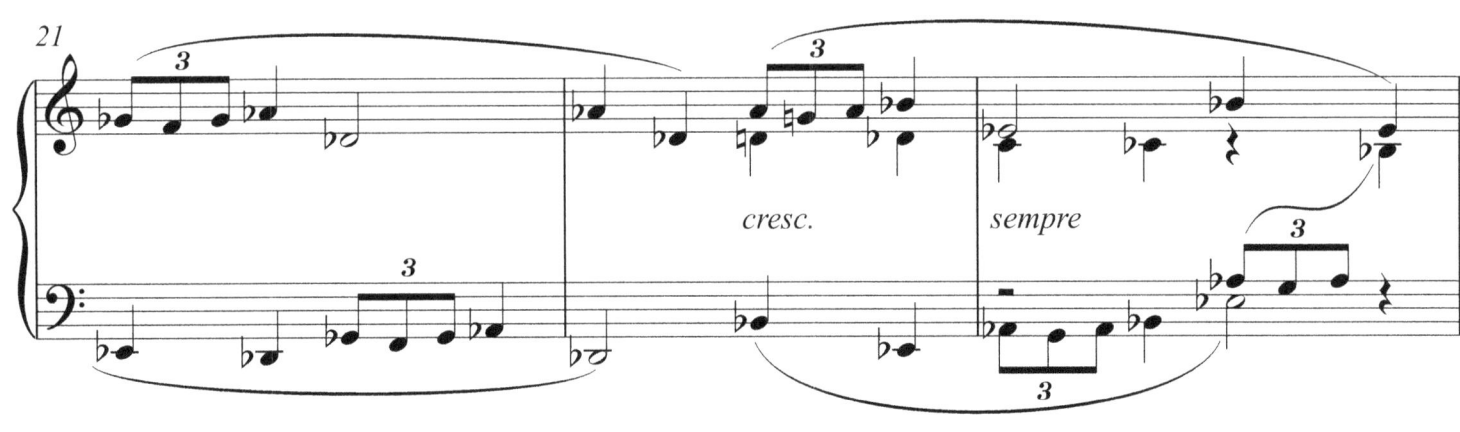
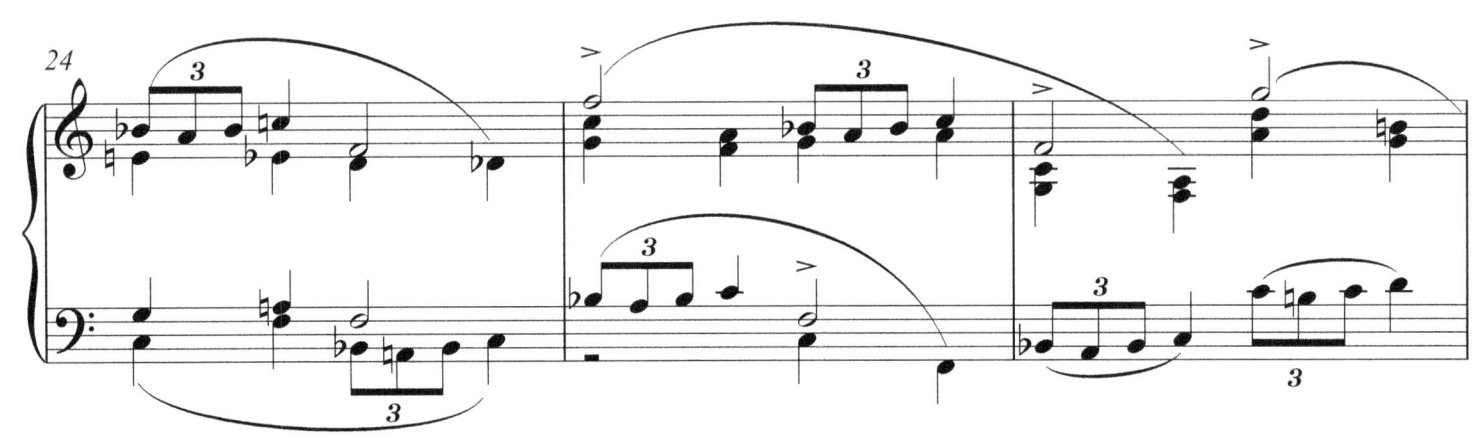

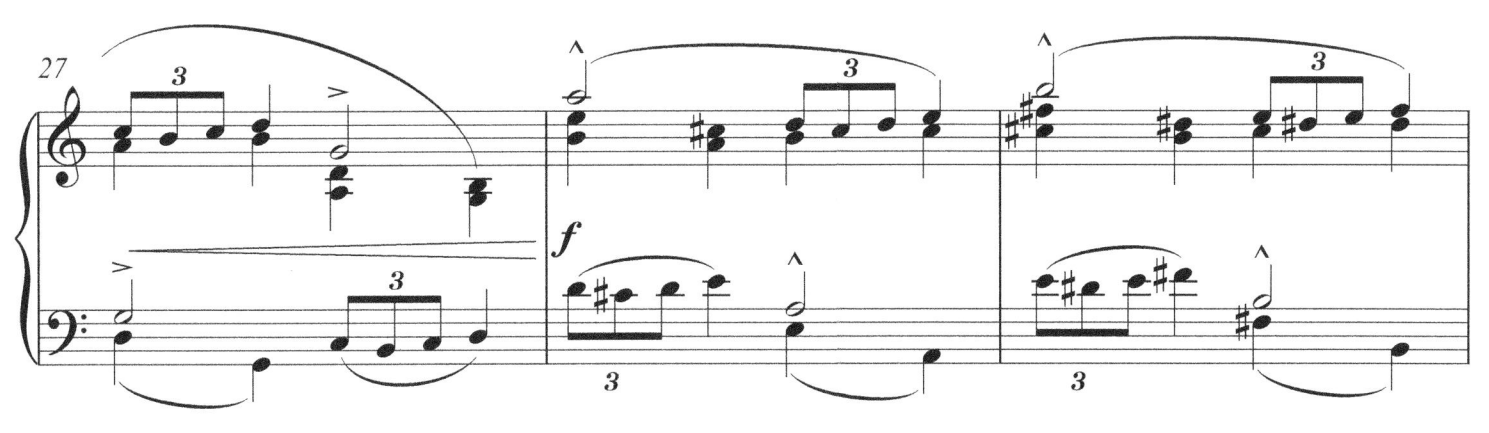

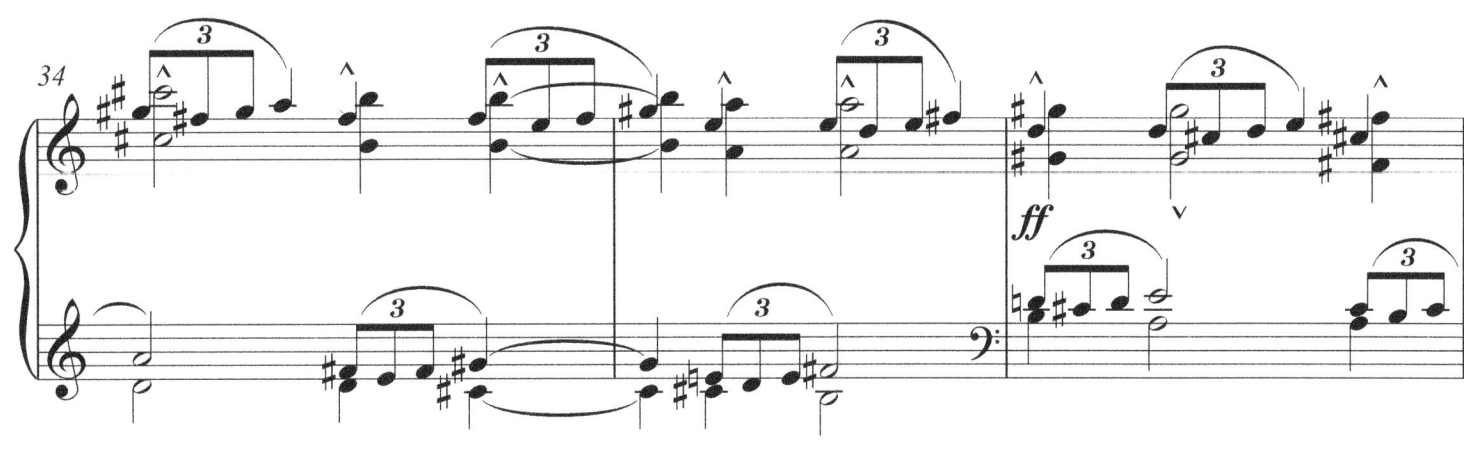

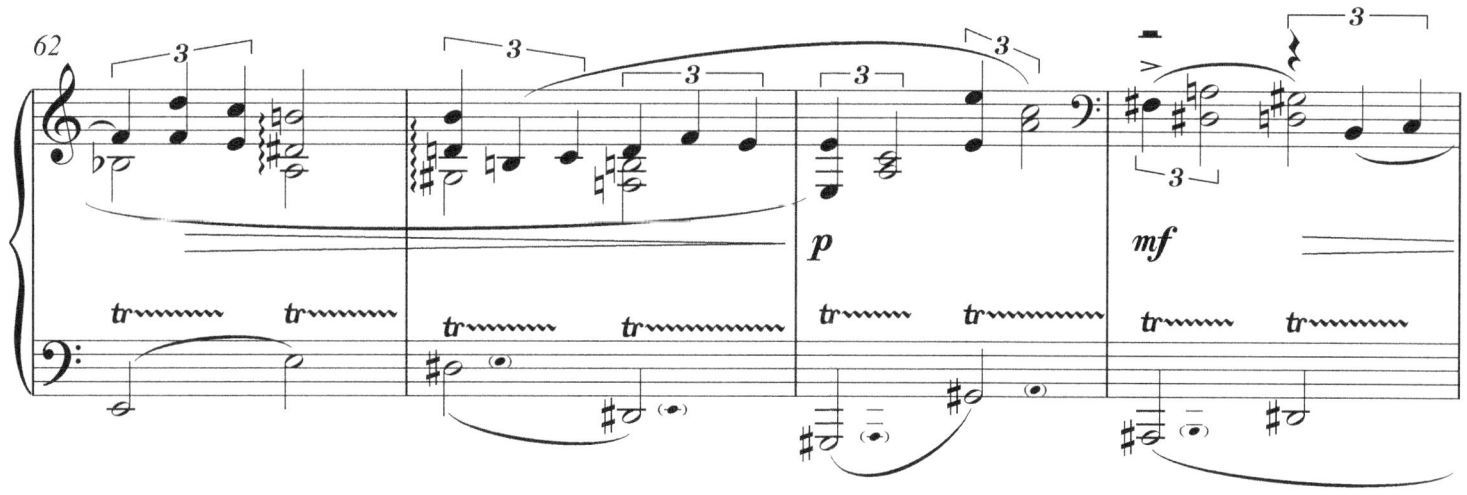
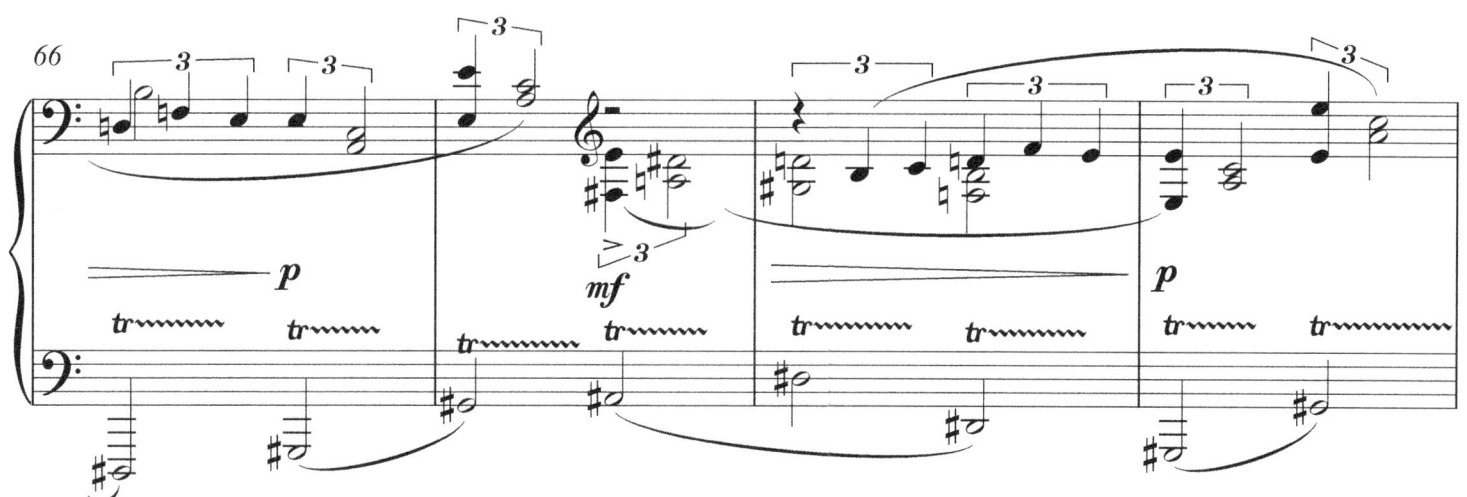

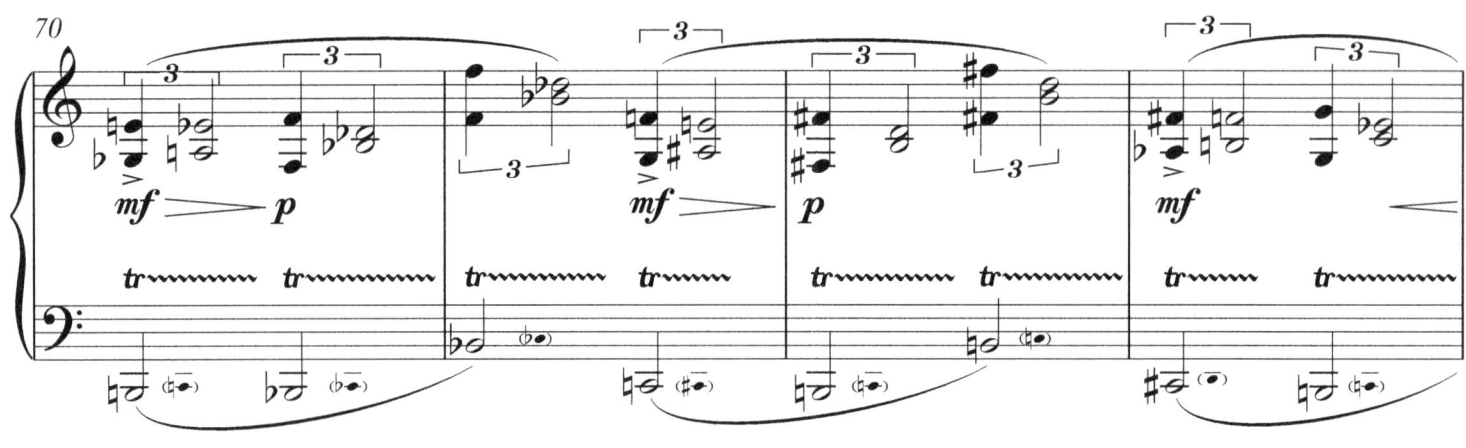

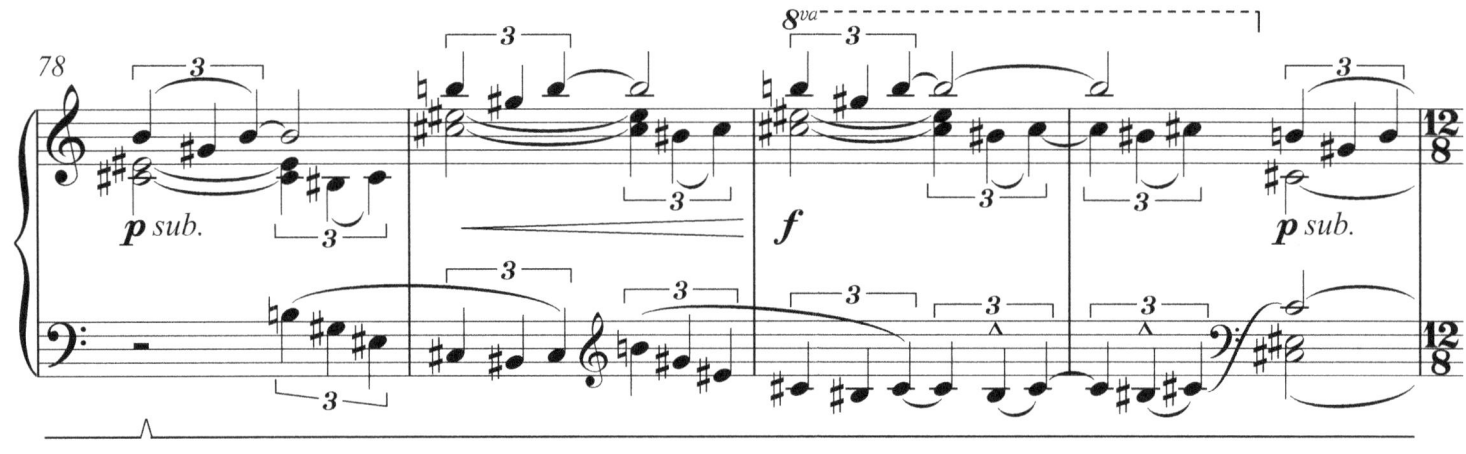

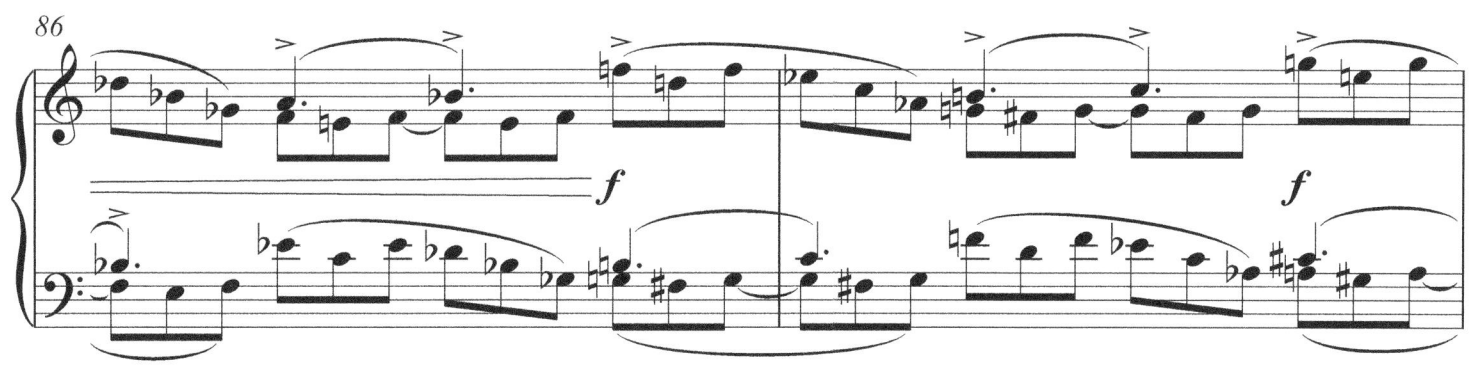

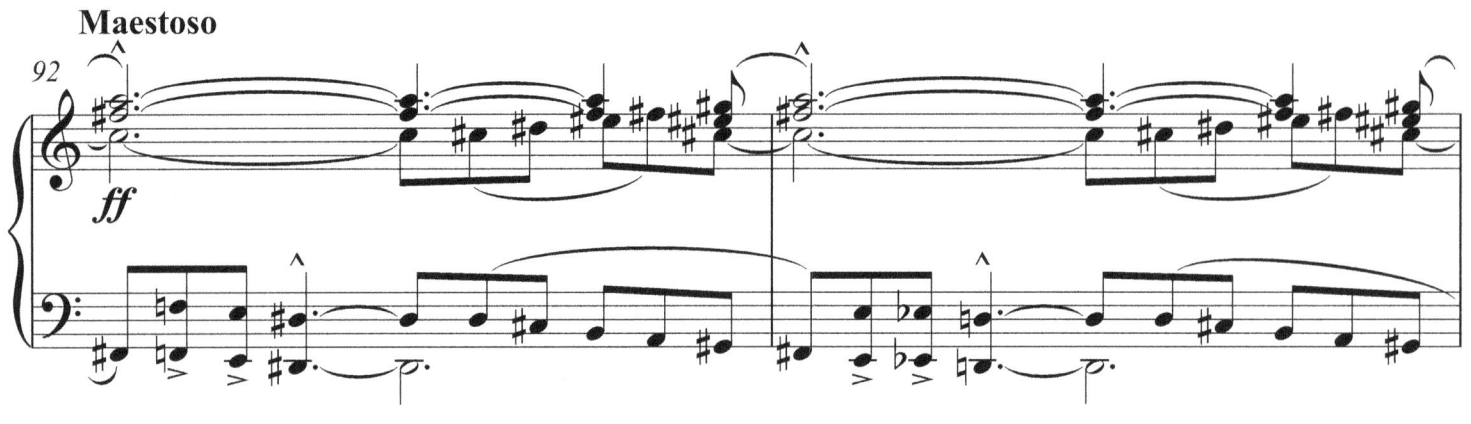
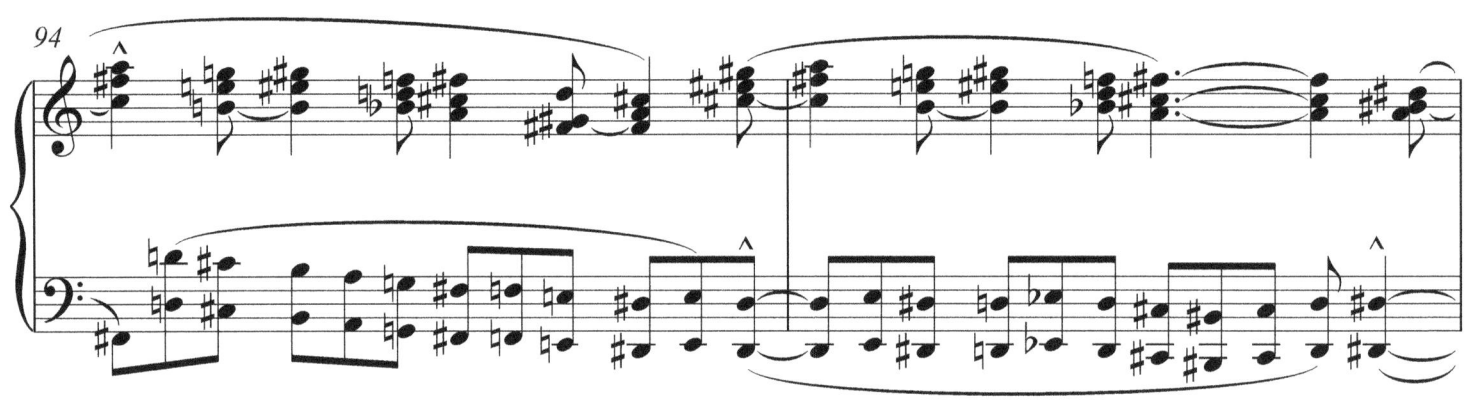
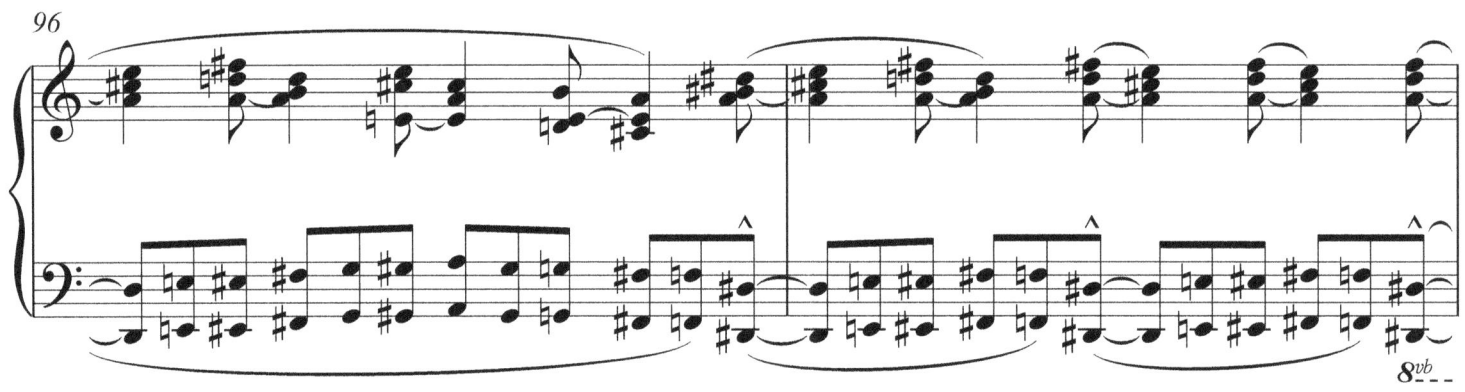

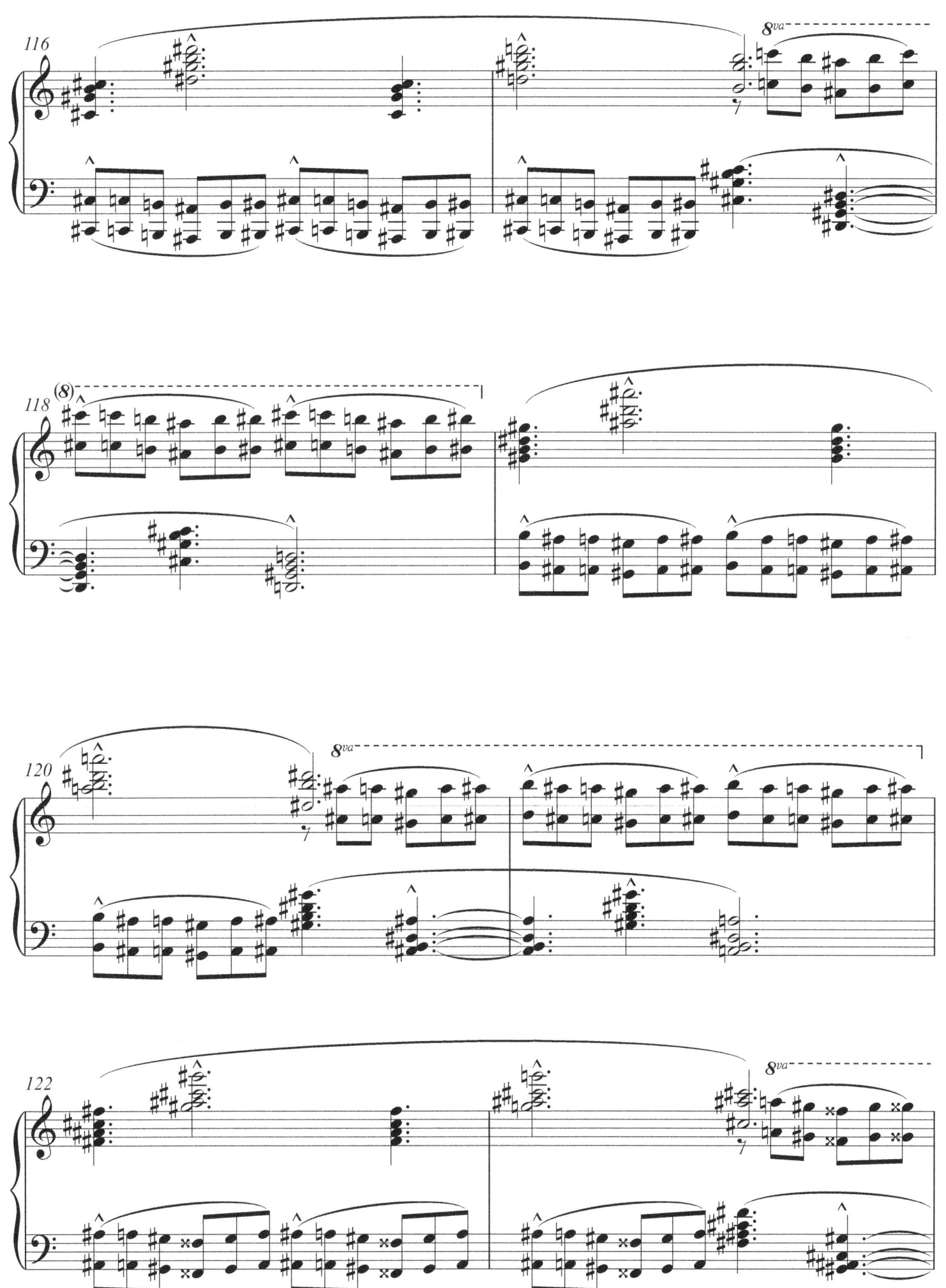

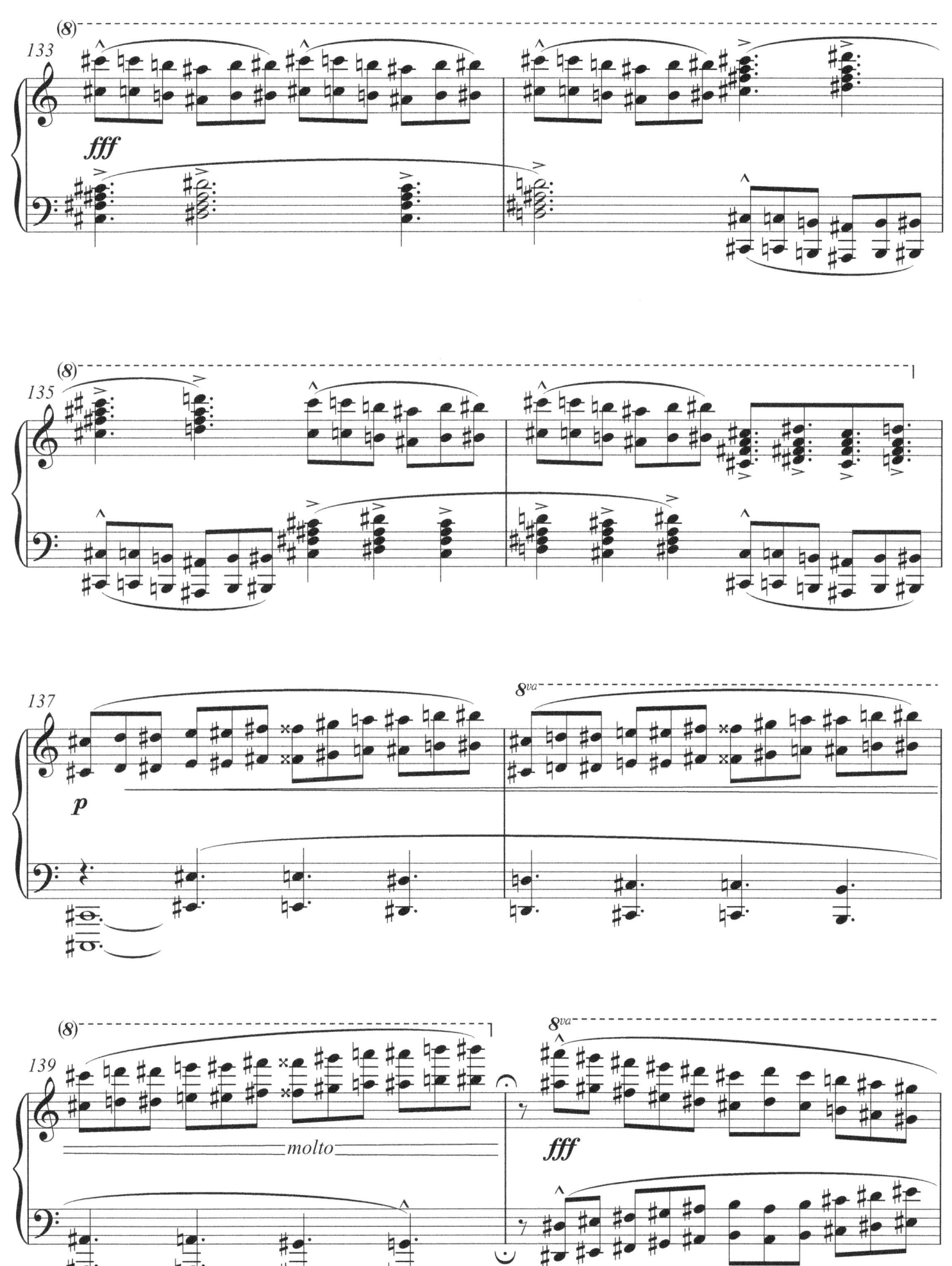

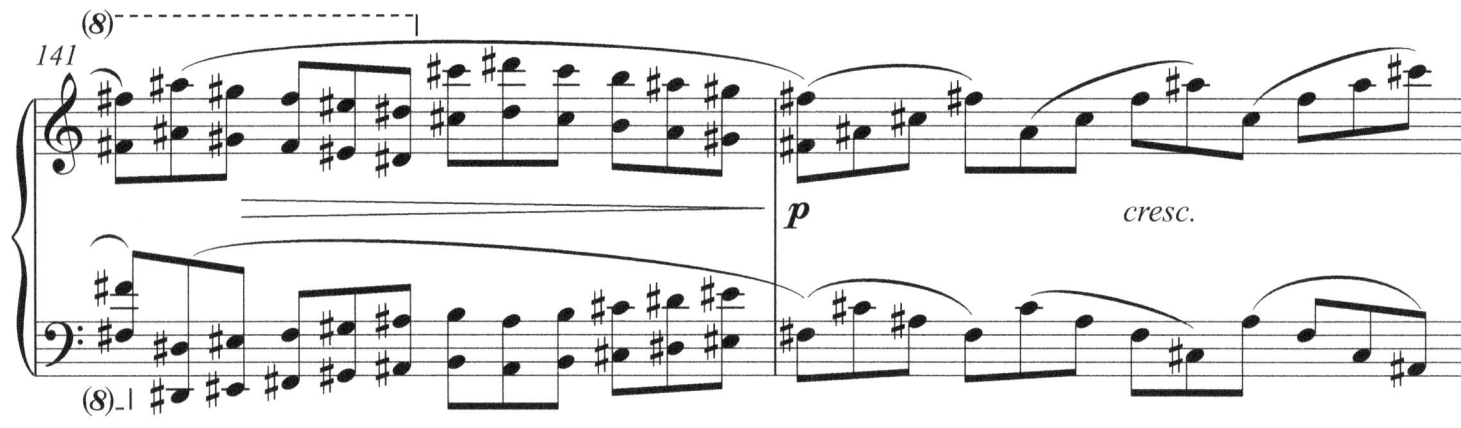

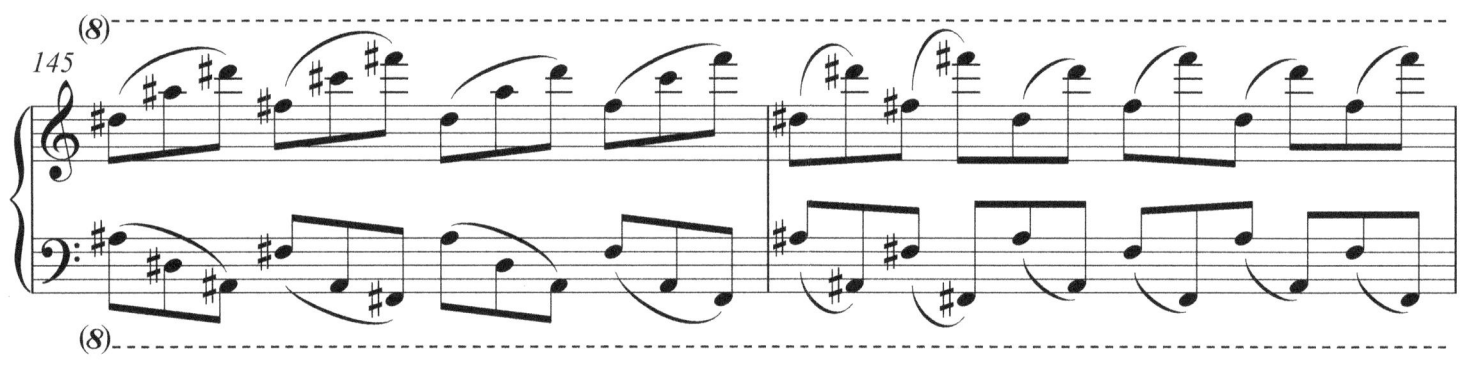
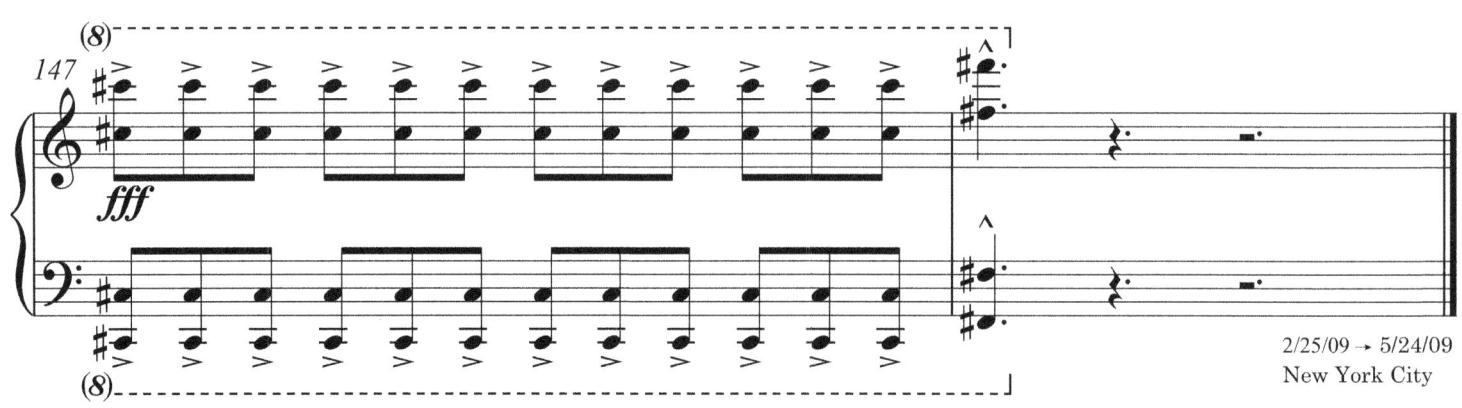

2/25/09 → 5/24/09
New York City

155

for Ray Warman — the inspiration

RAY'S BIRTHDAY SUIT
(Six Decades in Six Characteristic Pieces)

10 years old
Ray, a beautiful child, is taught
to embrace the Catholic Church.

I. RADIANT CHILD

DAVID DEL TREDICI

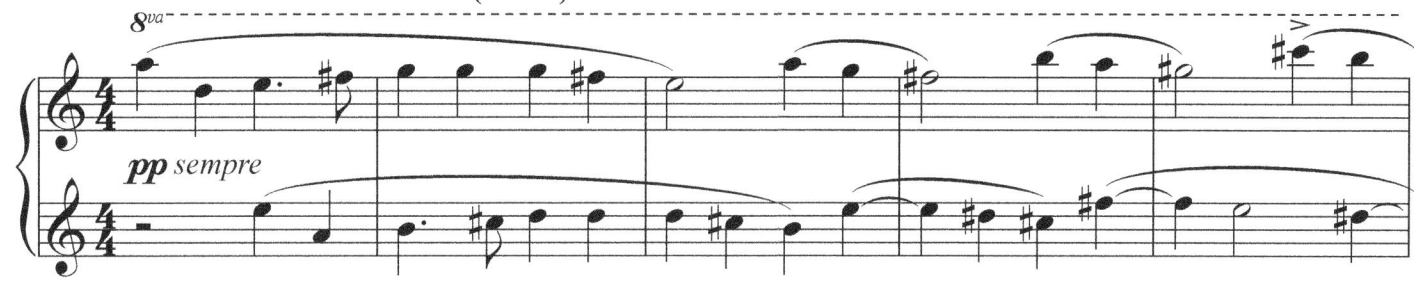

© Copyright 2016 Boosey & Hawkes, Inc.
International copyright secured. All rights reserved.

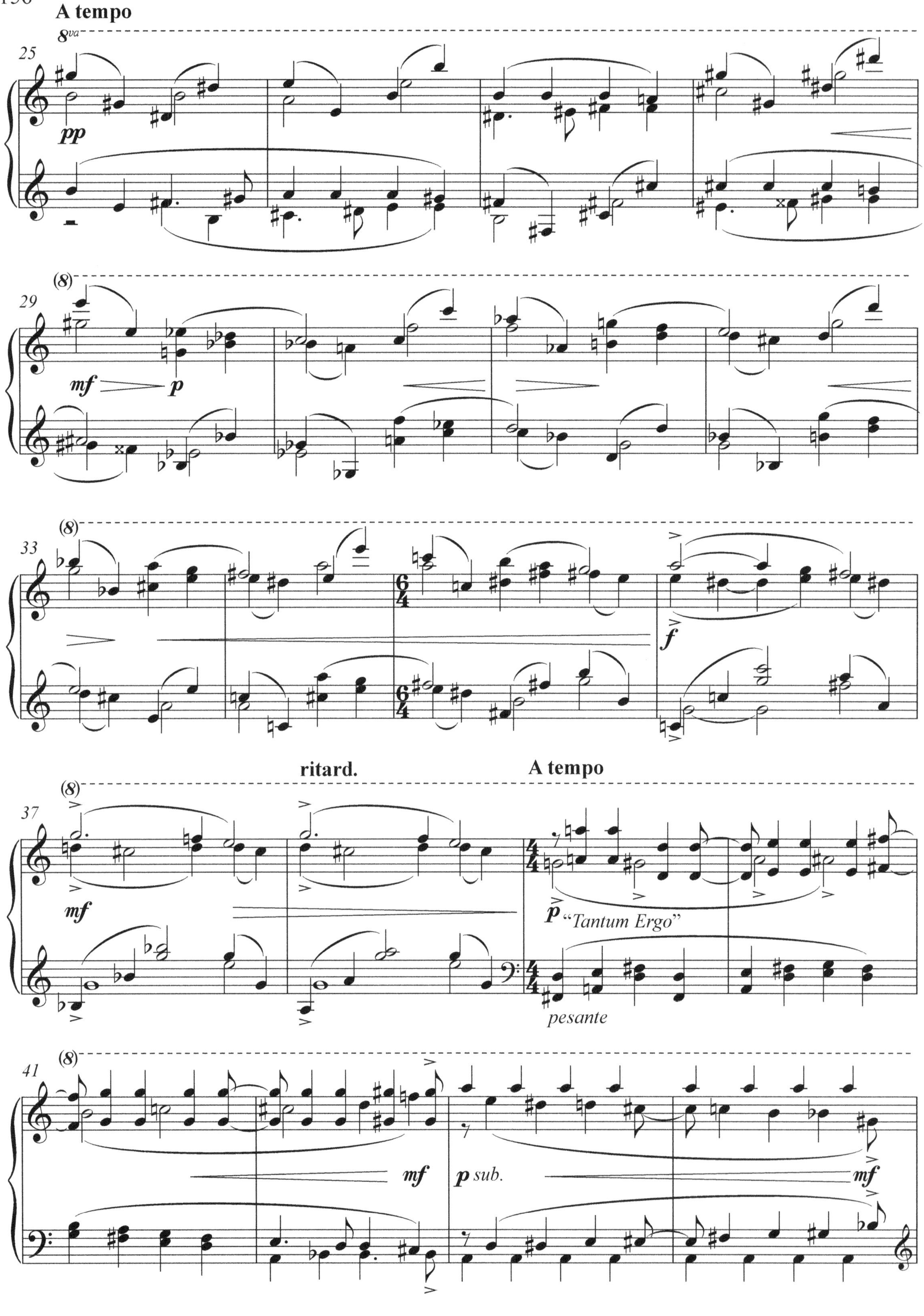
A tempo
8va
25
pp
29
(8)
mf
p
33
(8)
f
37
(8)
ritard.
A tempo
mf
p "Tantum Ergo"
pesante
41
(8)
mf
p sub.
mf

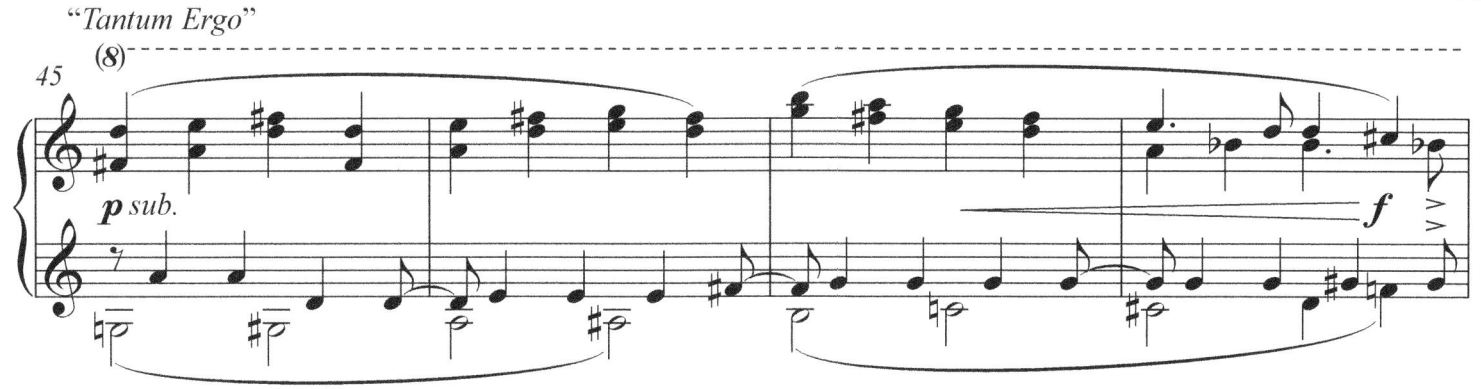

158

ritard.

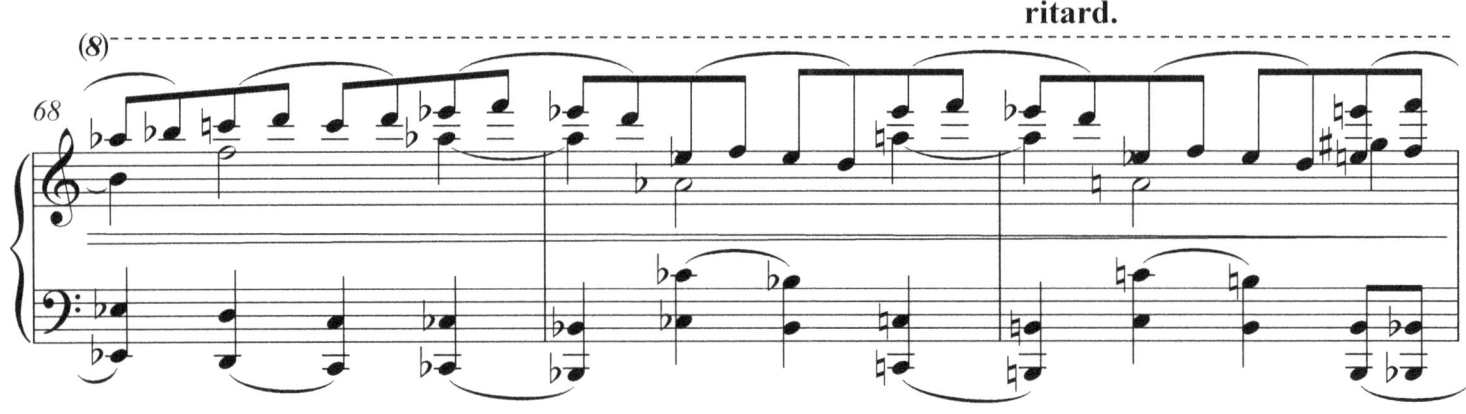

A tempo

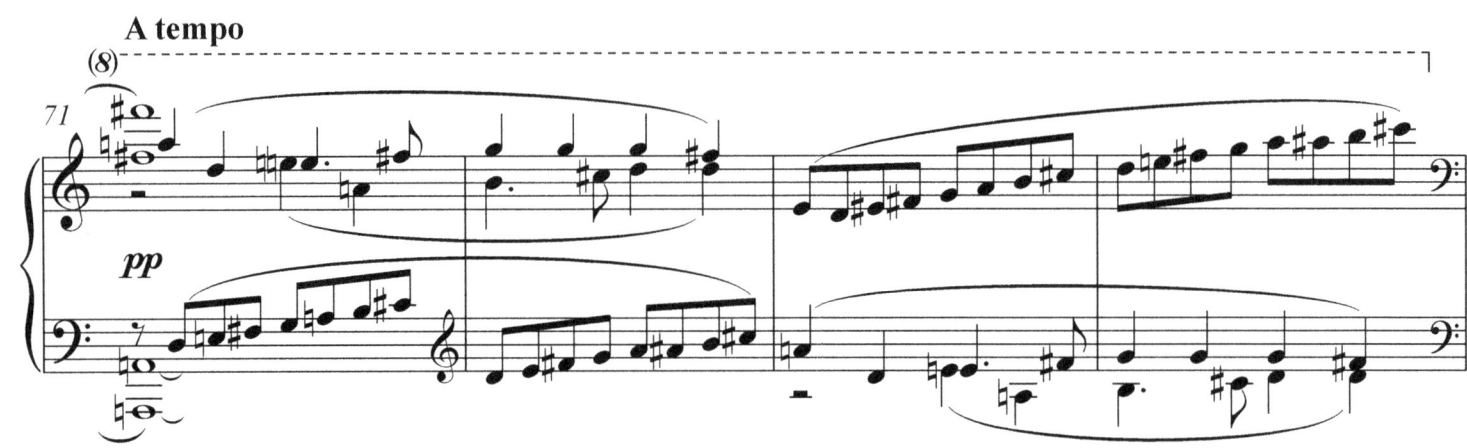

II. YALE FUGUE

(for Seth Slade)

20 years old
Ray, the Yale man, enters a new world
that will forever change his life.

Whiffenpoof Song (Part I)
Half tempo (← 𝅗𝅥 = 𝅘𝅥 →; 𝅘𝅥 = 92)

Whiffenpoof Song (Part II)
Half tempo

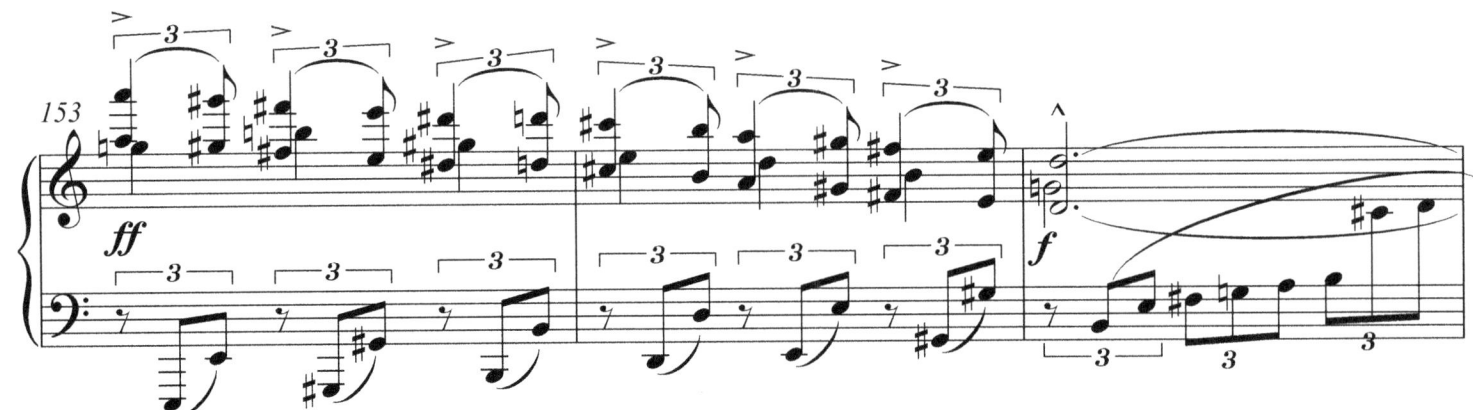

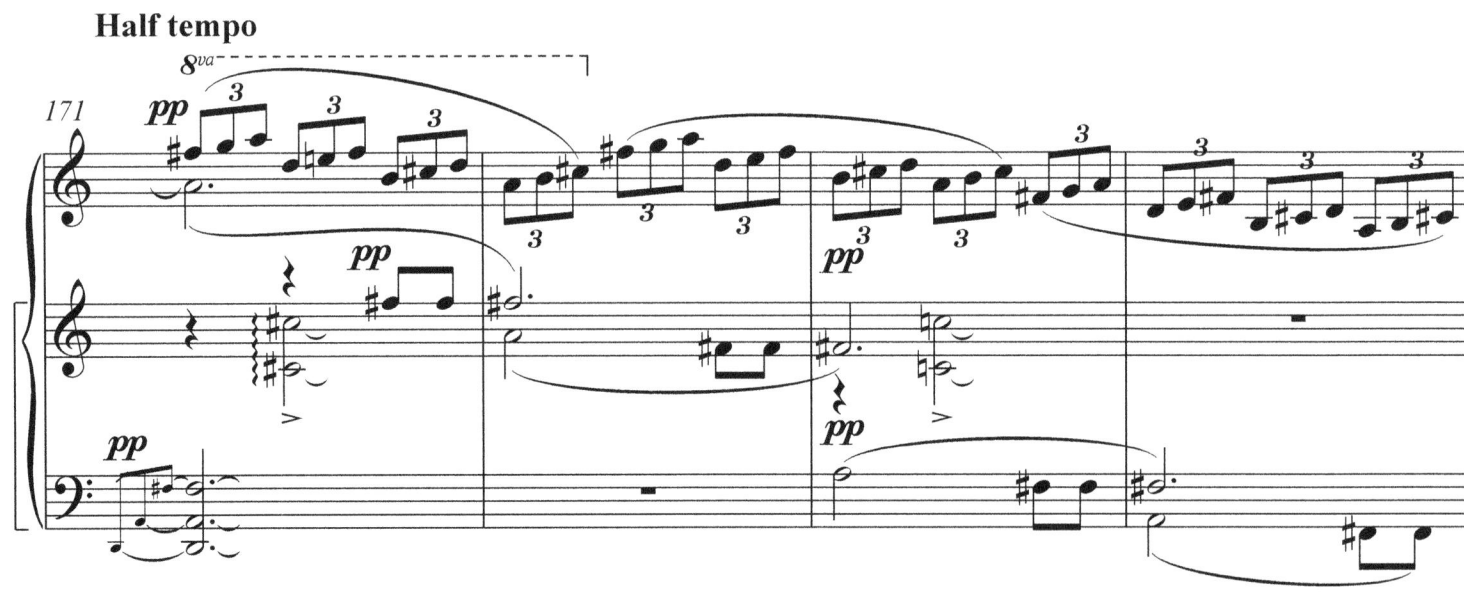

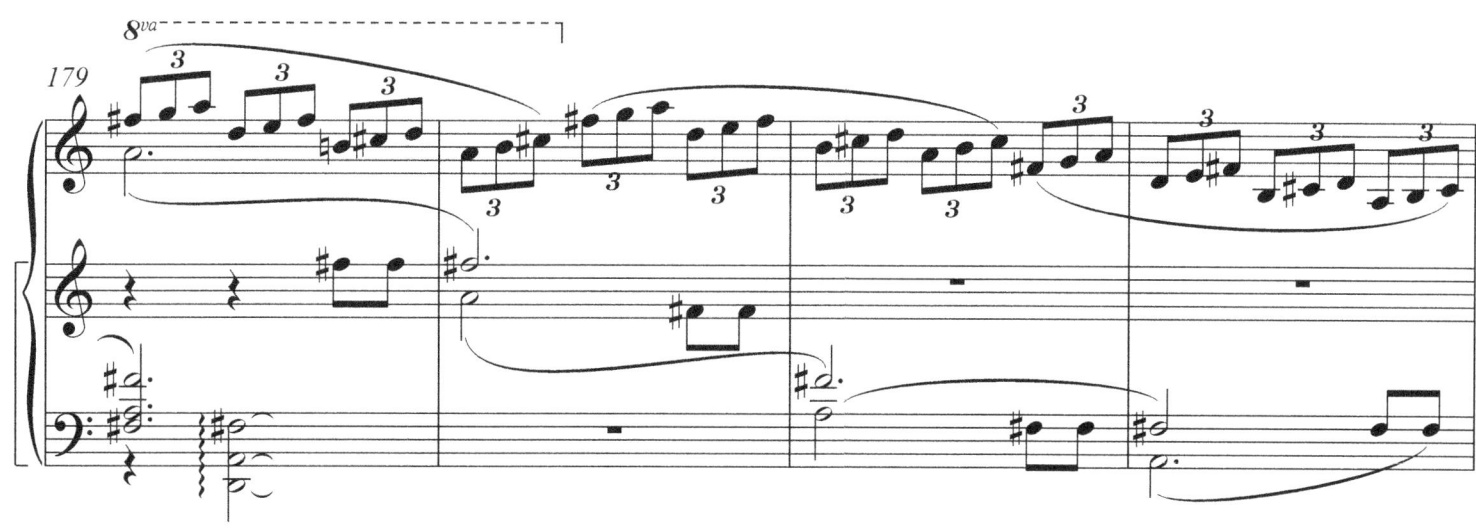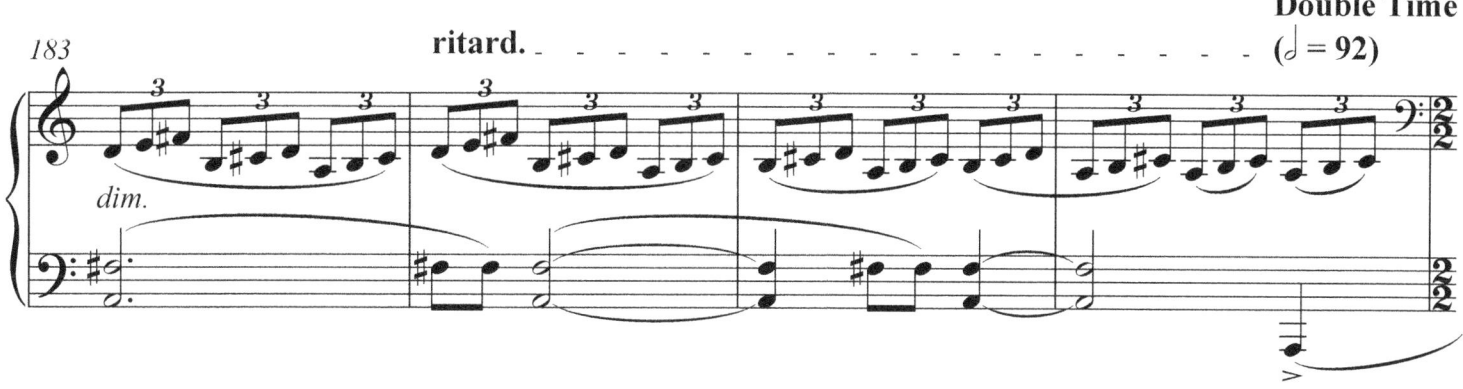

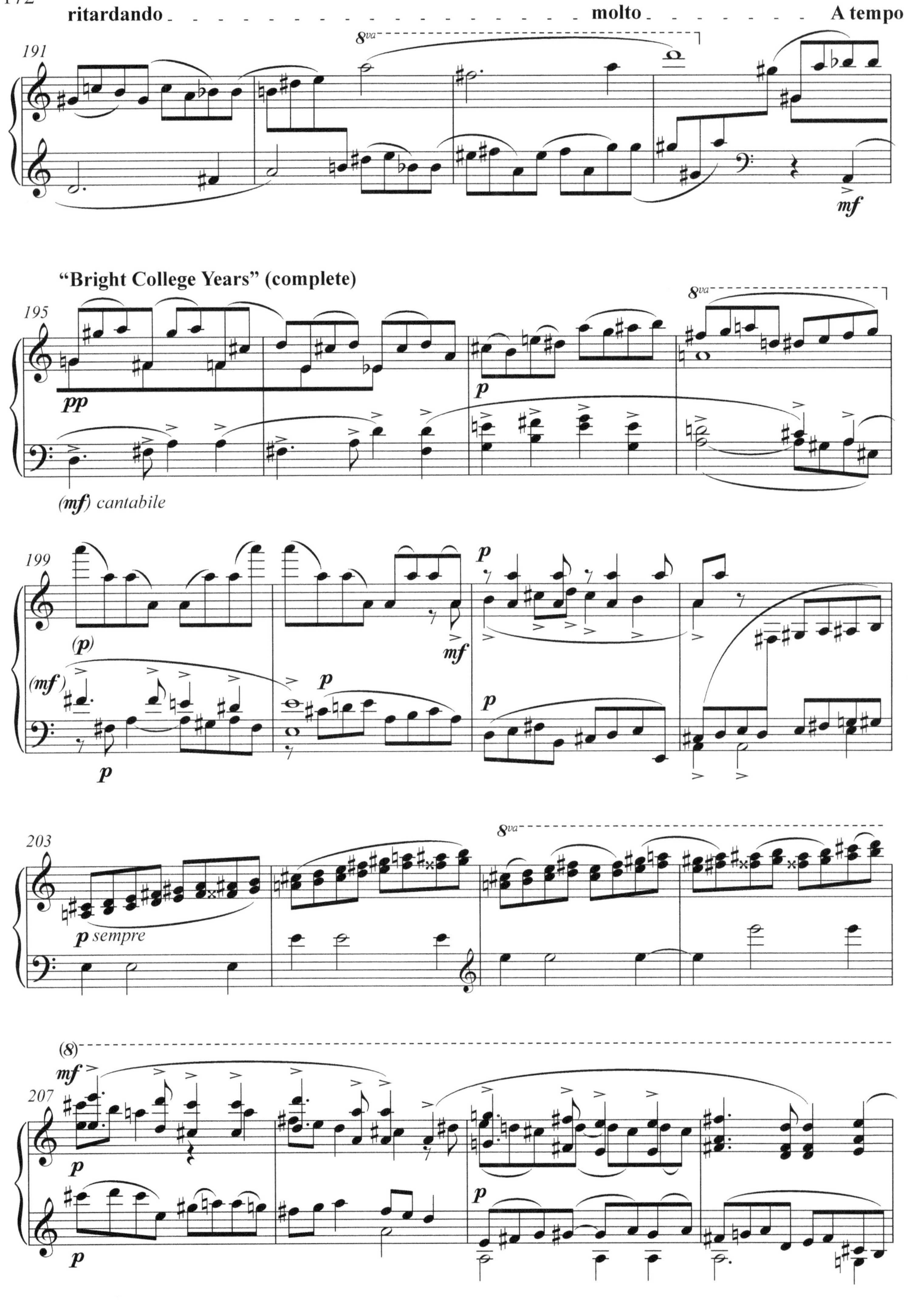
ritardando
molto
A tempo
191
8va
mf
"Bright College Years" (complete)
195
8va
pp
(mf) cantabile
p
199
(p)
(mf)
p
mf
203
p sempre
8va
(8)
207
mf
p

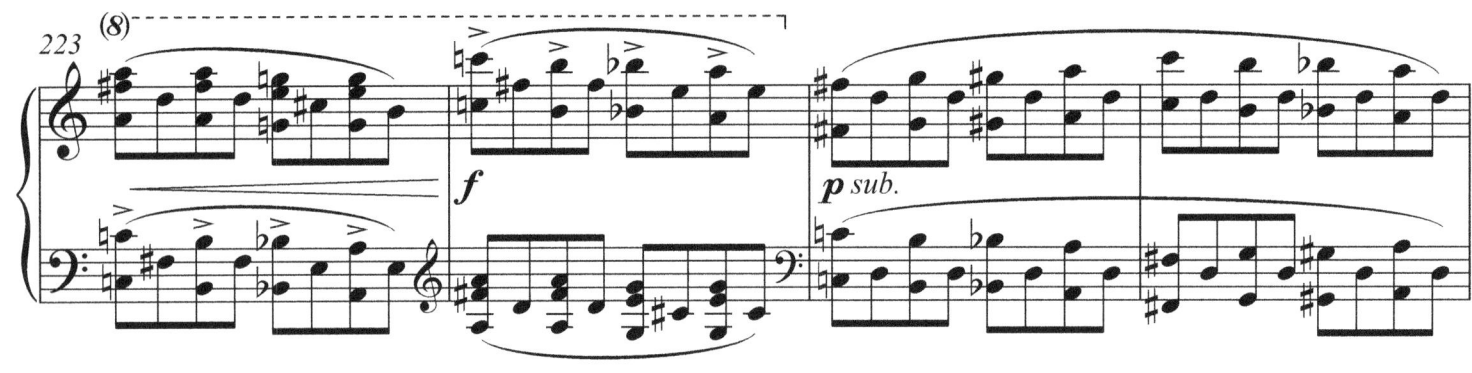
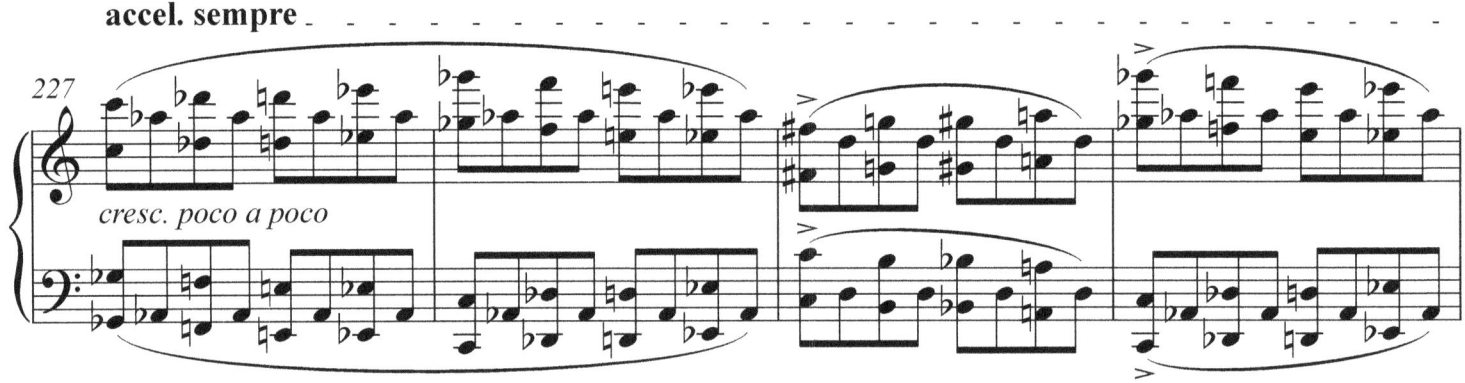

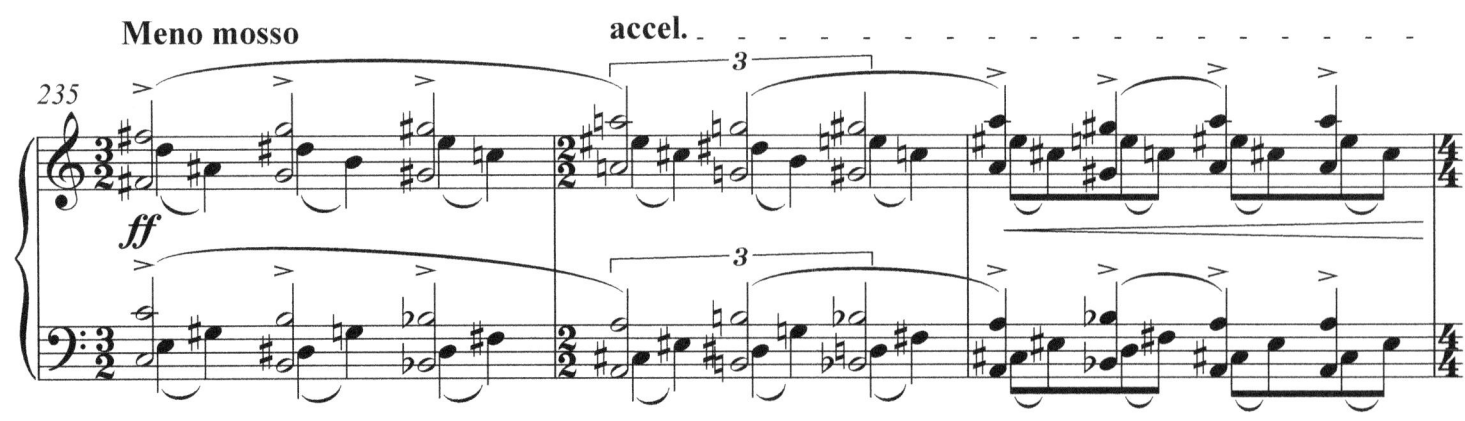

III. LAWYER ETUDE

30 years old
Ray, the hot, hard–working young lawyer takes on Gotham City.

Allegro passionato

178

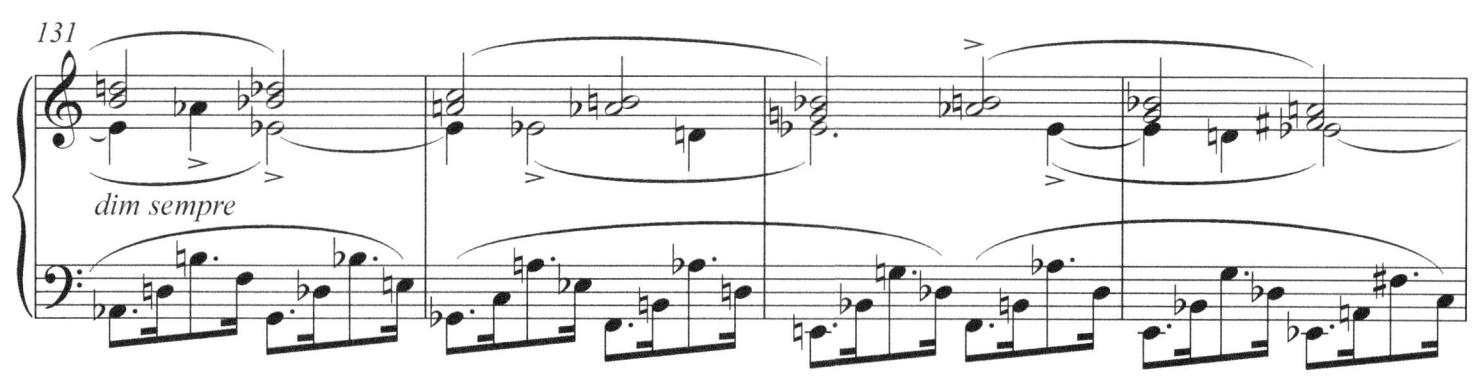

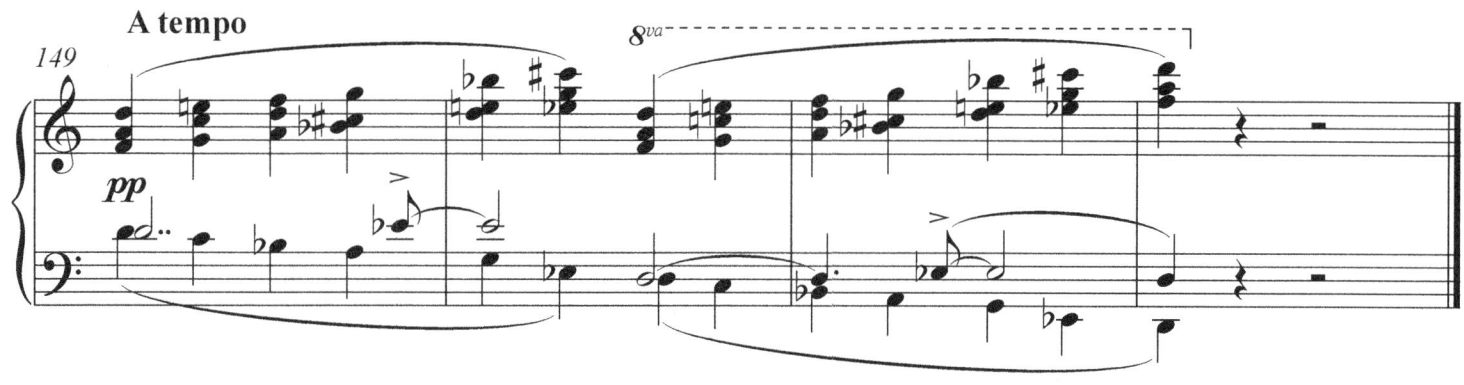

IV. DOMESTICATED / SEDUCED

40 years old
Ray, married and domesticated, hears a new and seductive call . . . (whack!)

* Throughout this piece, the page-turner takes a paddle and strikes the piano *(whack!)* as indicated — ***f*** *sempre*.
  (The word *whack* is never spoken.) In two places a tremolo effect is requested.

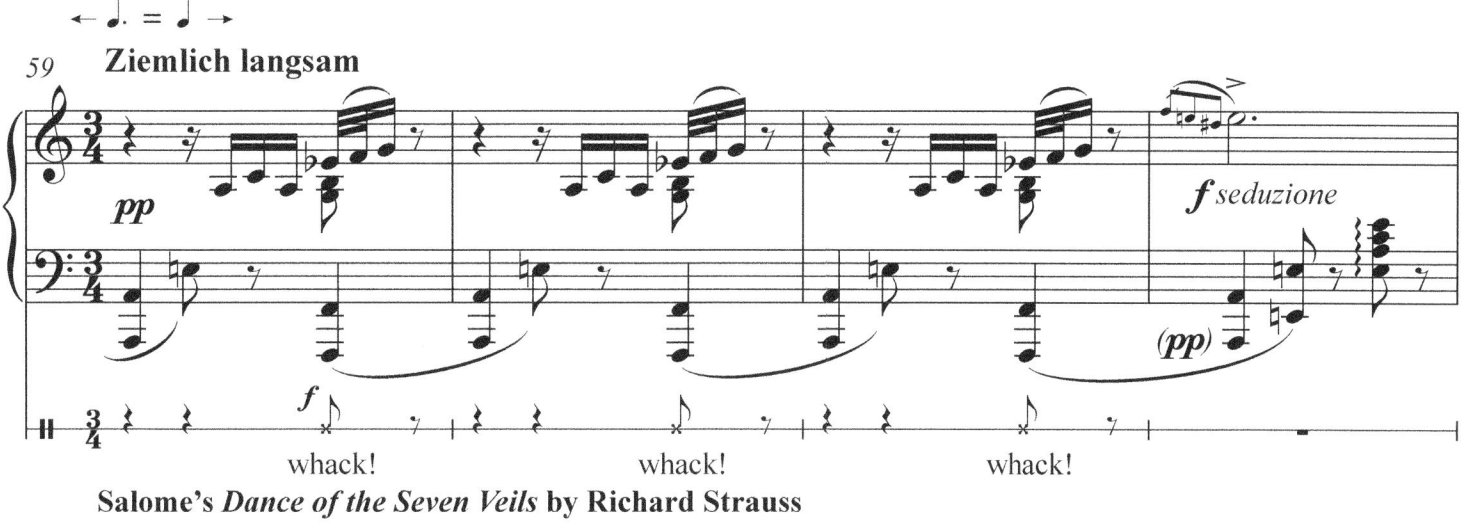

Salome's *Dance of the Seven Veils* by Richard Strauss

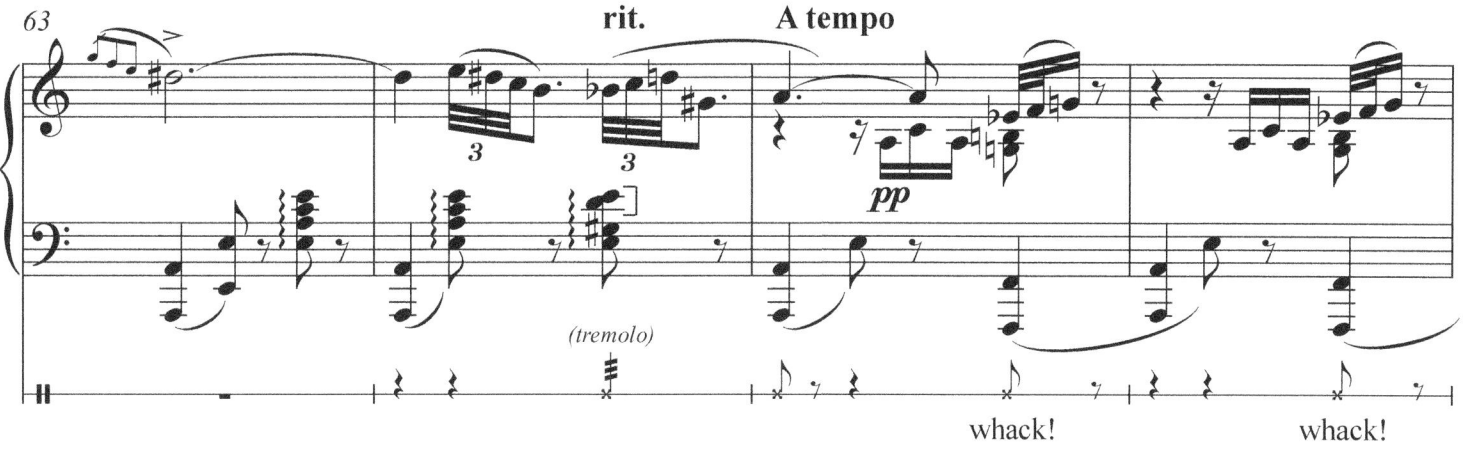

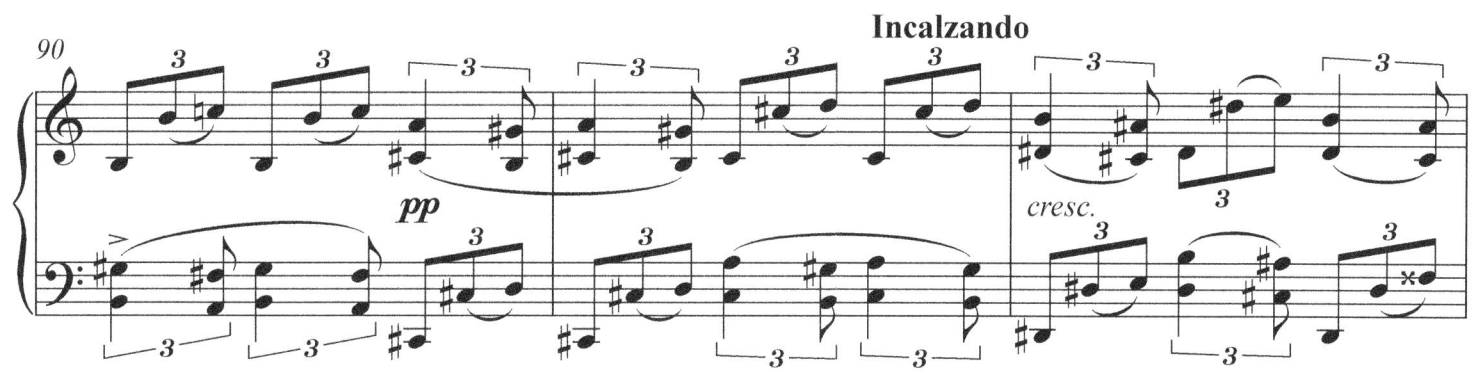

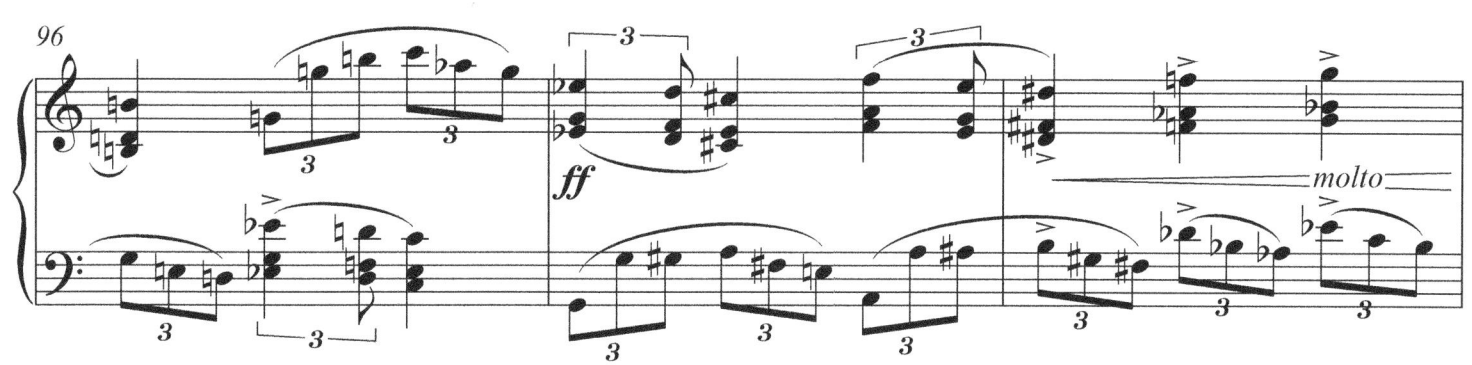

Ray's Birthday Suit

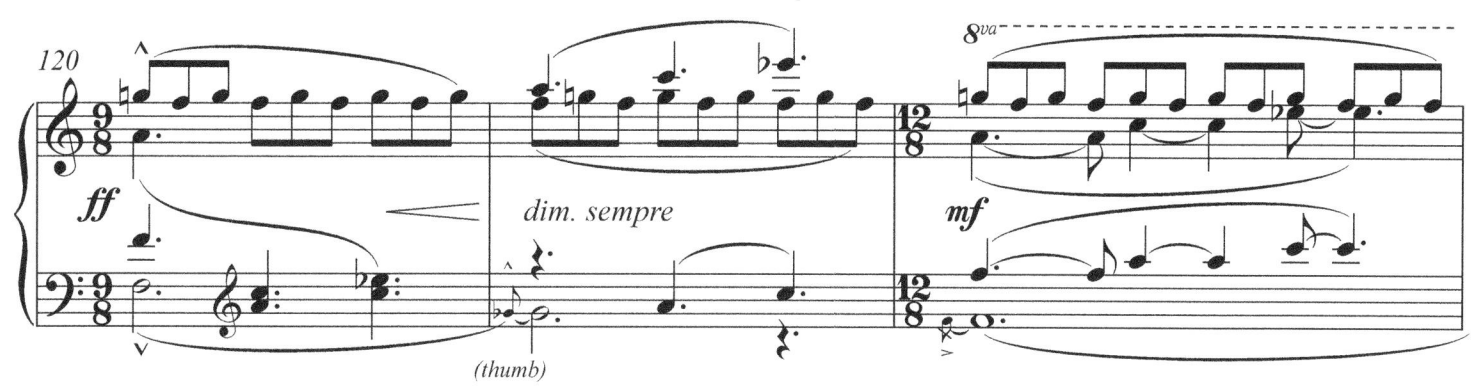

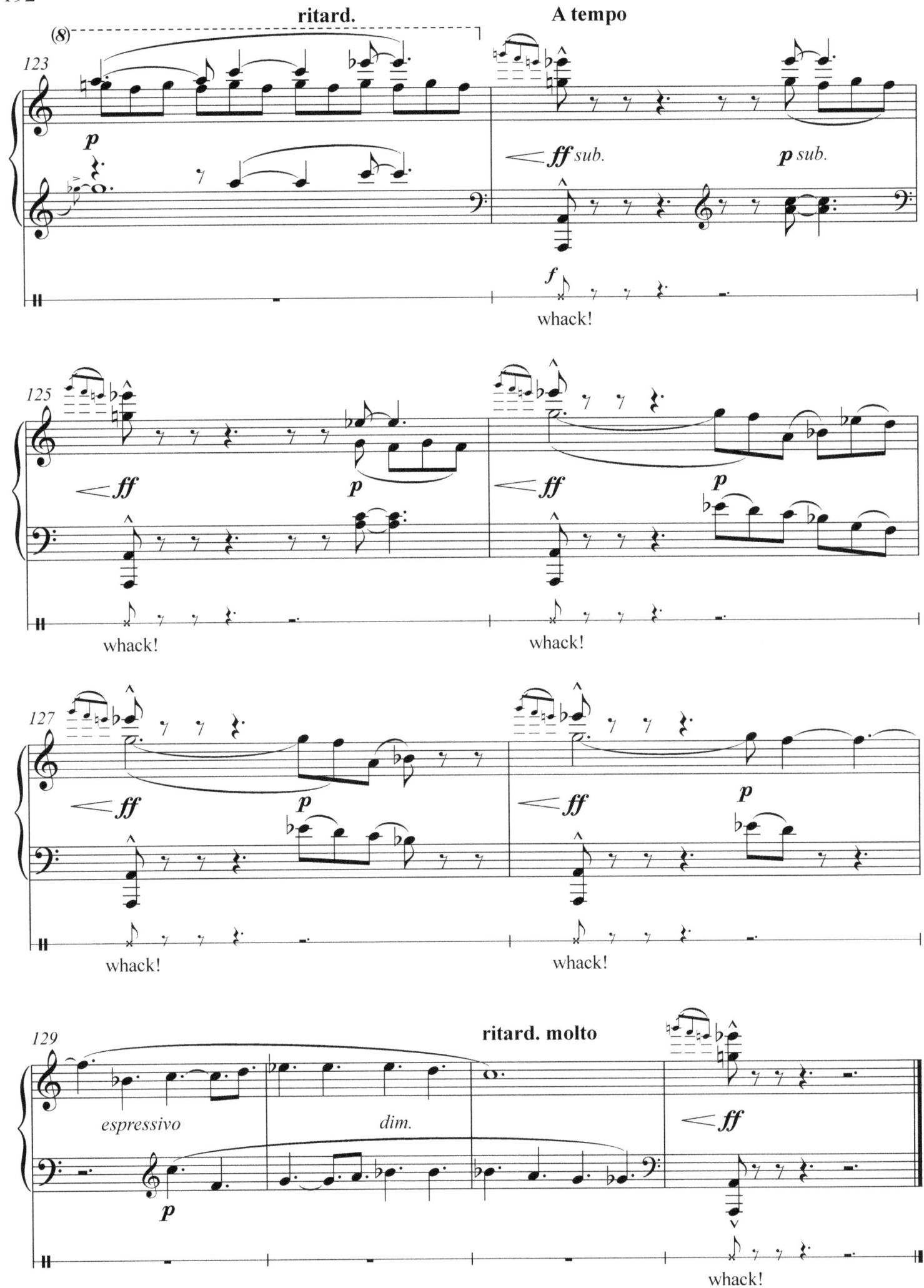

V. LOVE DUET

50 years old
Ray meets David, his first male lover.

*Theme from *Final Alice* by David Del Tredici

più e più animato

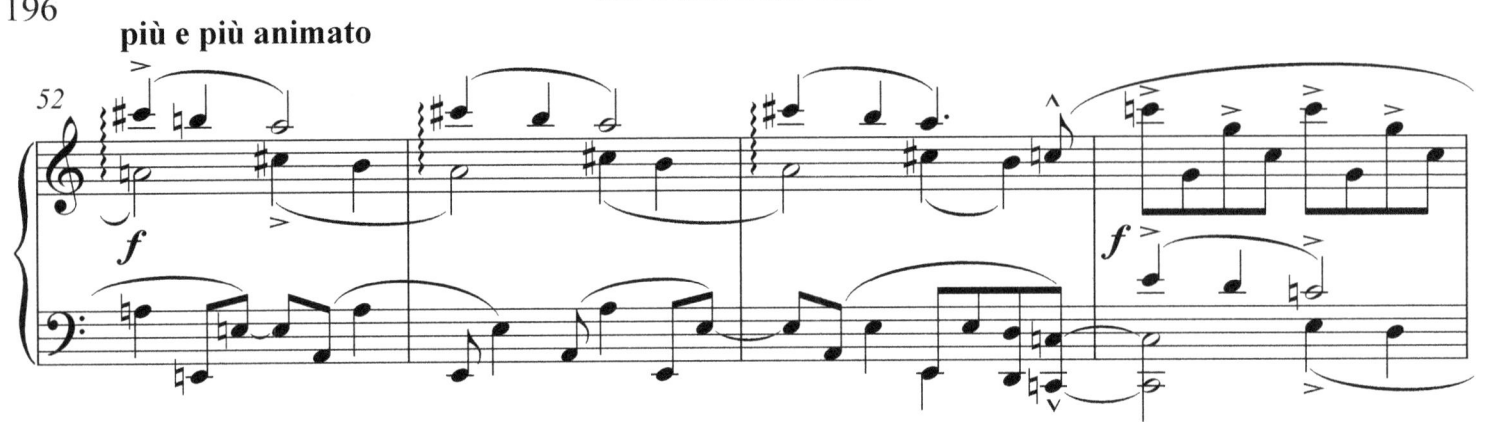

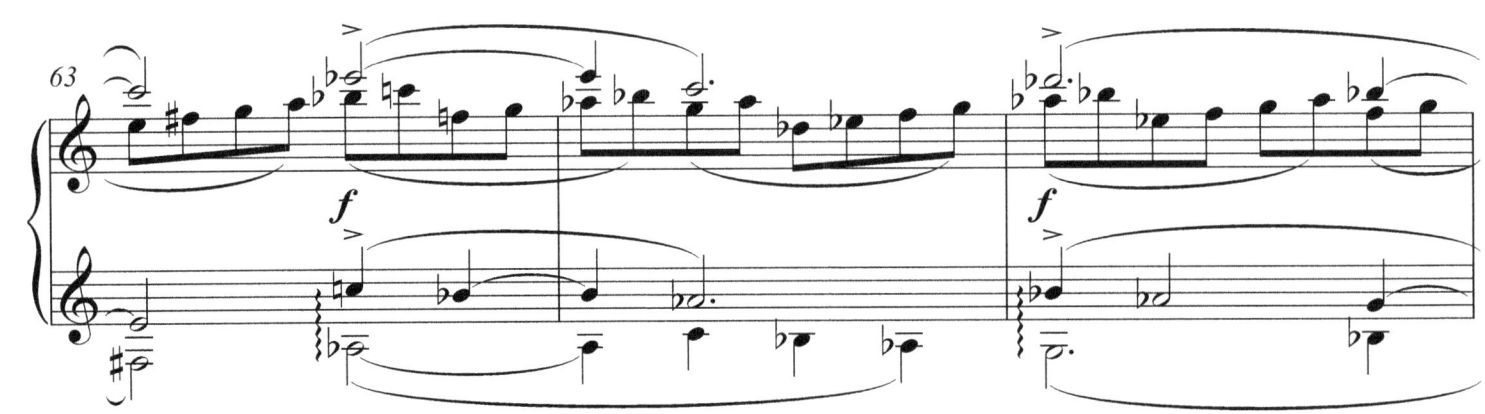

VI. A GRAND OCCASION

60 years old
The great birthday finally arrives. A joyful noise is heard throughout the land.

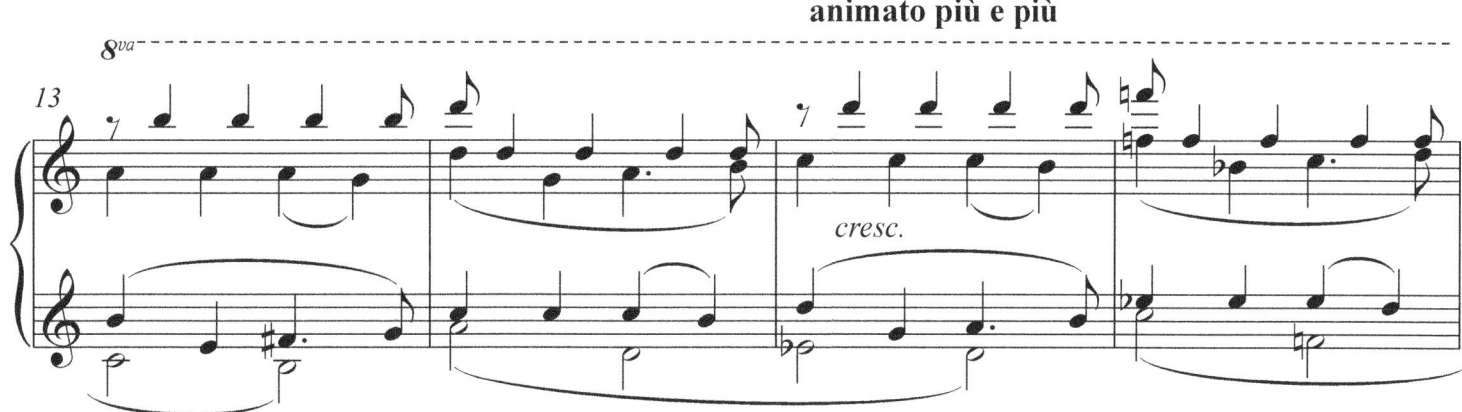

200

Ray's Birthday Suit

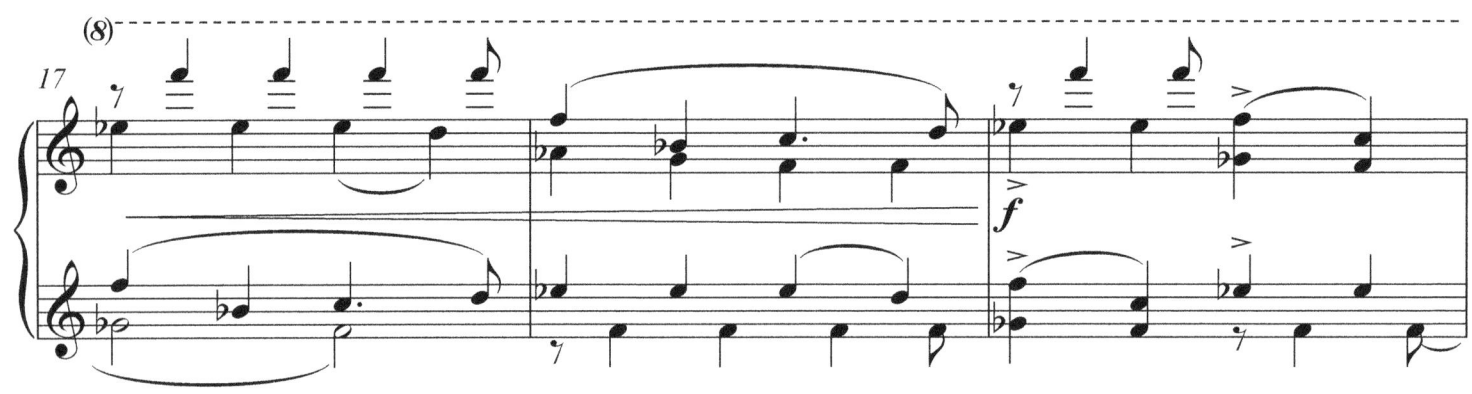

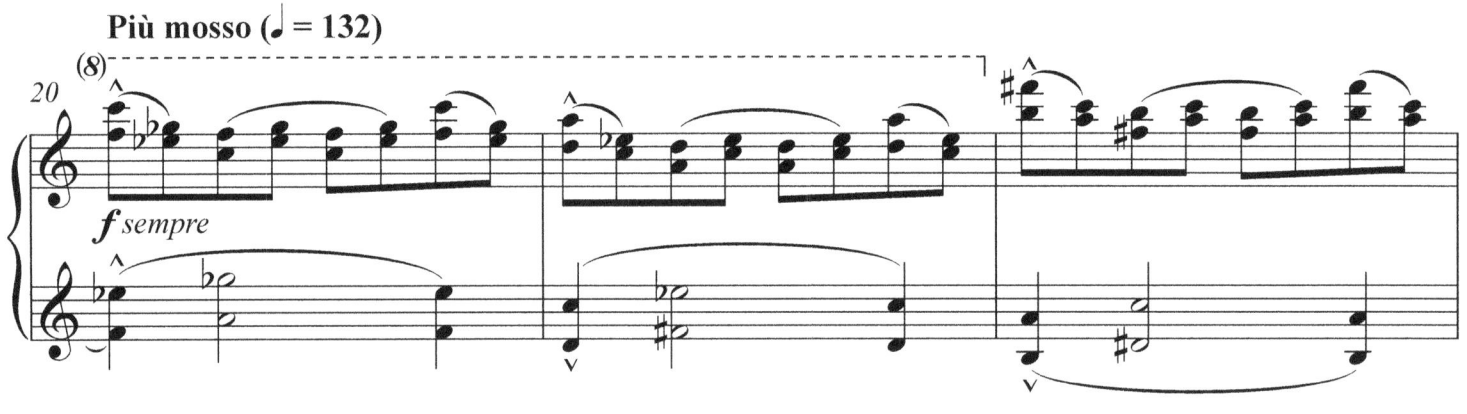

202 Fugue: Allegro (♩ = 92)

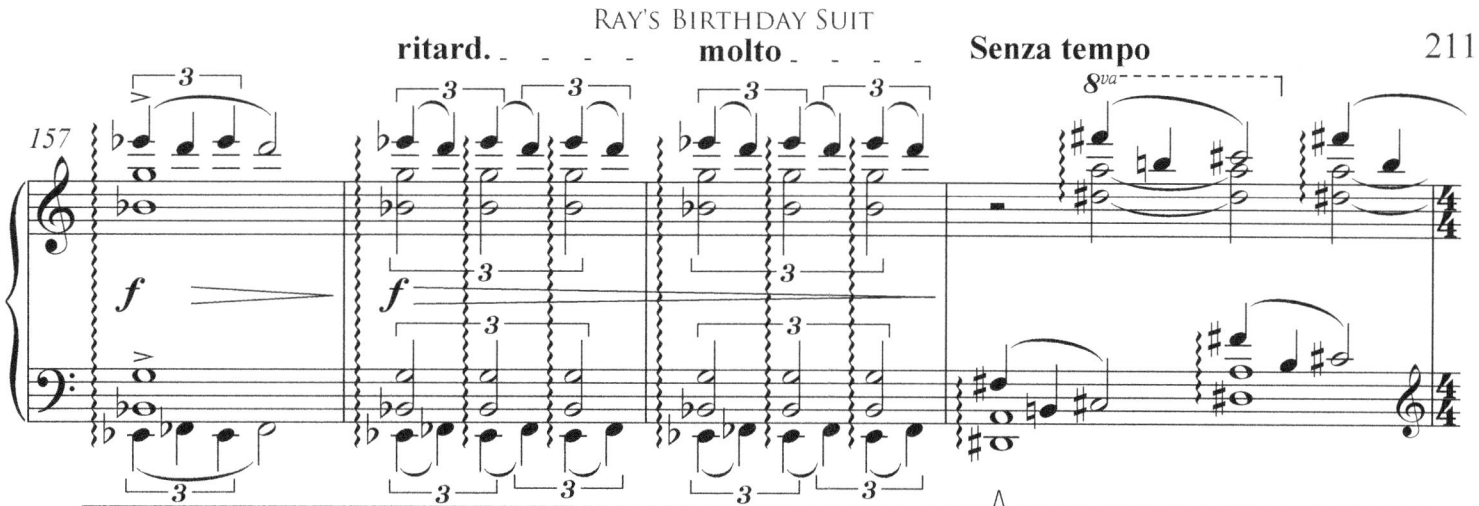

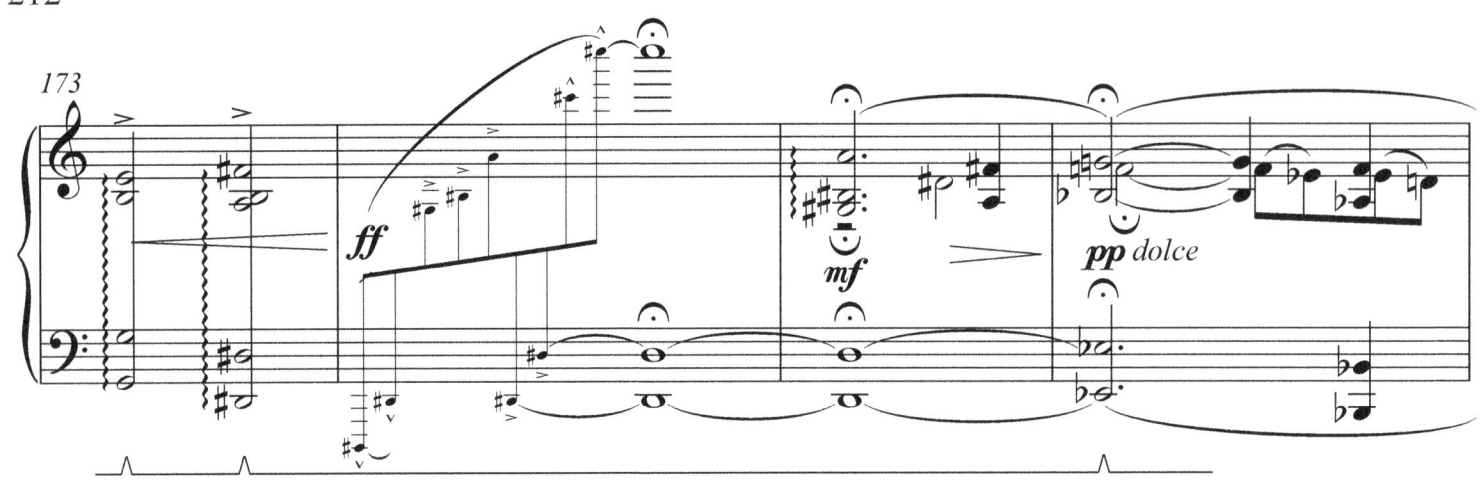

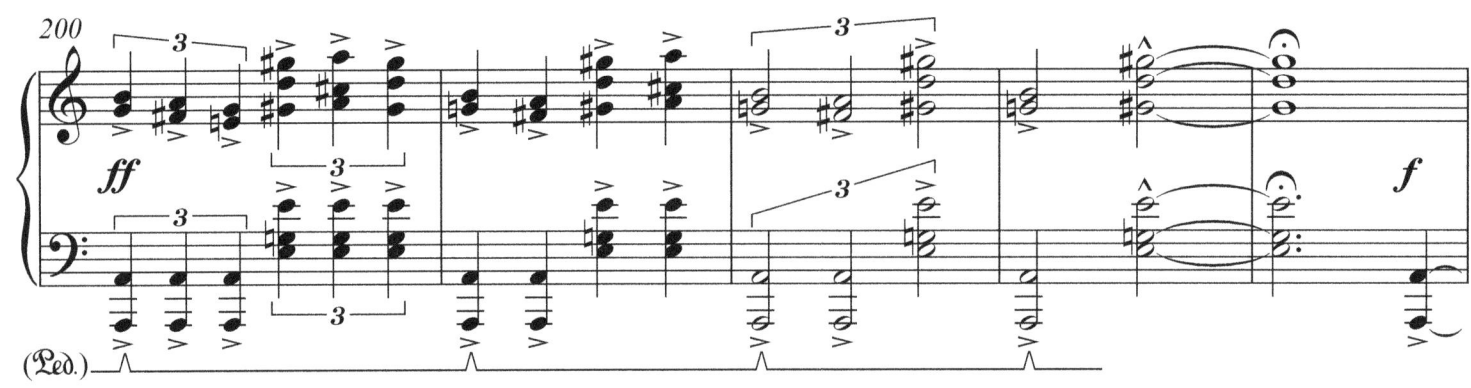

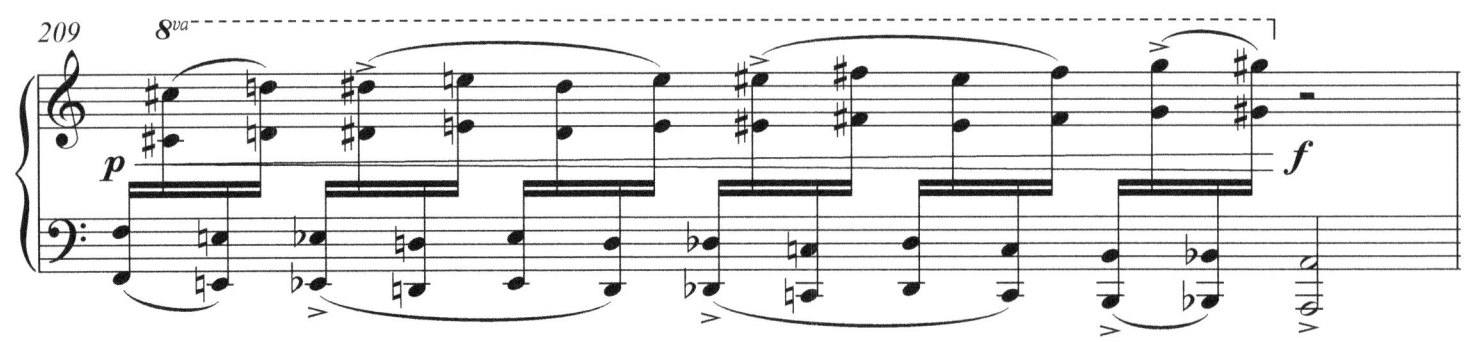

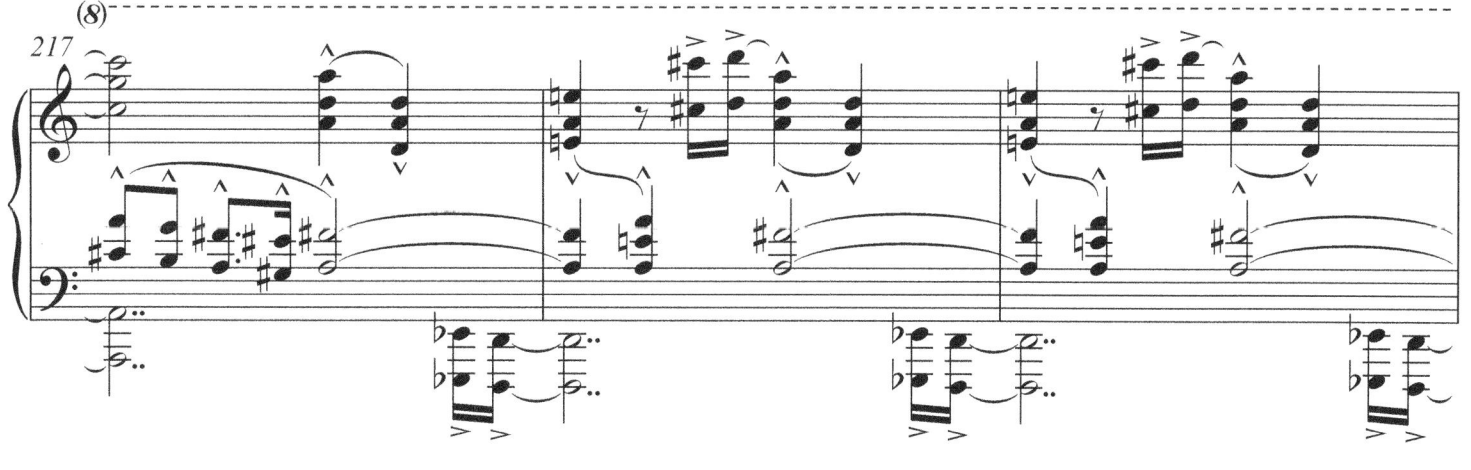